S0-AEH-501

Conversations with Lee Smith

Literary Conversations Series

Peggy Whitman Prenshaw
General Editor

Photo credit: David G. Spielman

Conversations
with Lee Smith

Edited by
Linda Tate

University Press of Mississippi
Jackson

www.upress.state.ms.us

09   08   07   06   05   04   03   02   01   4   3   2   1
∞
Library of Congress Cataloging-in-Publication Data
Smith, Lee 1944–
    Conversations with Lee Smith / edited by Linda Tate.
        p.   cm.—(Literary conversations series)
    Includes bibliographical references and index.
    ISBN 1-57806-349-3 (cloth : alk. paper)—ISBN 1-57806-350-7 (pbk. : alk. paper)
    1. Smith, Lee 1944– —Interviews. 2 Novelists, American—20th century—Interview.   I.
Tate, Linda.   II. Title.   III. Series.
    PS3569.M5376 Z464   2001
    813′.54—dc21
    [B]   00-050349

British Library Cataloging-in-Publication Data available

Books by Lee Smith

The Last Day the Dogbushes Bloomed. New York: Harper and Row, 1968. Reissued by LSU
  Press, 1994.
Something in the Wind. New York: Harper and Row, 1971.
Fancy Strut. New York: Harper and Row, 1973.
Black Mountain Breakdown. New York: Putnam, 1980.
Cakewalk. New York: Putnam, 1981.
Oral History. New York: Putnam, 1983.
Family Linen. New York: Putnam, 1985.
Fair and Tender Ladies. New York: Putnam, 1988.
Me and My Baby View the Eclipse. New York: Putnam, 1990.
The Devil's Dream. New York: Putnam, 1992.
We Don't Love with Our Teeth. Portland, OR: Chinook Press, 1994. Limited edition.
Saving Grace. New York: Putnam, 1995.
The Christmas Letters. Chapel Hill, NC: Algonquin, 1996.
News of the Spirit. New York: Putnam, 1997.
Sitting on the Courthouse Bench: An Oral History of Grundy, Va., interviews conducted by
  Grundy High School students under Smith's supervision and edited and introduced by Smith.
  Chapel Hill, NC: Tryon Publishing, 2000.

Contents

Introduction

"How does a girl from Grundy, Virginia, become a successful writer?" So begins the first published interview with Lee Smith, conducted by Edwin T. Arnold nearly twenty years ago.

It's a question Smith has been answering ever since.

The fourteen interviews and feature articles collected here—selected from numerous interviews, articles, and documentaries about Smith—tell the story of one girl's discovery of her hometown as a potential "literary place." Over and over again, Smith identifies her reading of James Still's 1940 novel *River of Earth* as a defining moment in her development as a writer. Until she read the ending of this landmark Appalachian novel—a scene in which the Baldridge family considers a move to Grundy in their perpetual search for economic survival—Smith had imagined far-flung places and outrageous scenarios in her early efforts at writing.

But when she read Still's work, a light went on, and Smith began to understand that she might have something to say about her home. This discovery would become the key to Smith's success as a writer. As she immersed herself increasingly in the stories of Grundy and its people, she moved beyond her early novels, which were commercially unsuccessful, and in 1983 she erupted on the literary scene—seemingly out of nowhere—with *Oral History*. Based on an old legend that had circulated for years in Grundy and Buchanan County, the novel was named a Book of the Month Club selection and brought long-overdue attention to Smith. When she began to pay closer attention to the voices of her hometown, her own voice emerged.

"Suddenly," she tells Jeanne McDonald, "lots of the things of my life occurred to me for the first time as stories: my mother and my aunts sitting on the porch talking endlessly about whether one of them had colitis or not; Hardware Breeding, who married his wife, Beulah, four times; how my uncle Curt taught my daddy to drink good liquor; how I got saved at the tent revival; John Hardin's hanging in the courthouse square; how Pete Chaney rode the flood. I started to write those stories down. Twenty-five years later, I'm still at it. And it's a funny thing: though I have spent most of my life in universities, though I live in Chapel Hill and eat pasta and drive a Toyota, the stories which present themselves to me as worth the telling are most often those somehow connected to that place and those people."

The daughter of Ernest Smith, who owned the dimestore in Grundy, and Virginia "Gig" Smith, a schoolteacher from Chincoteague Island on the other side of the state who had come to teach in Grundy and never left, Smith grew up as a town girl. She describes her position to Daniel Bourne: "I grew up in the town, but I still had all these deep mountain experiences, these talks with my older relatives. Our house was down along the creek, in Grundy, and all the hollers run up from it. But I was always fascinated with the mountain kids, and went up with them and spent the night there. I had cousins that grew up in a company town and I would stay with them. But I was always the town girl, always writing, the one whose father was weirdly bookish, the one who was always sent away to school."

Despite her relative privilege in the community, she was popular and well-liked by her classmates and neighbors. Her interviews are liberally sprinkled with uproarious tales of her childhood—from the literary advantage of growing up in a dimestore to her first public writing attempts in the newspaper she and her best friend Martha Sue Owens wrote and published, from her experiences as an adolescent with Holiness and Pentecostal churches to being named Miss Grundy High, complete with the prize of Samsonite luggage and a steam iron. Her interviews also recount how she left home to go to boarding school at St. Catherine's in Richmond and then to Hollins College, a period in her life which is richly described in Nancy Parrish's important study, *Lee Smith, Annie Dillard, and the Hollins Group: A Genesis of Writers*. At Hollins, Smith studied with Louis Rubin, became part of a lively community of women, many of whom (such as Dillard) would later emerge as important writers in their own right, and performed with Dillard and others in a go-go band called the Virginia Wolves. Her interviews tell of these and other early adventures—a study-abroad program in France where she was placed on probation for failing to catch the late subway and a *Huck Finn*-inspired raft trip down the Mississippi River.

Smith also describes her early efforts as a writer and her first marriage to poet James Seay. In these early novels and this first marriage, Smith had not yet come into her own, and she describes again and again her struggle to keep publishing after her first publisher broke its ties with her after her first three novels failed to sell well. Her story of finding a new agent, editor, and publisher is a compelling one, and the work that emerged from that experi-

ence—beginning with *Black Mountain Breakdown*—marks Smith's emer-
gence as an Appalachian writer.

As we listen to her life unfold through these conversations, Smith becomes
a strong voice, a strong woman, a strong presence. Smith has written a number of essays reflecting on her practice as a writer and has participated in a
number of "self-interviews" (in which the interviewer's questions are either
eliminated to give the piece the feel of a monologue or in which she's been
given a set of questions and then asked to write a response). While these
pieces have their merit, it is through conversation with others that she lives
and breathes. Social at her core, defined by her love of talk and her penchant
for a story, Smith—like her most memorable storytelling characters, from
Granny Younger to Ivy Rowe—comes alive through her own voice. Reading
a conversation with Smith is like sitting on the porch with your first cousin,
all the old stories tumbling out in a rush. "As they say in the South," remarks
McDonald about her own visit with the author, "Lee Smith has never met a
stranger. Five minutes after you meet her, you are exchanging intimate secrets and discussing weighty things—metaphysical issues, humanity, the
really important stuff. Smith demonstrates an empathy and involvement with
the concerns of others that are so sincere, you realize immediately that she
herself has been on the same emotional plateau at one time or another. Her
lively blue eyes are as friendly and approachable as a cool lake you can wade
into, and her smile and expressions seem completely implicated with everything you are telling her."

As when talking with Smith in person, the reader gets to know her life and
its stories, its highs and its lows. Smith talks about her early divorce and her
subsequent marriage to second husband, journalist Hal Crowther, her struggles as her parents die and she sells the home in Grundy, her drive for writing
even as she raises two sons. Through novels such as *Black Mountain Breakdown, Oral History, Fair and Tender Ladies,* and *The Devil's Dream,* we
watch not only the growth of Smith's characters, but now with the soundtrack
of the conversations she was having all along, we hear the growth of Lee
Smith—the writer, the storyteller, the Appalachian woman searching for and
ultimately finding her voice.

We hear echoes of Smith in Crystal Spangler, the main character in *Black
Mountain Breakdown,* who is literally immobilized by her passivity. While
Smith's own story in no way resembles the particulars of Crystal's, Smith
reveals in these interviews her own struggle with the assigned gender roles
of her region. In a conversation with Elisabeth Herion-Sarafidis, Smith re-

calls, "I was never quite like Crystal, but as a girl and a woman in my early twenties, like so many other young southern women, I did try really hard to fit into certain notions, certain roles. And at the time I was writing that, I was trying to get out of this and could identify, really empathize with Crystal." Smith describes the novel as a "cautionary tale," telling William Walsh that "I was at a point in my life where all my friends, women I had grown up with, were suddenly floundering, because we were following someone else's ideas of who we ought to be or what we ought to do."

But it was in the preparation for and the writing of *Oral History*—a process which Smith describes so thoroughly in these interviews—that she began to understand that the power of her voice lay at home. "When I first started writing about the mountains," she tells Claudia Loewenstein, "I remember specifically it was like a crusade. When the first fast foods started to go into Grundy, on the road of the river bend right up from my dad's house, and satellite dishes then began to dot the hillside, I realized this was all changing; it's changing in my lifetime, and I really began to consciously interview the older people I know and write down what they said and the way they expressed themselves and search out people who could tell me a lot about the way things were and had been." Her relatives, neighbors, and friends, she found, "loved to talk," as she explains to Peter Guralnick, and for Smith, taping these recollections became "my hobby, my avocation. I began to get addicted to 'going around.' " From this copious research, Smith created a rich and memorable novel which McDonald aptly describes as "the virtual prototype of the modern Appalachian novel."

In one of her next novels, *Fair and Tender Ladies* (seen by many as her masterpiece), Smith says that she created the remarkable Ivy Rowe at a time when she herself needed a strong role model. At the time she wrote the novel, her mother was dying, and Smith was tending to other ill family members as well. "With Ivy Rowe," she tells Virginia Smith, "I really needed to be making up somebody who could just take whatever 'shit hit the fan.' " In this novel, Smith began to articulate an idea she returns to again and again in her interviews. The novel is "just one woman's letters to other people her whole life long," she tells Irv Broughton. "It's *about* writing in a sense. It's about writing as a way to make it through the night." For Smith, too, "it has really just been like salvation to me," as she describes in conversation with Guralnick. "Because real life is real chaotic, and you can't control what happens to anybody—even the people you love the most. Terrible things are going to happen to them. Terrible things are going to happen to you. And you can't control any of it. But to write is to order experience, to make a kind of ordering on the page, no matter how fragile it is. And it is, of course, profoundly, deeply satisfying—even though it's not real. It's like prayer, I think."

Having found her own voices and having given Ivy a voice, Smith then moved on to *The Devil's Dream*, a multigenerational tale of the evolution from traditional mountain music to commercialized country music. She tells Renee Hausmann Shea: "In thinking about how women's horizons have expanded in Appalachia and in the South, it seemed to me that country music was almost too obvious a metaphor for finding one's voice as a woman. Singing your own song and being in charge of how it's actually produced, recorded, and distributed is a certain metaphor for women getting in control of their lives." Just as Smith herself found her voice as a writer when she went home to her mountain roots, so too Katie Cocker—the Dolly Parton-type star of the novel—reconnects with her mountain heritage. Having gathered her family for a reunion album, Katie "finds herself singing a traditional family tune that goes way, way back," as Smith tells Shea. "She doesn't plan to sing it. It's just there." In reflecting on her own development as a writer, Smith tells Loewenstein, "I hope we've gone from that [Crystal Spangler] to Ivy Rowe or Katie Cocker, who are able to write their own story or sing their own song. But it's taken me a long time to see that that's possible myself. It took me a long time to get to Katie Cocker."

Along the way, Smith has given voice not only to her own life and the tales of the folks from her hometown: she has also given voice to the entire Appalachian region. "Lee Smith taught us to be proud of who we are," says one fan cited by Guralnick, who himself states, "It was her embrace of her own past and the particularity of her experience that made her proud of who she was, and she could well be seen at the center of a movement, loosely defined as New Southern Regionalism."

Smith celebrates this pride in her writing, in the priority she places on letting these mountain characters tell their stories in their own voices and dialects and in her delight with women's artistic expression in all its forms. Just as Virginia Woolf's Mrs. Ramsay becomes an artist figure in her creation of the perfect dinner party, Smith too realizes that the *process* of artistic expression is what's important, regardless of the end product. "It's like the knitting of the sweater, the making of the quilt," she tells Pat Arnow, and it is the making of a cake in "Cakewalk" or the writing of letters in *Fair and Tender Ladies* that constitutes women's art. "That something is art," she tells

Arnow, "even though it is not perceived as public art. It's the difference between monumental sculpture and needlepoint."

In recent years, Smith's commitment to expression in the Appalachian region has been evidenced in her work with regional writer's workshops, including the lively program at the Hindman Settlement School in Hindman, Kentucky, as well as its adult literacy and GED programs. Smith loves to talk; she loves to tell stories; she loves to make characters come alive. But perhaps even more profoundly, Smith loves to *listen*—this is what makes her use of Appalachian dialect and folklore flawless—but it also allows her to nurture other storytellers and writers. "Watching people express themselves in language is like watching them fall in love," Smith says to McDonald. "I love to work with older writers," she says of her work with Hindman's adult literacy program. "This experience in Kentucky puts the emphasis on communication and how thrilling it is to read and write." With the help of Lee Smith, these older members of the mountain community—folks like Knott County ballad singer Florida Slone—"are able," as McDonald describes it, "to express on paper the scores of stories that have been stored in their heads for years." Of particular reward to Smith was her discovery of Lou Crabtree, who, when in her seventies, enrolled in one of Smith's workshops, mentioned she had written a great deal over the years, and then shared her stunning work with Smith. Through Smith's support and encouragement, Crabtree subsequently published a collection of her work, *Stories from Sweet Holler,* and thus another writer joined the circle of strong Appalachian women voices.

Through her novels and stories, Smith brings to life the communities of the Appalachian mountains, and in these conversations with her, we hear her own voice growing bolder and clearer. We listen as Lee Smith tells the story of how a girl from Grundy, Virginia, became a successful writer, how she found her way home and claimed her own voice. Finding the way home, Smith asserts, is important for all of us, even if we eat pasta and drive Toyotas. "We've become very interested in our roots and traditional ways of life," she tells Shea, "because I think we're in danger of turning into people who live alike, and sound alike, having condominiums, and don't know our grandmothers. I think people are very interested in Native American, Appalachian, and African American writers because their writing connects us with something beyond ourselves. To hear our mother's stories and our grandmother's stories can connect us back to something that can give us a firm footing, which contemporary life hasn't given us with its nomadic quality, high divorce rate, and so forth. I think a lot of us have gone back to feel more secure.

The stories are the way back. And much more often than not, it's the women who tell them, who keep alive what's important from the past."

It has been a true privilege to collect these conversations, to help bring to life Smith's voice as an Appalachian woman and as one of America's most compelling contemporary writers. From the day I first encountered Lee Smith's work, reading *Oral History* while sitting on a porch high atop North Carolina's Mt. LeConte, I've been hooked. Many, many thanks to Lee for her work, for her generous and infectious spirit, and her enthusiasm for this project. Because the interviews are unedited, they do contain inevitable repetition, but this repetition—Lee's favorite stories told again and again—only serves to bring her more fully to life.

Thanks also to all those interviewers who have talked with Lee and shared their conversations with us. There were far more interviews than I could include in this volume, and much appreciation is owed to everyone who has helped to bring Smith's work to greater public awareness. Special thanks is due to the publishers and writers who gave their permission for pieces to be included in this volume.

My deep thanks go to my colleagues in the field of Appalachian Studies, who have helped me to claim my own place and voice. Helen Lewis has been for me, as for so many others, a mentor and teacher who has helped me to make a new path by walking. Rachael Meads worked with me to bring an appreciation of traditional Appalachian culture to our community in Shepherdstown, West Virginia, and I am especially grateful to the students at Shepherd College who have joined us in our journeys to celebrate mountain culture. I deeply appreciate all of the Appalachian writers and musicians who have welcomed me into their fold, and I am especially indebted to two friends who have shared so strongly with our community their voices as mountain women: Hazel Dickens and Ginny Hawker.

Thanks to my friend and colleague Will Brantley, who helped me to envision this project; Seetha Srinivasan at the University Press of Mississippi who encouraged me to pursue the idea; and to the Press's Anne Stascavage, who attentively shepherded the volume through every stage of the editorial process.

I wish to extend special gratitude to Dolores Johnson, Beth Darby Upton, and Jan Adkins-Bills. This book drew its first full breath at our weekend at Laura's Folly in Garrett County, Maryland. Thanks also to Jennifer Soule, my favorite clipboard girl, who joined us in spirit that weekend. For their neverending support and encouragement, I thank my parents, Jim and Bonnie Burrows, and my sister, Julia Burrows. And as always and for everything, I thank my companion, George McCarty.

LT
August 2000

Chronology

1944	Born on November 1 in Grundy, Virginia, to Ernest Lee Smith and Virginia Marshall Smith
1963–1964	Attends St. Catherine's High School, Richmond, Virginia
1964–1967	Attends Hollins College, Virginia
1964	Studies abroad in France
1966	Travels down the Mississippi River on a raft, accompanied by several friends
1967	Receives B.A., Hollins College, Virginia
1967	Marries James Seay on June 17
1967	Wins Book-of-the-Month-Club Fellowship for *The Last Day the Dogbushes Bloomed*
1968	Publishes *The Last Day the Dogbushes Bloomed*
1969	Son Joshua Seay born
1970–1973	Lives in Alabama and writes for *The Tuscaloosa News*
1971	Son Page Seay born
1971	Publishes *Something in the Wind*
1973	Publishes *Fancy Strut*
1974	Moves to Chapel Hill, North Carolina
1979	Receives O. Henry Award for "Mrs. Darcy Meets the Blue-Eyed Stranger at the Beach" (*Carolina Quarterly*)
1980	Publishes *Black Mountain Breakdown*
1980–2000	Leads workshops on writing novels at the Hindman Settlement School Writers Workshops, Hindman, Kentucky
1981	Publishes *Cakewalk*

1981	Receives O. Henry Award for "Between the Lines" (*Carolina Quarterly*)
1981	Divorces James Seay
1981–1999	Serves as Professor, English Department, North Carolina State University, Raleigh, NC
1983	Publishes *Oral History*, which becomes a Book-of-the-Month Club selection
1983	Receives Sir Walter Raleigh Award for *Oral History*
1984	Receives North Carolina Award for Literature
1985	Publishes *Family Linen*
1985	Marries Hal Crowther on June 29
1988	Publishes *Fair and Tender Ladies*
1988	Receives Weatherford Award for Appalachian Literature for *Fair and Tender Ladies*
1989	Receives Sir Walter Raleigh Award for *Fair and Tender Ladies*
1990	Publishes *Me and My Baby View the Eclipse*, which is named a New York Times Notable Book
1990–2000	Numerous stage productions adapted by other writers and musicians, from *Oral History*, *Fair and Tender Ladies*, and *The Devil's Dream*, performed throughout the United States
1990–1992	Named as a Fellow at the Center for Documentary Studies, Duke University, Durham, North Carolina
1990–1992	Awarded a Lyndhurst Grant
1991	Receives Robert Penn Warren Prize for Fiction
1992	Publishes *The Devil's Dream*
1995	Publishes *Saving Grace*
1995–1997	Receives Lila Wallace/Readers Digest Award and uses the award to work with literacy and GED students at Hindman Settlement School
1995–2000	Serves on board of directors for the Hindman Settlement School

1996   Moves to Hillsborough, North Carolina

1996   Publishes *The Christmas Letters*

1997   Publishes *News of the Spirit,* which is named a New York
         Times Notable Book

1999   Participates in stage production, *Good Ol' Girls,* a collabora-
         tive musical revue, an all-woman show that Smith describes as
         a "feminist country music musical"; written by Lee Smith and
         Jill McCorkle, with music by Marshall Chapman and Matraca
         Berg and adapted and directed by Paul Ferguson

1999   Receives Academy Award from American Academy of Arts
         and Letters

2000   Publishes *Sitting on the Courthouse Bench: An Oral History of
         Grundy, Va.,* interviews conducted by Grundy High School stu-
         dents under Smith's supervision and edited and introduced by
         Smith

2000   *The Last Girls,* novel in progress

Conversations with Lee Smith

An Interview with Lee Smith
Edwin T. Arnold / 1983

From *Appalachian Journal,* 11:3 (Spring 1984), 240–54. Copyright
© 1984 by Appalachian State University. Reprinted by permission of
Appalachian Journal.

Arnold: How does a girl from Grundy, Virginia, become a successful writer?

Smith: Well, first of all I would like to qualify "successful." I don't know
in what sense you mean that. It's interesting because *Oral History* has been
widely and really well received, and I was astounded because I've been writing fiction seriously for twenty years, and that hasn't happened before.

Arnold: *Black Mountain Breakdown* was reviewed pretty widely, wasn't
it?

Smith: Pretty much so, but nothing like *Oral History* has been. So I don't
know. I'm just somebody who has been writing seriously for a long time,
and at this point when you say "success," I don't know what that means.

Arnold: You don't have any theory as to why this book has been successful, or has been reviewed so well?

Smith: I really don't. I think that technically it's a better novel than my
other novels have been because it's more adventurous, in a sense. It's more
experimental in terms of point of view, and it's also a bigger book. It's more
ambitious; it has a broader scope. I think, too, that there are a lot of people
who are interested in regional things right now, and that the novel has sort of
fed into what people are interested in.

Arnold: But you're getting terrific reviews from such seriously urban,
whatever, publications like *The Village Voice,* which goes so far as to com-
pare you to Faulkner.

Smith: Which is ridiculous. I don't understand it. I think it has something
to do with the old thing you always tell your students: the more specific to
the particular detail you are, then the more universal the story will be. And
this is as regional a book as you could find. It concerns as specific and small,
as isolated a culture as there is today. And somehow dealing with small
specifics does give things a more universal appeal. That's always true. So I

1

don't know. It has something to do with this very regionalism, the reason
that people like it.

Arnold: When did you start writing?

Smith: I started writing when I was a child. I was always writing when I
was ten or eleven or twelve. And then I went off to school my last two years
of high school. I went to St. Catherine's School in Richmond, Virginia, which
is sort of a strange thing to do. I didn't know anybody who went off to high
school except an older cousin of mine. My parents just sort of sent me off,
under some duress, I have to say. [laughter] But while I was there, I really
did encounter some very good English teachers. I always just wanted to write,
and I went to Hollins because of its writing program, and because it was close
to home, too. It was a close-to-home place that had a good writing program.
I continued to write at Hollins, and that's where I got very interested in it, I
guess. But it was always all I ever wanted to do.

Arnold: Did you use regional material then?

Smith: Oh, no. I think that when every writer starts writing, you think you
have to write about something glamorous, something exciting. I was writing
about all kind of things I didn't know anything about, and it was only after I
was in college, maybe my sophomore year, my junior year, that I began to
read Eudora Welty and Faulkner and Flannery O'Connor—writers who used
the kind of material that I had available to me but which I really hadn't
thought was the stuff of fiction. And my teachers had been telling me, in my
freshman year, "This is o.k.; you got a C+ here, but you really ought to
write what you know." But the big problem with that was that I just didn't
know what it was I knew until I began to read some of these people.

Arnold: So you didn't think there was anything in Grundy, for example,
to write about?

Smith: Yes, that anybody would be interested in reading about it. I think
it partially goes back to that old problem of distance. You have to be distant
enough to get a perspective. And I don't think I did anything that you could
consider specifically regional, specifically based on that kind of material,
until *Black Mountain Breakdown,* probably. At least I had realized that I
wanted to write about small-town life in general and family and so on, but
they weren't specifically mountain families until I wrote *Black Mountain
Breakdown.*

Arnold: *Fancy Strut* is in Alabama.

Smith: Yes, Alabama, where I then lived. I worked for a newspaper in

Alabama and had to cover this big majorette contest, and so. on. And my first book [*The Last Day the Dogbushes Bloomed*] is in any small town, I guess. And the second book [*Something in the Wind*] is in any college town. Actually it was Chapel Hill. So it wasn't until *Black Mountain Breakdown* that I decided to really write about the mountains, and I think that's because it does take a long time to get enough distance, to get a real sort of aesthetic purchase on things.

Arnold: I have been told that for the characters in *Black Mountain Breakdown,* there are counterparts in Grundy and that area. Is that true?

Smith: Yes, that's true, but not the main characters. One thing I really don't write is autobiographical fiction, I guess because I've been writing so long. What really interests me, frankly, is making things up. But it's true for the minor characters—and there are a lot of them—people who are just mentioned, people who made a lot of money in the coal business and did such and such with it. You know, there are details like that.

Arnold: How about somebody like Agnes?

Smith: No, Agnes is entirely fictional, and so is Crystal, and so is Roger Lee and all the main characters. But, you see, Agnes is a *kind* of woman I think you find in small mountain towns. I knew several women when I was growing up who were like Agnes in certain ways. She's my favorite character, by the way. I just love Agnes.

Arnold: I like Agnes, too.

Smith: I guess one reason I wrote *Black Mountain Breakdown,* though— which is a weakness in the book, I think—is that I really did want to capture all those characters—the minor ones—and all these *things,* like being in a beauty contest and being saved at the revival and just the way it was growing up in a mountain town at a certain period, because it's changed so fast. I mean, it's gone. And it seemed to me that this was material I'd been sitting on for fifteen years, and I really did want to write something about it. But I think maybe the main story line—the Crystal plot—may not be quite up to the materials that surround it.

Arnold: Do you feel that you tried to put too much in the book? Capture too many scenes?

Smith: No, I just think maybe that all the peripheral material in there is the best part of the book and that the story of Crystal herself is not quite as clear, not quite as resolved as it perhaps would be if I hadn't gone at the book with the idea of capturing the flavor of growing up in this certain time and place. Maybe I was more interested in the time and place than I was in the main character.

Arnold: In a number of your books, you've got the character of the young girl who doesn't quite know where she belongs and is trying to find out.
Smith: Yes.

Arnold: Now, is that autobiographical?
Smith: Oh, well, I think—I guess so, but it's also the stuff of fiction, and if you have a young girl who knows what's going on and is not trying to find out what she's all about, she's not going to be found in a novel. You've got to have a certain amount of conflict. No, I couldn't say that Crystal is autobiographical at all. I wrote the book for two reasons: one was to capture the way it was growing up in that time and place, and the second one was to really make a thematic point—another weakness in the book—that if you're entirely a passive person, you're going to get in big trouble. The way so many women, I think particularly Southern women, are raised is to make themselves fit the image that other people set out for them, and that was Crystal's great tragedy, that she wasn't able to get her own self-definition.

Arnold: In *Oral History,* Dory, who is a much more active and self-assured person, reminded me in a funny sort of way of Crystal.
Smith: She's trapped, too. They both seem to be. I'm not somebody who goes back through and tries to analyze anything, but a graduate student showed me this paper on "Images of Entrapment" in my work. The mountains themselves embody that, and Dory is certainly trapped in one way, and Crystal is trapped in another way.

Arnold: In both these books, the past is very important. Certainly in *Oral History,* in which it is a major theme, but also in *Black Mountain Breakdown,* where Crystal has her ancestor's journal, her diary, which she goes back to at certain times in the story.
Smith: Which she should have been able to get strength from, but she wasn't.

Arnold: How do you gain strength from the past?
Smith: I don't know. It didn't help Crystal. I really don't know. I thought it would for a while, and then Roger Lee threw the journal into the fire, and that was the end of that. I mean, it just seems funny. We're brought up to

think that we ought to be able to gain some sort of strength from the past, but it doesn't seem to work that way a lot of the time.

Arnold: But you've got characters who keep looking to the past.
Smith: Where else are you going to look, though?

Arnold: You're right. We think the past is supposed to tell us how to live our lives.

Smith: Yes, and I think that was one thing I was trying to say in *Oral History.* It's just the idea that you never know what happened in the past, really. When you go back to look for it, all you ever get is your interpretation of it. And it changes so that what really happened is not what anybody thinks happened by the time the story gets all weakened and changed.

Arnold: In *Black Mountain Breakdown,* the journal excerpts that you print are taken. . . .
Smith: They're from my great-aunt's diary.

Arnold: They are kind of ambiguous in the story. When I was reading them, I didn't always know what to do with them.
Smith: I didn't either.

Arnold: How did you choose which ones to put in and which ones not to?
Smith: I just put in the ones I really liked. I just put in the ones that seemed to me to be clearly a little girl in a specific time and place, clearly somebody who had a grasp on what her life was at the time, which was what Crystal didn't have a grasp on. But I don't know. I just put in the things I liked the best, that I thought were kind of strange and intriguing.

Arnold: Well, in *Oral History,* the whole idea of the past is certainly very important to the book, but one character you present—Bernie Ripman, the folklorist—is clearly a satiric character. I mean, you're satiric in your representation of him. Given that, how do you feel about the, what's a good word, the institutionalization of the past? How do you feel about courses studying folklore?
Smith: Oh, I think it's wonderful. I mean, that's what I'm doing when I'm going around doing all the research that comes into the book. But I feel that no matter how much you do and how much you record people and so on, you never really know exactly the way it was. I particularly love things like the *Foxfire* books, where somebody tells me *how* they used to make jelly or *how* they tested the oven with a piece of white stationery to make sure it was

right, you know, this kind of stuff. But I'm also endlessly fascinated by the
idea that it is always the teller's tale, that no matter who's telling the story, it
is always the teller's tale, and you never *finally* know exactly the way it was.
I guess I see some sort of central mystery at the center of the past, of any
past, that you can't, no matter what a good attempt you make at understanding how it was, you never can quite get at. But I think institutionalizing the
past needs to be done. Things need to be preserved insofar as they can be.

Arnold: But when I read that book, I, as a reader, have to laugh at Ripman
and his concept of the past.

Smith: Oh, yes. He's funny.

Arnold: In the effort to record it that way, he falsifies it, takes the vitality
out of it. What Jennifer gets for Ripman's class is not the truth nor even an
approximation of it.

Smith: Yes, that's right. You've got to try to record it, but as soon as you
write it down, the vitality is gone. Again, this is what I mean about the central
mystery of the past; there's a sort of paradox there.

Arnold: But in *Oral History,* when *you* are retelling the past in the early
parts of the book, you do it in almost a folktale way. I mean, you tell it
through the voice of the old woman, the old people, and there is magic and
myth in it.

Smith: Yes. See, I did all this research, all this reading, and I'd been taping
my relatives for years and I knew all this material that I wanted to do something with, but I felt that it would be really dumb to try to write anything that
would attempt to say, "O.k., this was the way it was," because of the paradox
of the past that I see every time I try to deal with it. And so I thought the
only way to do it was in fiction, through fictional voices.

Arnold: The past seems stronger than the present in the book.

Smith: Yes.

Arnold: Do you think that's true?

Smith: It's true in terms of the book, because one of the things I was
showing or trying to show in that book is that—well, it's just like the way
that the land changes in the book. All these things used to grow there and
then gradually the lumber companies came in and the coal companies came
in and the floods took place, and now it's not as strange and strong and

beautiful. The landscape has changed. And the language is another thing that interested me enormously, just the language in the first sections, all these wonderful terms and phrases and incredible strength and eloquence in the spoken language that changed and has become diluted toward the end through t.v. and everything else. So everything gets weaker, I think. I mean, I like Sally; I like the last narrator. I think she's very strong and she's meant to be a positive image of a woman as the speaker at the end, but she's in a hurry: she has to get dinner on the table and this and that, and she just hasn't got the narrative feel because she doesn't have the words, she doesn't have the time. . . .

Arnold: But she *does* have the words, too, doesn't she, to a certain extent?

Smith: To a certain extent, but I feel it's a weakness in the book that the first part of it is stronger than the last part of it. But then I finally decided that I wouldn't worry about that so much because those early characters were so isolated and so—well, they really are kind of mythological.

Arnold: The earlier one.

Smith: Yes, the earlier ones, and there was just nothing to be done. The later ones are still interesting, but they are not of the scope, I suppose, with the earlier ones. So I don't know what's to be done about that. I perceived it as a weakness in the book.

Arnold: But at the same time, when I read the book, I thought that representation was more or less intentional.

Smith: It wasn't as intentional as I would like to believe.

Arnold: But you meant that what happens to Pearl and her attempt at escape. . . .

Smith: Well, her attempt at a grand passion. . . .

Arnold: . . . to be trivial.

Smith: It is trivial compared, say, to Almarine's grand passion.

Arnold: But can't we have grand passions today?

Smith: Yes, I think we can. I think Sally has one for her husband, for instance; I think that's a grand passion in a sense.

Arnold: Is it that we are just too close to the later characters? Do they need to be distanced in order to gain that grandeur? I mean, is there any way that Pearl's affair, in fifty years, could become legend? Well, in fact, it's already becoming the stuff of legend by the end of the book, isn't it? I don't want to push that, but it is, isn't it?

Smith: Yes, yes, it is. But I don't know. I guess I was making the point that once life is homogeneous, once it gets all pasteurized and evened out and everything, that the grandeur isn't nearly as possible.

Arnold: *Black Mountain Breakdown* as well as *Oral History* seems to be saying something about the cultural changes that are taking place in Appalachia. In *Black Mountain Breakdown* you give the descriptions of the coal mines and mining in general which have a kind of—we're going to overuse this word—"grandeur" to them but are horrible at the same time. And then you tell about how when all the money comes in, the people begin to change, to turn away from their heritage. In *Oral History,* you have Ghosttown, an amusement park, being built on the site of the Cantrell family home. So what are you saying here? Are you regretting this change, despite the good it sometimes brings?

Smith: I guess I'm regretting, sure. I mean, I'm regretting in a way. But I think I'm more or less just observing. It's like, well, I'm such a fan of country music, for instance. I remember we were living in Nashville when the Opry moved from the Ryman out to Opryland, and everybody was bemoaning this, the loss of the historic Ryman and all. But the history of country music is totally commercial. That's the way it is. I mean, it's hard to make a living in the mountains. In Appalachia, it's all sort of like that. So I'm as fascinated, say, with Opryland and Ghosttown and theme parks as I'm fascinated with the history of the Ryman theater. I'm just sort of observing that it has changed.

Arnold: But they are taking tradition and they are cheapening it in some way, don't you think?

Smith: Well, they're changing it. They're exploiting it, but the whole history of Appalachia, just as the whole history of country music, has been one of exploitation, of the land, of the whatever, and I think if you are going to try to faithfully observe that, write something that pretends to depict that kind of life, then that is what happens.

Arnold: Then you are not one of those Appalachian writers who is protesting against that kind of commercialization?

Smith: Well, I'd like to, but I don't think there's anything you can do about it, except for signing petitions against Duke Power or supporting greater planning for strip mining—there are specific things you can do, but the changing is a process that you can't stop because it's all equated with progress in this funny and terrible sort of way, and you have people who want some more money, who want to send their kids to school. The whole idea of selling out is just much too simplistic for what goes on. I'd like to see things be preserved and not changed and so on, but I think it's going to have to be through institutionalization. That's where it's going to have to be preserved because there's no way to stop the movement of the culture, which is away from these ways of doing things.

Arnold: Of course, that's true. And at the same time, before the outside forces came in, when you have all the so-called "romance" and "grandeur," at the same time you had. . . .

Smith: At the same time you had babies dying right and left, and you had people who were poor and miserable. It's very easy to depict this in some sort of picturesque way, like John Fox does. It's very easy to sentimentalize it and depict it in a sort of romantic view through the smoky haze that hangs over the mountains and all, but that's a hard life, and these changes that have come in have come in invariably under the rubric of "economic progress" or what was construed, was believed, what was sold as a bill of goods, as economic progress. I don't think there's any way to change what's happened or what's going to happen except to make state parks and make Centers for Appalachian Culture.

Arnold: To go back to the idea of exploitation, this has been one of the themes of Appalachian studies, that "outsiders" have come in and that the "outsiders" have taken advantage of these native people. But in your books, you have some of the locals actually cooperating, actually taking part in the exploitation itself.

Smith: Sure.

Arnold: And that's true.

Smith: Sure. That's really what happens. That's a non-romantic look at it, but it is what happens. It's like Pappy [in *Oral History*] who wants them to tape his songs, and he's a true artist figure. He's a true artist as opposed to Richard Burlage who's a would-be artist, but he's more willing to sell out than Burlage. I don't know. I get really involved in the characters and the story, and it's hard for me to talk about whether I have any of what my class calls the DHM, the Deep Hidden Meaning. What I'm trying to do all the time is just tell a story, essentially, and if the other stuff comes in, it just has to sort of creep in, I think.

Arnold: A few minutes ago you talked about watching Roger Lee take Crystal's journal and throw it into the fire. Is that the way you write: wait and see what the characters do?

Smith: I think it out as fully as possible ahead of time, just because I find it saves me so much time in revision. I have a real clear idea of each character so I know what would be consistent for that character to do, and I know how it's going to end. But then when I'm writing along, I will see things that happen that the characters just kind of do. They'll maybe surprise me a little bit.

Arnold: You don't go so far as to sketch out a character; you don't write down a full description?

Smith: Oh, yeah, I do pages. I write on yellow pads and I'll do maybe twenty pages on even a minor character. And it's all stuff that usually never gets into the book, details that—I imagine what their whole family is like and how their parents got along with each other and if they watched t.v. what did they watch and just all the stuff until the character is literally walking around in my head so that once I start writing the novel it saves an awful lot of time and revision. They're just not going to do anything inconsistent.

Arnold: How long did it take you to write *Oral History?*

Smith: Well, that's a kind of a loaded question because it actually took me about four months, which is just real short. On the other hand, it was material that I had been thinking about and reading about and getting hold of for about ten years, more the last two years, before I really settled down to write it. Also, it's from a short story named "Oral History" that I wrote first, which was just about the girl coming to tape the relatives and leaving the tape running and somebody going back to get it. And I published the short story in *The Carolina Quarterly,* but it was intriguing to me because I kept wondering what would have been on the tape. So then I decided to write the novel filling in what would be on the tape. But, see, before I even thought of writing the novel, I had the ending and beginning for it, and I knew kind of where it was going to go, and I knew all the sorts of legends and customs like how to kill hogs that I knew I wanted to put in it somewhere, so it was really very easy once I sat down to do it. Also, it's very easy for me in a way because I do all this preparatory work first so that by the time I write the novel, it's almost beside the point. I do all the stuff on the characters and I pretty much know what's going to happen.

Arnold: But you do actual research. At the beginning of *Oral History,* you list the specific sources that you've used.

Smith: And I particularly like to put them in there in case the people who read that novel would be interested in going back and finding out the real thing.

Arnold: In a couple of the books, you've got girls from one class who are intrigued by boys from a lower class, from a very different culture, and the boys often seem to have more strength than the boys from the upper class. Is that fair to say?

Smith: Yes. I really think there are social classes there to be dealt with. In *Black Mountain Breakdown,* the kids from the Holler as opposed to the kids in town. That's just there to be dealt with. Also, when you're in a certain stage of growing up, you really are drawn to somebody who seems exotic and different, and if you are trying to set something in a small mountain town, then you'll usually have somebody drawn to somebody of another class, from a variation of the culture, from a different way of life.

Arnold: But these characters who come from the different culture do seem to be stronger or more vital. Say, for example, Mack Stiltner is a better person or a stronger character than Roger Lee.

Smith: He's not a better person, I don't think, because I meant Roger Lee to be a good person, just sort of limited in certain ways. But Mack was kind of limited in certain ways, too.

Arnold: I don't know about Roger Lee. I guess it's because he's a politician and all of the old stereotypes start working in my mind. I feel sorry for him.

Smith: Yes. I think he's just as nice as he *can* be, given certain human limitations. You know, several people have accused me of being really down on intellectuals, have said that any time I have a fairly well-read person, he's always weak and doomed. [laughter] I really don't know quite what to say about that. But in terms of, say, *Oral History,* if I had to say, I'm much more like Jennifer who comes with the tape recorder or Richard Burlage than I am like anybody else in the book, clearly. But people who are not what we think of as intellectuals are often stronger. I mean, they may be terrible and wrongheaded, but they are able to be stronger in their opinions, more decisive in their actions, because they don't know the alternatives.

Arnold: They see one side. They don't see as many sides as the rest of us who just sort of sit.

Smith: Right, but I don't mean that to be a put-down of learning or intellectuals or anything like that. It just seems to me from my observations that that's the way it is.

Arnold: Is that, in a sense, romanticizing the other class?
Smith: Maybe to some extent it is, yes. You mean, not giving them credit for complexity. It does seem that a lot of times when people do "get culture" or "get learning," it does tend to water down other aspects.

Arnold: O.k. In your many notes, where you sketch out the character of Mack Stiltner, what happens to him? He becomes a success in his music career, we know, but what happens to him after that? Did you get that far?
Smith: Oh, yes. I do them all the way through. Yes, I would imagine that he gets to be a success and then he starts taking some drugs. Again, he was a figure who seems to me to be like a lot of people who go to Nashville and have a hit record or two and then they have a pretty hard time.

Arnold: Elvis? [pointing to an army picture of Elvis which is pinned to Lee Smith's office wall]
Smith: Yeah, yeah. I'm a big Elvis freak. I was thinking for a while, quite seriously, about writing a novel that would be about a woman in Memphis who had just known Elvis slightly and had a big Elvis fixation. Which would be a good thing to do except that so many people had done something similar, before I got around to it. [laughter] On top of my Appalachian stuff I've got my Elvis stuff, but I don't think I'll do anything with my Elvis stuff.

Arnold: But Elvis has never been done right. Did you read the Goldman biography?
Smith: It was terrible, *terrible.* The whole approach to what Goldman obviously considered the redneck South and the whole put-down and his total not understanding. But I imagine Mack Stiltner being kind of a success and having kind of a hard time and then maybe being born again at some point, sort of the way they do.

Arnold: Do you feel a kinship with other Appalachian writers? Perhaps I should ask if you consider yourself a regional writer. From what you were saying earlier on, you deal with regional material but you deal with it in such a way that it takes on universal significance. Are you an Appalachian writer?
Smith: That's kind of hard. That's kind of like saying do you consider yourself a Southern writer.

Arnold: I could ask that, too.

Smith: Well, yeah, I do because I would have to, because that's the material I've dealt with quite a lot. On the other hand, the first three novels and a lot of the stories are not specifically Appalachian. You know, you have to write about what you have a sense that you really do know, and that's what I felt I knew enough about to write about. I'm just fascinated. When I was doing *Oral History,* I'd just get drunk on all this language and these legends and all this kind of fascinating material. However, I've put everything that I know about all that into the last two novels. So I'm going to write another novel, but it's going to be, maybe it's going to be *in* the mountains but it's going to be contemporary. It's going to be about a family and the focus is going to be on versions of family love rather than an attempt to deal with the land and the setting and the lore, because I've said everything I know about that, just about.

Arnold: Well, you have been writing about family in the other books.

Smith: Yes, that's just a kind of central theme that really interests me, how families work and what happens to them. I'm sure those themes will resurface, but this family that I'm going to do next is going to live in a town sort of like, maybe, Bristol. I might move them out, just a little bit.

Arnold: Do you keep in touch with other Appalachian writers? Are there those you admire?

Smith: I have a lot of friends who are writers because I've been doing it for so long, so I keep in touch with those writers who happen to be friends. There are people I really want to meet—Harriette Arnow, for instance— because I have taught her book *The Dollmaker* for years. And I'm a great admirer of James Still and of John Ehle and of Gurney Norman, and there are people who are Appalachian writers who I would love to meet, but they are not people I know.

Arnold: The writer who has been getting an awful lot of attention lately is Bobbie Ann Mason. Have you read her?

Smith: I love Bobbie Ann Mason's work; I think she's wonderful. Again, I've read all of her work, but I don't know her. I have a real horror of groups of writers getting together and talking about their work. You know, every now and then I like it, but it seems to me not a good thing for a writer to do.

Arnold: Bobbie Ann Mason deals with some of the same concerns that you do: the family and the disintegration of the family, the disintegration of everything. You can't hold on to the past in her stories, either.

Smith: Like in the story "Shiloh." You do keep trying to, because you think that you ought to be able to, but you can't quite do it. But I think that she is so interesting. In terms of themes, we pretty much deal with a lot of the same things and also with the same kind of people. Her prose style though is so much more controlled, it's just beautifully controlled. It's a—and I'm not saying this as a put-down—kind of a *New Yorker* prose style approach to this kind of material which gives the stories incredible tension. Bobbie Ann Mason, it seems to me, is a writer of major importance, in terms of contemporary writing. I wonder what Bobbie Ann Mason would say if she were asked if she considered herself an Appalachian writer? But another writer that I think is just phenomenally good is Cormac McCarthy. God knows, is he good. And I think he is one of those people who is going to emerge from this whole fifty-year period as being of major importance in American literature. And you have to consider him. He's from Knoxville, and he has this sort of unspecified, vaguely Southern, vaguely mountain locale. Would he consider himself an Appalachian writer? A Southern writer he would have to. It seems to me that, still, the South is the source of a lot of very good fiction. It's very difficult to do the deep South anymore, unless you stand it on its ear like Barry Hannah does. If you're from the deep South and that's what you know, it's very hard to write and not be trite. It's not quite as hard if you're from the mid-South, from the mountains, and it does seem to me that there's an awful lot of good writing that's coming out of that region now.

Arnold: You said a while ago that *Oral History* was a bigger book, that you were trying more things in it. Do you still feel the need to try new things or do you feel that now you've done the big book and now you need to move back to a smaller work? I mean, you tried various approaches in *Oral History* with different narrators and writing styles, although you also did a little of that in *Black Mountain Breakdown* as well.

Smith: I don't know. Increasingly I've been interested in the technical possibilities that are opened up by manipulating point of view, and I think in my new book I'm going to have it told by different narrators. I think it was when I was teaching Virginia Woolf last year, and when I read *The Sound and the Fury* again, that it was visited upon me how the story itself is greater than the sum of its parts, and if you use the different points of view, then the story takes on all kinds of dimensions that it doesn't have if you restrict it to one. Of course, that doesn't work for short fiction, but it works for novels. I think really that *Oral History* is the first novel I've written in which I can see the whole thing in terms of a novel rather than a series of isolated episodes that I just sort of strung together and said okay, that this is a novel. It was one single story. It wasn't just simply the expansion, because most of my novels really have been where I wrote a short story and then expanded it. But in this one I wrote a short story and split it up and put it on the beginning and the end. But it's *all* new stuff in the middle. [laughter]

Arnold: Going over three generations certainly increases your perspective.

Smith: Well, again, I'm a lot older now, too. I'm a lot more interested in time and the passage of time. You know, the older you get, the more of a perspective you have on all that. And there are things that I used to be able to do that I can't do well any more, like write well from a child's point of view. But I'm too old now and I've got my own children and I'm firmly in the adult camp. Doris Betts has said that short fiction is for young writers, and I think that there's something to that, the idea that as you get older what comes to interest you is *whole* lives. And it does make it easier to consider a novel as a single thing.

Arnold: Your books have this underlying thread of comedy, some more than others.

Smith: Well, you never can quite tell. I really thought—well, when I was writing *Black Mountain Breakdown,* I was taking this serious theme, the idea that if you're simply a passive person you'll end up like a vegetable, but I really didn't intend for anybody to take it realistically. I mean, I meant the book in a sense almost like a cautionary tale, and I just didn't think for a minute that it was realistic. You know, I'd been reading a whole lot of South American writers [laughter] and I really didn't think, like in A *Hundred Years of Solitude,* that I had to be particularly realistic. And everybody was taking it as a very realistic story. I mean, I don't really believe that people become paralyzed and turned into vegetables and stuff like that. I saw this as almost as comic as it is tragic. As I say, it's a real fine line, and sometimes I think that I've gone one way and it appears that I've gone the other.

Arnold: But there are some wonderfully funny scenes in those books.

Smith: Well, yeah. I think I tend to see life fairly tragically. If you do that, you've got two choices: you can either go in the closet and sit in the dark or you can make jokes, right? You can take that other approach to it.

Arnold: You've had two of your novels, I think, condensed in *Redbook.* How do you feel about seeing these three hundred page books cut down in that way?

Smith: Well, from a practical standpoint—of course, it's all over now because they're not going to condense any more fiction; *Redbook* has changed its policy—but, it's great because you need the money. I mean, it's wonderful.

Arnold: But they do it, right?

Smith: They do it. I mean, you sign over everything, and they do it. I've had three of them in *Redbook.*

Arnold: Which one did I miss?

Smith: There was the first one [*The Last Day the Dogbushes Bloomed*] and *Black Mountain Breakdown* and *Oral History.*

Arnold: Good grief. I missed *Oral History.*

Smith: Just as well. It was *terrible.* They changed the title to "The Mystery in the Hills." And *Oral History* is a book that's so complex in the relationship between the people and what goes on that to have everybody to come and just speak for three sentences, it's simply incomprehensible. But on the other hand, [laughing] I have this nice new Toyota which I really needed right at the time that came out, so what can I say? Also, naming it "The Mystery in the Hills" I thought was better because nobody would think it was *Oral History* when the book came out.

Arnold: The *Redbook* version plays to the old stereotypes?

Smith: Yeah, the Gothic Appalachian stuff. But I thought the serious reader wouldn't read anything named "The Mystery in the Hills" anyway. Still, I can't put *Redbook* down because they're one of the—have been in the past—one of the few places where serious but middlebrow fiction is published, which is a category I would have to put myself in.

Arnold: How do you define "middlebrow" in terms of your fiction? I mean, you're a serious writer. You're not pandering to an audience.

Smith: No, no, but I just tend to write about families and children and—I don't know exactly. I mean, I tend to put Anne Tyler at the absolute *top* of that category. Her material is material that the average reader can read and like, and if you're a more than average reader you can see all the wonderful things that she does and can appreciate them, but you don't have to know that to really like to read her. A writer like William Gass or a writer like Donald Barthelme does have a specialized audience. I think *Redbook* was so good for so long because they were publishing really good stories. I think there needs to be a place for that. And also they would consider stories just sent in by their readers and publish them. I first read Bobbie Ann Mason in *Redbook;* long before *Atlantic* found her or *New Yorker* found her, she was in *Redbook.* So I can't put them down entirely for chopping up *Oral History* and calling it "The Mystery in the Hills."

Arnold: It loses a certain integrity, one might say.

Smith: Oh, it does, it does. I guess the key to that is, if it's ever going to see print the way you want it to be. And it was already going to come out from Putnam the way I wanted it to be.

Arnold: Do you have a good working relationship with Putnam? Do you find that what you have written is what finally sees print?

Smith: Oh, yes. It's absolutely wonderful. I have the world's best editor. She's just wonderful. I mean, she's just *wonderful.* She *reads.* She's very literate, and she has such a feeling for language. She will call you up long distance and discuss an adverb, whether it should be there or not. She's absolutely terrific. I couldn't say how good she is. In fact, if she hadn't been such a good editor, I don't think *Oral History* would be as good. There was one section that she took out, and I'm so glad that she took it out.

Arnold: What was that section about?

Smith: Well, everybody likes to think that these books are all written and you just do it, but you don't. You really do have an editor. It was a section from Red Emmy's point of view, and it portrayed Red Emmy as not a witch at all, but completely crazy. She had been raised by a fundamentalist preacher and all this kind of stuff. It gave a lot of reasons for why certain things happened, but it was also unfortunately very much like a bad Faulkner imitation, which I did not see at the time. Because she was crazy, and it was very disjointed, sort of like bad Benjy. My editor, who is so tactful, said that she felt that it would be better to leave a central mystery at the core of the novel, which is whether Emmy was a witch or not and whatever happened to her. So we don't have that section in there any more, and God knows I'm glad we don't. Because some reviewers have very graciously—it's also dumb— compared me to Faulkner, as you noted. If that section had been in there, it would not have been a compliment but a criticism of a bad imitation of Faulkner, which would then have colored the critics' reading of the whole rest of the book since it was a fairly early section.

Arnold: Would it also have contradicted what we were saying earlier about the past being so mysterious in the book? Would it have explained too much?

Smith: Oh, it wasn't that wrapped up, but it did give some basis for her actions. It showed you exactly how she was crazy and what her own obsessions were and why she did certain things. So I was really glad. Faith Sale, my editor, is a totally non-directive kind of editor. She'll say, "I just feel that, perhaps. . . ." [laughter] She's Barthelme's editor and Pynchon's editor, and she's very good. She never says "Do this" or "Do that" but she'll just say that she feels that such and such, and she's [whispering] *always right.* She doesn't say much about a lot of stuff, but if she does make some kind of comment, it's worth thinking about. There are some things she said that I didn't change, but sometimes she's just so on the money that you know it right away.

Arnold: Last question. In *Black Mountain Breakdown,* you wrote that Crystal reads two books by Faulkner and loves them. You don't give the titles. Which two books are they?
Smith: Oh, I have no idea. [laughing]

Arnold: No, you have to tell me.
Smith: I don't know, my goodness.

Arnold: *The Sound and the Fury?*
Smith: I would think so, yeah. I don't think she would be quite up to *Absalom, Absalom!,* which is my favorite. But I would think maybe *The Sound and the Fury* and, maybe, *Sanctuary.* [laughter]

Arnold: I wondered if there was a connection between Crystal and Caddy Compson. That would work.
Smith: So would *Sanctuary.*

Arnold: So would *Absalom, Absalom!,* if she could have read it.
Smith: If she could have read it. But I don't think she could have gotten through it.

An Interview with Lee Smith
Dorothy Combs Hill / 1985

From *Southern Quarterly*, 28.2 (Winter 1990), 5–19. Copyright ©
1990. Reprinted by permission of *Southern Quarterly*.

DH: We have listened throughout the symposium to discussions of your book
Oral History, which seems—unlike your new novel, *Family Linen*—to be a
departure.

LS: *Oral History* was a departure. The whole time I was listening to this
discussion today was strange. It's weird to hear people critiquing your work.
It was particularly interesting to me because all the papers were about *Oral
History,* and I never felt like I wrote that anyway. It's the only thing I have
ever had that sense about. I wrote it very fast, and I still feel like I cheated. I
had never used research in anything I had written before. I kept asking my
editor, who kept reassuring me, "It's all right." But I loved the folklore. I
loved all the research. And I loved these little legends, like what to do if you
have an ugly daughter: you put her out in the first spring rain and then she
will get pretty. As soon as I read that, I knew I would have a scene about
putting the ugly daughter out in the first spring rain. I love to read about
processes, how to do things. I was fascinated by several accounts I had read
of a hogkilling. So I knew I would have a hogkilling scene. And I knew,
when people birthed a baby, they put an ax under the bed to kill the pain.
See, I didn't make any of that up.

DH: So you didn't make it up, and that's why you feel you were cheating?

LS: Yes. I just sat down and tried to find a form that would allow me to
put as much of this in as I could. I wasn't sure how to deal with it. And it
went very, very well. I almost felt as if it were being dictated to me.

DH: In a recent interview Jayne Anne Phillips says she thinks the artist is
a sort of conduit, that real writers serve their material—allow it to pass
through them and so have the opportunity to move beyond the daily limitations of being themselves.

LS: I don't believe that artists are some kind of special people who are in
touch with spirits and all this stuff. Writing is a lot of work. As for *Oral
History,* that's great material. Anyone who is going to write a book and use

that material is automatically going to be pretty good. And a lot of it *is* luck, happening onto a form that pleases you. I think you can have talent, but I do not believe that you are just seized by some spirit. I think you have to rewrite everything five times.

DH: People in your work are in fact sometimes seized by a spirit, like Mrs. Darcy.

LS: *They* can be. *I'm* not. That's where it starts getting difficult.

DH: Who are the artist figures in your work with whom you identify?

LS: That's interesting because it was touched on today. One paper stated that artists fare very badly in my fiction, and I don't think that's true. It's just that I hate people who have pretensions of any kind, and a lot of artists, even very good artists, are very pretentious people. So it's not that I don't like artists, but that I don't like pretentious people.

I think a lot of people, particularly women, function as artists in ways that we are not trained to understand or appreciate. Some years back I went to the North Carolina State Fair, and I was looking at the ornamental cakes in the exhibit. These cakes were incredible! I wrote a story about them. My favorites were twin sheet cakes: one was Mount St. Helens before it erupted; the other was Mount St. Helens erupting!

Let me follow this line of thought a little farther. In *Family Linen,* the character who is the most important character to me—and the most successful, well-integrated person—is Candy, who is a beautifician. She functions as an artist in the book in the way that women often function in Virginia Woolf, women like Mrs. Dalloway or Mrs. Ramsay. They create the moment—the time and the place—for everybody else, where things can happen. Well, Candy does everybody's hair. So she participates in everything that marks the passing of time in town, every kind of ritual. I think that is a very important thing. I think all these lives that are involved with people, particularly where women function, are not understood—not who they are, not what they are doing. They are creating order.

DH: So the artistic moment is created when people and their roles intersect with ritual?

LS: Yes.

DH: It seems to me, looking back through all your work, that you have two opposing figures. You have these rigid people—rigidly in control and anti-life—who tend to have classical Greek or Latin names, like Stella and

Sybil and Florence. Then I noticed that the others, the lifebringers, tend to have organic names like Florrie, Candy, Poole.

LS: This is fascinating, but I don't accept this theory at all! When you name characters, though, you do try to give them a name that is connected to them in some way. You try to give them a name which will be indicative of their personality, which will be implemented in some sense as the story unfolds. Anne's paper was interesting today on that topic [Jones, Anne Goodwyn. "The Orality of *Oral History*." *Iron Mountain Review* 3 (Winter 1986): 15]. I didn't do anything that conscious, though, in determining names.

Let me say something here in my own defense: I can do this stuff, too! In my own English classes I teach and analyze other people's work, get theories that make it all fit together. And I think I'm right! But that's a different process.

DH: Let's go back to *Family Linen.* After the ease of writing *Oral History,* was it harder to start on *Family Linen?*

LS: It's always terrifying to start anything. This was particularly painful. It was terrible because I had told my school that I was going to take a semester off to write a novel. I had told Putnam's that I was going to do this, and they were really nice. They had given me an advance. But I had no idea what I was going to write. I realized that it was too soon—I really didn't want to do it. Yet there I was. I had the semester off, and I had to do it.

DH: When did you read about the North Carolina murder which gave you the idea for *Family Linen?*

LS: I had read about it some time before. And I remember Reynolds Price had said he thought it would make a great novel—we were discussing it right after it happened. But I didn't have anything down on paper. I'm not that kind of writer. I think there are several different ways to go about a novel, in terms of actual writing. There are some people who write drafts. My friend Elizabeth Cox has said that she works like this. She will write a draft, and then another draft and then another draft. And, the more she writes, the more the book becomes clear to her, as she goes, so that by the third or fourth draft the book is sort of emerging. That's not the way I go about it. I think it through for a long, long time, so that when I get the time I just sit down and write it. So the timing is crucial. And I was afraid it was off for *Family Linen.*

Frankly, I'm relieved that the reviews are all right, because I felt like I was rushing it, like it wasn't quite thought through. I felt like there were loose ends kind of going off, and there were. I had a lot of editorial help with that book, all in the interests of making it cohere. So I don't want to do that again. I want to take the time. I don't want to set myself up for something like that before I'm ready.

DH: It is my favorite of your books—except for *Oral History*. For one thing, the voices of so many different characters—you have mastered that.

LS: I think I am at a point now where I have really used up my own life, and I don't write fiction which is autobiographical in any sense at all. Not with *Oral History*, not with my stories, not with *Family Linen*. And I think it does free you up to imagine your characters more fully because they are tied to nothing. There they are. So it's a little different from writing when you are younger.

DH: Because when you are younger, you're working through things in your life?

LS: Yes, you are. Most young writers really *are* working through things, and the result is often not-so-hot fiction. But it's fiction that you have to write if you want to be able to write later. You have no choice. I mean, your material is simply given to you. You can't create it. You can only find it.

DH: In the entry Katherine Kearns wrote in the *Dictionary of Literary Biography Yearbook: 1983,* she quotes you as saying that in Crystal you faced down a lifelong struggle with passivity. And that you think it is something good southern girls are taught, to fulfill other people's expectations and forget about their own.

LS: Yes. What interests me most in writing are the characters. I have a lot of trouble thinking of plots, but I love to create the people. I think each person that you create is coming out of some aspect of yourself. And with me—I lead a kind of staid life, actually, and oftentimes the characters will do things I would never *dream* of doing, or be ways I would never dare to be. Like the wild alcoholic housesitter in *Family Linen*. I loved him; I loved doing him. I love to write this sort of thing. And I think it's because I would never have a chance to live like that.

As for Crystal? Sure, I think I've always had—and I think a lot of women have—a tendency to be passive, because our expectations have been set out for us by other people—our mothers, our men. It is something I was thinking about a lot at the time because, at the age I was when I was thinking that book up, I had come to a point—and a lot of my friends had come to a point—where that was failing us. I think you go through your twenties fulfilling other people's expectations. Then suddenly you realize—well, *why* am I doing this stuff? And all of a sudden you think, well, what if I *didn't* serve a green vegetable? What would happen? We were all at that point—everybody was at that point. I suddenly realized that no one thing was going to hold as the most important element for anybody's whole life, and I got interested in exploring the alternatives. That is the only book I ever consciously wrote with a theme.

DH: What did happen when you didn't serve a green vegetable?
LS: Nothing! Nobody died. Nobody got scurvy.

DH: I think *Fancy Strut* already shows some sense of disappointment with a conventional life.
LS: Yes. Oh, yes.

DH: And that makes it sort of a mean book.
LS: I don't know. I don't think so, actually. It's funny—a lot of times the things that I satirize are human foibles that you also have to love. One of the characters that I satirize in that book is one I loved—Miss Iona Flowers. I was working on the *Tuscaloosa News* in Tuscaloosa, Alabama. There was a lady who had retired as the society editor of the newspaper, and, in her later years, she had become disillusioned with the way society was going in Tuscaloosa. She felt it was falling below certain standards. So she had ceased to attend any of the events she wrote up. She just wrote them up the way she felt that they should have happened! She'd dress everybody according to her standards and have everything very elegant. She had just died when I started working there, and my favorite thing to do at lunch was to go in the morgue and read what she'd written about these various events. So perhaps it *was* mean to satirize a dingbat old lady like that, but I always liked her. Even though I did a number on her!

DH: At the end of *Family Linen* you allow Lacy to have a vision of her own past. A reclamation. That vision seems to be a true one—the kind that would make a person whole.
LS: I think it's a positive ending.

DH: I do, too. Redemptive.
LS: I hope it doesn't make the novel weaker. All my students go crazy with the stories I assign them. "Why can't we read a happy story?" I keep telling them happy endings aren't really the stuff of fiction. I don't know—

that was a very happy ending to arrive at. I wonder if it should have been darker. Yet I don't know if it could have been any other way.

DH: But Lacy was able to do something that Crystal had not been able to do: imagine her own life. Lacy reclaims her own past. Why did you start the book with Sybill?

LS: Well, she's the one that had the dream. And the dream was what got it all started.

DH: Why is she one of your frigid characters who try so hard to keep order?

LS: Because that would be the kind of person that would have headaches. I needed somebody to have a headache, and I was just trying to think of the kind of person that might have headaches.

DH: You've said that the *New Yorker* once told you they would like to publish your work if you would write about a different class of people.

LS: That's right! I finally figured out what they mean. What they want are persons who are more *aware* of themselves—who are seeking while they are going through their experiences. More analytical. I think Bobbie Ann Mason writes about basically the very same kind of material I do, but there is a way in which her characters think more clearly, and there is a higher stylistic gloss on the story. There is a lack of polish in my stories, unfortunately.

DH: I suspect your heart is with your messy and temporal characters, who are alive and so don't have a high gloss either. Your characters who write in over-mannered, glossy styles, like Richard Burlage or Miss Elizabeth, are often pompous and pretentious.

LS: I love to write like they do, but I can't do it straight. I have to write it inside a book. I will have people inside a book writing diaries, or someone inside a story writing stories—like Richard Burlage's diary—because I love to write like that, in that florid, extravagant way. But I don't think it is possible anymore to do it straight.

DH: Would you say something about the extent to which your editor influences the final text?

LS: I think we all like to think that novels spring full-fledged, and that's anything but the truth. I have had, essentially, two separate writing careers. I started writing when I was very young, and I wrote three novels and just sent them off! I was very naive and very foolish. I didn't go to New York, I didn't have a personal relationship with my agent or my editor. I was incredibly lucky to be published at all. My editor was an older gentleman, a sweet and wonderful gentleman, who hardly edited me at all. I'd just send these things up to New York and eventually they'd come out. We didn't work together over the manuscript or anything. All three books lost money for the company, Harper & Row. So when I wrote *Black Mountain Breakdown,* Harper & Row wouldn't publish it. Having three unsuccessful novels had put me in a much worse position than a first-time novelist would be in. They said, "No, thanks." My agent said, "No, thanks." So there I was.

And then I went a long, long time—seven or eight years—before *Black Mountain Breakdown* was eventually finished and published. By that time— and I really didn't think it would ever be published—I had already applied to go back to school in special education at UNC and do something else entirely because I felt I was very indulgent to go on writing when nothing was getting published. It's very difficult. I try to tell my students, especially my students who are older and take it up late, that to be a writer means you are somebody who is *writing,* not somebody who is publishing. It's hard to keep doing it when nobody's publishing or taking it seriously, or doing anything to show the slightest interest. And meanwhile you're neglecting your kids, or your house or whatever it is that you give up, because you always give up something to do this.

Anyway, the second career started when I did hit upon a good agent, Liz Darhansoff, and she found me an editor at Putnam's, Faith Sale, who really actively edited *Black Mountain Breakdown, Oral History* and *Family Linen.* And I *need* to be edited. I'm the kind of writer who is not very conscious of what I'm up to, and I'm not a very good critic. I think I'm not a great critic of my own work, and I really need somebody to tell me certain things. I think that probably most writers are that way. I read a lot of things by established writers that could really benefit from editing, but I think that people get scared to edit them after a point.

Faith Sale, my editor now, makes me question certain choices. [Addressing audience.] I'll just tell you about one that I think was a very good choice, since you're studying *Oral History.* Originally, I had a whole section written from the point of view of Red Emmy, who was the witch. It was a very disjointed stream of consciousness thing, because she was crazy. My idea about Red Emmy was that when she was a girl, she was an orphan who had been sexually abused—by a preacher, actually. Everything that happened to Emmy was clear in the narrative. It showed that she wasn't a witch at all, that the way she was was probably understandable, given all that she had been through. Faith Sale suggested I should take all of that out. She said the book would be a lot better with an unexplained mystery at its core. Her idea was to *never* explain Red Emmy, to let her just exist there, and if she *is* a witch, we leave her as a witch. Faith felt strongly about it, and she added, "Plus, that's a bad Faulkner imitation." And it was. So I took the section out, and I think, in retrospect, that doing so was a very good decision. It left mythic elements, making the book mysterious and mystical in a way that it would not be if every single thing in it had been explained away.

DH: What is your next novel?

LS: I just don't know. I'm writing short stories. The short story is my favorite form. I love it. It's very hard to get any of them published, and if you do you only make $30.00. But I think there's a resurgence in the short story right now. I keep reading collections that I think are wonderful. I've just read Ellen Gilchrist's book, *Victory Over Japan,* which I had not read before and which I think is extraordinary. And others—Andre Dubus, Richard Bausch, Elizabeth Spencer, Bobbie Ann Mason, lots of others. The way they are writing them now, it seems to me, is not so tightly structured—you know, plots are not as important. The form of the short story is becoming less tyrannical, I think.

DH: I think we had better see if the audience has any questions in the time we have remaining.

Questions from Audience

Q: Do you consciously put ritual occasions in your work?

LS: I don't know. It's a good question. I do tend to have weddings, and funerals and processions—sort of set pieces of various kinds. For one thing, I think there is a set way that people are expected to behave on these occasions. You put your characters there, and there's a good chance that they will do something else that shows what they're really like.

Q: What do you think of as rituals?

LS: Oh, having dinner with real napkins and candlelight. Having your baby christened. Funerals, weddings, any sort of thing that is a celebration of the passing of time and making an occasion out of things. And I think it's very important to do that. I mean, I think it's important in my own life, and so I guess it has its place in my fiction, too.

Q: Do you object to labels like woman writer or southern writer or Appalachian writer?

LS: They're all true! I think there are people who resist being called southern writers because they find it in some way limiting or derogatory—and this goes for woman writer or Appalachian writer. All those labels are applied to me, and they apply to me. I think you have to write out of your own experience, or it's truly not valid. So everything I write will be set in the South, unless I go someplace else! And I will probably write mostly about women because I understand more about how they think. It takes me a long time to make up a man. It really does—it takes me a whole legal pad! I want to write more about men, actually. I think this is a weakness in my work. But I am just saying that I am a woman. And I think the subjects that women have often written about—which are deep kinds of rituals and families and relationships—I think that those things are as important as slogging through some battle. I really do. As important as some traditionally male thing. I don't think that there is a degree of subject matter which is inherently lesser or greater, so it is fine with me to be called all those things—woman writer, southern writer, Appalachian writer. They're all true.

Q: Are you part of a new group of southern writers? Your picture was in a recent *Newsweek* article on a new breed of southern writers.

LS: I think that whole thing is silly. Because there have *always* been a lot of writers in the South. In the South people are born into and grow up on narrative, on anecdotes. If somebody asks somebody a question, they'll answer it with a little story. They'll say, "Let me tell you a story about that!" That's the way they relate information. There are a lot of writers in the South and a lot of good new books coming out of the South. Every now and then somebody will decide to write a story in *Newsweek* or *Time*—"A new southern . . ."—and make like it's a big new deal. Well, it's not. We've had terrific southern writing all along. I do think that the givens of the southern experience—like the concern with the past, the interest in religion, the importance of the family—can become trite. What is interesting now is that there are people doing different stylistic things with it.

Q: What is your interest in beauticians and beauty shops?

LS: My feeling is that in many small towns—and not only in *small* towns, but in Chapel Hill, too, for instance—the beautician is operating as a psychiatrist. When a woman comes in, the beautician remembers not only how to do her hair, what kind of rinse she uses, but also where her husband works, how old her children are, how they're doing, how her back feels . . . and this beautician is able to talk to her and do her hair at the same time. That's really *hard.* I think the beauty shop serves a function in the community, too. It is a place where life is ritualized. And it's also a place where news is disseminated.

Q: But what is your interest? Just the ritual?

LS: I guess I'm also interested in the difference between image and reality and the faces we present to the world. Especially for women.

Lee Smith
William J. Walsh / 1987

From *Speak So I Shall Know Thee: Interviews with Southern Writers* (Jefferson, NC: McFarland, 1990), 256–62. Copyright © 1990 William J. Walsh by permission of McFarland & Company, Box 611, Jefferson, North Carolina 28640, <www.mcfarlandpub.com>.

Could you discuss your background?

I was born in 1944 in Grundy, Virginia, which is in the mountains of Southwest Virginia. I was an only child of parents who were forty when I was born. I don't think they ever expected to have children. I read a whole lot, the way an only child does. I wrote a lot of little stories to just myself as I was growing up. My father ran a dime store in Grundy, a Ben Franklin, and he still runs it today. He's in his eighties and he still goes to work every day.

Your first novel, The Last Day the Dogbushes Bloomed, *was published in 1968, when you were twenty-three.*

I wrote that book when I was a senior in college. I wrote the first draft as an independent study. We could do something like that and get three hours credit. I was just really lucky to get it published. It's the kind of book that if it were happening today I don't think would be published. It's what they call in the trade a "quiet novel." It's sort of a quiet, tasteful, little novel.

How did The Last Day the Dogbushes Bloomed *come about being published?*

There used to be a contest that they don't have any more that was co-sponsored by the Book of the Month Club and the College English Association. It was for college seniors, and I was one of twelve national winners, and they put out an anthology with each of our work in it, which was great. It was my first publication. An editor saw it and liked it, and asked to see the manuscript. So I was real lucky.

Who were you studying with at that time?

Louis Rubin who teaches here at Chapel Hill. He was my teacher for four years at Hollins College. Richard Dillard, a wonderful writer, was one of my teachers, also. Hollins was a great place to go to school in creative writing. I had a lot of friends who were writing and are still writing. There was a whole lot of interest in it and everybody was very supportive of your writing and

29

you didn't have to feel weird. (*Laughing.*) You know, for girls in the South, at the time I was writing, it wasn't exactly the thing you did. And it wasn't what I was raised to think I should be doing. I was more geared to marry a doctor . . . you know what I mean? So this was a very supportive environment.

Of your friends in your group, has anyone gone on to write?
Oh yeah. Annie Dillard, who won a Pulitzer. We had graduate students, too. Henry Taylor, who just won a Pulitzer. (*Laughing.*) This was a wonderful little group. Rosanne Coggeshall, a poet, Anne Jones, who wrote *Tomorrow Is Another Day*, which is a feminist critique of Southern women. Most of the people in the group are still writing, which is real unusual. I feel lucky because with this group I felt I had a base and always thought of myself as writing. I did that before I got married and had kids. I thought of myself as a writer first. I teach a lot of continuing ed-type students, and a lot of times the women will come in who want to write, but they have always thought of themselves first in these other roles. Then it's really hard. It takes an awful lot of nerve to begin to think of yourself differently at thirty-eight.

What kind of effects did having your first novel published directly out of college have on you?
In one way it was really bad, because it made me think that it was all going to be that easy, and it hasn't been. In fact, I've had two separate careers so to speak. After *The Last Day the Dogbushes Bloomed* was published I wrote the next two books and just sent them to the same publisher and they just published them, but without any publicity or promotion, or anything. I was just sort of sending them up to New York from the deep South, not thinking much about it, not bothering to make a personal contact with people, not pushing myself in any way. Then, when all those books lost money, which they did, I sent the fourth book and they said, "Sorry, honey." And that was it. I hadn't made any contacts, I didn't know anybody.

What was the fourth novel you sent them?
Black Mountain Breakdown. It went to something like eighteen publishers.

Even after you had published three novels?
Yes, because at this point you're a proven loser. If you've published three books and they've all lost money, then from their point of view you're in a much worse position as compared to a first-time novelist that nobody knows.

You should have submitted it under a pseudonym.

(*Laughing.*) No, I didn't even think of that. But I lost my agent, too, at that point. It had been very easy for my agent; I would just send it to him and he'd send it to Harper and Row. That's all he ever had to do, so when this one turned out to be hard to publish he said good-bye. So I didn't have an agent or an editor.

That brings up something I wanted to discuss. There's a publishing gap of about nine years between the third and fourth books. You went from 1973 to '80 or '81.

I guess it's closer to eight years. It seemed long. And I had decided to quit writing because I had always had little Podunky jobs so that I would have time to write. Suddenly it just seemed indulgent because I wasn't getting anything published. So I had applied to Chapel Hill to go back to school in special education. At least I could make some money teaching to support myself.

How did Black Mountain Breakdown *finally get published?*

I came up with an agent, finally, after several disasters. I was determined to make a personal contact so I went to New York to talk to agents. I found a woman I really liked, but she ran off to Tibet to find herself (*laughing*) for her fortieth birthday, and never came back. I mean that was it. So I had to start over again. It was really terrible. But I have a friend, Roy Blount, and he hooked me up with the agent I now have. She sent this book to a lot of places and finally she found an editor, Faith Sale, who liked the book, but she wanted revisions. But then she changed publishing houses. She moved to Putnam. So it was a long time. I was lucky to end up with her, because she's a great editor. It was a whole second career with a major hiatus in between.

Do you go back and read over your older material?

(*Laughing.*) No. The trouble with me is that I'm always pushed for time. I apologize again for it being so hectic around here. I don't have the kind of life I think a writer should have. I have a hectic life with kids strung out all over the place, and I don't have time to go back. I don't keep a journal—that's another thing writers should do. I don't approach it as rationally as I wish I did.

In Black Mountain Breakdown *the main character, Crystal Renee Spangler is pretty much a passive main character, in the sense that she doesn't do anything, and that's a difficult thing to pull off and still keep the book inter-esting.*

I'm not sure I pulled it off. That's one of your first rules of writing—to not have a passive main character. You want an active one. At the time I wrote that, it was really the only book I ever wrote that I had a theme in mind. It's almost a cautionary tale, because I was at a point in my life where all my friends, women I had grown up with, were suddenly floundering, because we were following someone else's idea of who we ought to be or what we ought to do. I decided to write a book about this tendency that women, particularly Southern women in my generation, have to be passive. I have Crystal modeling herself upon her mother's idea, then there are the various men, and so on, with the result that she doesn't have enough of an identity herself.

I'll tell you one thing about that book that I shouldn't admit, but I will. In the original version there was no rape. My idea was that certain kinds of women can be that passive just by the way they're brought up. There is a scene where she goes into the toolshed with Deever and he says something to her, just to scare her and make her think her daddy's weird. In the original version he didn't rape her. It went to so many publishers, and finally, when Faith Sale did want to publish it, she suggested the rape. So I put it in, because I really wanted the book to be published (*laughing*) because at that time I didn't want to go back to school in special education.

As a result, the rape provides Crystal with more motivation for her actions being passive.

Yes, it does. I think it was a good idea. An idea of repression works real well. Another thing I was doing at that time was reading a book on family therapy and it said that what is a quirk in one generation will become a neurosis in another generation, then it might become a psychosis in the third. I was thinking of staying at home and holding up. I had that in mind. Do you know what a breakdown is in banjo? It's the same refrain played over and over again, but it's augmented each time. So it was the family and the country music. That was my idea. No one ever got it, so I'm delighted to have a chance to tell you that.

When I've talked to people about your work, the novel everyone seems to identify you with is Oral History, *which was very critically acclaimed and has sold well. Do you see this as your best work?*

I do. But it's real weird. I wrote it very fast, and never revised it. It's because it's the material I love the most; it's where I'm from, I mean, that really is the way I grew up hearing language like the language in that book. Though I tried to use the older turns of phrase in the beginning sections. That really approximates the way I grew up and all these stories I would get different people to tell me. I like the material, but it's really weird, because it almost feels like I didn't write the book. These things that you hear about that are so striking—like if you have an ugly daughter then you put her out in the first spring rain to get beautiful. So that makes a great scene, but it's not like I thought that up. Or the hog killing. So the book was almost conceived of as a series—set pieces bringing to life my favorite little bits of lore. I just lucked out. I never had a notion that it would hold together as a novel, and maybe it doesn't. Maybe the format allowed it to get away with some things.

What are you working on?
  A new novel. It's fun, because it's the same kind of material as *Oral History*. It's an epistolary, one woman's letters over her life. It's about writing more than anything else. She was born in 1900.

This is The Letters from Home?
  Yeah, but I changed the title to *Fair and Tender Ladies,* because she writes to her sisters, daughter and granddaughter, so it's about her letters to other women.

You've been working on this for about three years now.
  Yeah. It's the longest I've ever worked on anything. I'm through, but I haven't typed it. I'm in there typing now. I write in longhand, which is not as impractical for me as you would think, because it means I can do it anywhere. That is important.

You teach writing and are involved with editors and publishers. How difficult is it for a first novel to be published?
  It just depends on the novel. I mean, I've heard the horror stories, but I've seen manuscripts that I thought were excellent which have not yet been published. On the other hand, most of my students who have written good novels—the novels are coming out. If they're good, there's still a big demand for good fiction. The difference is when my first novel came out they were publishing eighty percent more fiction, serious fiction, than they are now. It's just that the market for serious fiction has declined so horribly that they really

can expect a lot of rejections, and no matter how good their novel is, they can expect to have it turned down a number of times, unfortunately.

I think people are of two minds about the proliferation of the MFA programs and writing in the university. I think it's helpful for the young writer. They can get feedback on their work, they can get readers and they can talk to people about writing, because the actual publishing has just gotten to be so hard. It used to be people were sitting in a log cabin out in America writing novels. Then they'd send them to New York and they'd be published. Now, it's more of finding a community of like-minded writers and finding feedback and encouragement from that as well as from publishing and not publishing your material. Also, you have to think of yourself as a writer if you are a person who is writing, not necessarily if you're being published.

Does the sense of a community hold true for the established writer also?

I think it does, and that's why so many writers are attached in some capacity to one school or another, and why they like to go around giving readings. It used to be that a publisher would publish your good work along with your bad work, and they would nurture a young writer and watch the young writer grow. They don't do that any more. It's too expensive. An exception to that rule is Algonquin Books here in Chapel Hill. What they do is find young, promising writers and they edit them quite a lot and help them. They'll read a manuscript and think how it could be, and urge them that way, nurturing them in the way the old editors used to do in the New York houses, but who no longer do.

Shannon Ravenel is the fiction editor. She's really good. In fact, I sent my first novel to her first when she was at Houghton Mifflin. She was young then. I was young, too. She didn't take *The Last Day the Dogbushes Bloomed.* She didn't publish it, but she sent me a three page single-spaced comment on why she wouldn't publish it and what she thought was wrong with it. I rewrote it according to everything she said. Then the next person did take it.

That's why I believe that since Faith Sale has become my editor my writing has improved, because she questions everything. She doesn't stop if something is just okay. She wonders if it would be better if you did so and so. It makes a huge difference. With the first three books, I was literally sitting in the deep South sending them to New York, and they would just publish them. I never had an editor who would talk to me about them and suggest changes.

As a writer what has been the biggest drawback?

Like most writers, I've never been able to make a living writing. I do it for the love of writing, but it is a shame.

You've reached a great deal of success with your novels. They're selling very well and I've talked with some book dealers who say they're pushing your books.

I'm breaking even now. In order to write *Oral History* and *Family Linen* I took a semester off from teaching. Putnam paid me what I would have made teaching. By the time the book came out I had already spent the money on living expenses. I know it's possible to make a living because there are people with movie deals and big paperback deals. My books have gotten good reviews and are certainly selling. At first, it was like working for the company store; Faith took me on, but I was never paying back my advances. Then *Oral History* did well and it paid for the other books, the ones that lost money.

Your writing deals with people caught up in soap operas and Phil Donahue. How would you describe your writing style? Is it the New South?

I don't know. I guess. New South—yeah, I guess so. I've been living in a university community for a long time and teaching on the college level for five years now, and I could no more write an academic novel than fly to the moon. I just couldn't do it.

Your main characters are women. . . .

I think my characters are too much alike, which is one reason this new novel is so different. The work I've done in the last ten years, particularly with the short stories and *Family Linen,* the women tend to fall into two groups: They're epitomized by the two women in the story "Cakewalk" where one woman, Stella, has shallow-oriented values. She's the one who sells make-up. Florrie is natural. She loves children and she's sloppy and she's an artist in her own kind of feckless fashion. There's a beautician character in *Family Linen* who is like her. It seems to me that I have these two types of women that appear in various disguises. So now, I'm tired of them. You do something for awhile before you figure out what you're up to, and I do think I have this polarizing of two sets of characteristics that are found in women in the South today.

Much different than say Faulkner's women?

Yeah. That's one reason that with the novel I'm on now that I've gone back to early 1900s in the mountains, because it is possible to write about somebody who is more like a Faulkner-type character, which is a pure, unadulterated person.

What is it that motivates your characters to do what they do? Like in Family Linen, *burying the body in the well.*

That was out of the newspaper. That was real. There was a murder down
near Lumberton. Actually, it was worse. I toned it down for *Family Linen*. It
started with this middle-aged woman who had headaches, so she went to the
shrink. He hypnotized her and it turned out that when she was three or four
she had seen her mother kill her father and cut him up. But the mother had
put him down the outhouse in the real story. I couldn't deal with the outhouse
so I made it be a well. She's still alive—the woman who had the headaches.
In the real story she just called the FBI and turned her mother in. She didn't
give her mother a chance to say "Boo." And all these years her mother had
been head of the Episcopal Altar Guild. It was amazing. I get a lot of stuff
out of real life.

*Cakewalk was the first material of yours that I read years ago, and naturally
I thought you were a short-fiction writer. I then realized you had several
novels to your credit. I was wondering how the short stories came about.*

Well, I like the short stories better than anything else, but it's just really
hard to write short stories. For one thing, you have to put as much energy into
them as you do a novel. I like writing short stories better than anything else,
but they're hard to place, they're hard to sell. Mine are particularly hard to
sell, because they're not really arty, they're not really literary and there's
nowhere they can go. I like to write about domestic things, like parents and
children and families, and so that makes them not literary enough for many
places. But, yet, they're not pabulum, so they can't be published in the *Ladies'
Home Journal* or other places that publish schlock. They're not sophisticated
enough for the *New Yorker,* so they fall in between. I like to write short stories,
but if I can get an advance on a novel, I'll write one. The stories are very iffy.

Do you see another collection coming together anytime soon?

Probably so. I've done a fair number.

Previously, you were married to poet James Seay.

He gave a reading at Hollins College when I was there. (*Laughing.*) Actually, the first time I met him I was a go-go girl as a matter of fact. We had a
very long reading and in between we had this entertainment, which was just
English majors. We had this rock band called the Virginia Wolves. This is in
Roanoke, and I was a go-go girl with the Virginia Wolves when Jim came to
give a reading.

I'm interested to know what happened to the other Virginia Wolves?

Hmmm. One of them went on to be a real singer and another one is a
moviemaker. Jim and I met and started going out when I was a senior and
then got married at the end of my senior year.

What was it like being married to another writer?

It was good. One thing I had liked about college was this community of writers and support, and in my marriage that continued, because Jim was always teaching wherever we lived at various universities. He taught at the University of Alabama and at Vanderbilt. He was always teaching creative writing and had his students around visiting and other writers were around. That keeps you enthusiastic. It's very difficult to work in a vacuum. It's a hard balance, because you don't want to be talking about it too much with other people or have too much partying going on. It's stimulating to have a certain amount of contact with writers and writing in general. Being married to Jim really afforded me that. I was working on newspapers, and had I not been married to him, I would have been out of that atmosphere.

Where do you see your writing in ten or fifteen years? Or where would you like it to be?

I have no idea. I don't have the slightest idea. I'm really unable to focus on anything other than what I'm working on. I sort of have a short novel about the sixties I'm dying to write next. It's very difficult than what I'm working on now. I might even quit at some point. I'll just write as long as it fascinates me.

If you weren't writing what would you be doing?

I've always wanted to work with emotionally disturbed children. I've taught now at all levels, and I might want to go back to work with emotionally disturbed or handicapped children. But right now, I'm still fascinated with writing.

You started writing when you were a child and had always wanted to be a writer. When did you know that you could be a writer and that you were a writer?

I don't know that you ever know that. Every time you start writing something you're just in a panic, you're just terrified. You never really know that. I mean, it could fall through. I've figured it out now that when people ask me what I am I'll say I'm a writer. Like on an airplane when someone asks what you do, I'll say I'm a writer. But that's very recent. I used to say I did any old thing to not say I was a writer.

You put a lot of stock in the creative writing workshop. How does the writer best benefit from the workshop as opposed to individual instruction from a teacher?

Well, the instructor is only one person. You might benefit from individual instruction or the instructor might not get what you're saying. But if you have a workshop and if there's a consensus, which usually there is, you can pretty well trust it. I don't believe you can trust your own reaction to your work. You need readers to see what they think.

Even an established writer?

Yeah. I have three or four people who read my work, but it's not like a workshop. My editor and agent are two people I let see my work, and a couple of friends. I listen real hard to what they say, because if there's a consensus about something that needs to be changed, then I think you should listen.

What do you look for in your student's work?

An original mind and a sense of language. I mean, they can plot like crazy and it will still be really pedestrian. The other stuff you can learn, but you can't learn those two things.

What mistakes do you see occurring most often in their work?

An unwillingnes to revise. I think you have to decide if you are writing to express yourself or whether you're writing to create as good a story as you can possibly come up with. There's a big difference. Writing for self-expression is different from writing to learn a craft. You have to get tougher.

You worked for a number of years with the Tuscaloosa News. *How important was the newspaper work to you?*

Newswriting gives you a chance to go up to a total stranger and ask real personal questions. You hear all these great things. I'm still writing stories based on things that happened at the *Tuscaloosa News*—just people I would interview in situations I would have to write about. I got to walk into somebody's house that I would never get to get into. I think if you were in the police force it would be the same way. It's just an entrée into these other people's lives.

What was your childhood like?

I was by myself a lot because I was an only child and I was sort of sickly and imaginative. I was always having pneumonia and reading long novels. My family was a family of storytellers, particularly my Uncle Vern, my father and grandfather.

Is your work autobiographical?

No. I don't think it is. Although in *Black Mountain Breakdown* all the minor characters are. Like the teachers in the hospital really were my teachers, and my father did read some poetry to me. I really was Miss Grundy High and won some luggage. The details are autobiographical, but the plot and the main characters are not. I don't like to fictionalize real events. I either write nonfiction, which I like to write, or it's fiction. I don't like a combination of the two.

Of the characters in your books, who would you say is most like Lee Smith?

Richard Burlage in *Oral History*. I would like to say I am more like Candy in *Family Linen,* but I'm not. A lot of these characters I create because I want to be like them, but I won't ever be.

Do you have a favorite childhood memory?

It is Easter. Now when you buy Easter baskets in the dime store they come already done up, but they didn't used to, and so before Easter my daddy would have two nights where everybody who worked in the store would go home late. He had big boxes of the cellophane straw and big boxes of candy and baskets and they'd make their own baskets and wrap and tie them. I used to just love that. One of my favorite memories is of climbing down into this huge container of pink cellophane straw and falling asleep. I remember looking up through the pink cellophane straw. It was great.

I would imagine you must conduct a great deal of research for your material?

Yes, I do. Particularly *Oral History*. In the book I'm writing now I have notebooks full of what mountain life was like during the Depression or 1920, the Unionization, and what it most affected. I do other weird stuff. For *Family Linen* I went to a hypnotist. I got myself hypnotized. I learned how they did it so I could use the scene. Then I worked in the Kroger Plaza Beauty Coiffure for three weeks to learn all I needed to know about beauticians. I'm always going to doctors about illnesses I want my characters to have.

Is there anything I haven't asked you that you would like to discuss?

No. I do apologize for being late. I have to tell you about where I was. This is ironic. My older son keeps forgetting crucial things, so we went out to buy him a notebook and a pegboard to carry around so he would stop forgetting his appointments, and then I came home and you were sitting in the driveway. That's the way my life goes. (*Laughing.*) It's really embarrassing.

Artful Dodge Interviews: Lee Smith

Daniel Bourne / 1988

From *Artful Dodge*, 16/17 (Fall 1989), 38–52. Copyright © 1989. Reprinted by permission of *Artful Dodge*.

Daniel Bourne: Do you see yourself as much a part of the community you write about as gossip columnist Jolene B. Newhouse does in your story "Between the Lines"?

Lee Smith: Probably not as much, but I certainly do see myself as a big part of the community. Even though I have been teaching school for years and years, I don't see myself as an academic person but more as a part of Chapel Hill or a part of my hometown of Grundy, Virginia, when I lived there. I don't have a sense of myself as being in the academic community—whatever that means.

DB: Do you see Jolene B. Newhouse as an artist in the same way you are one?

Smith: Yes, she is. But I wasn't seeing myself in her character at all. I was just seeing her as a woman functioning as an artist. She's writing down the history, marking the ritual, naming the things that need to be named, paying attention to the things that need to be paid attention to.

DB: And she edits reality—

Smith: She edits reality, right. She doesn't just put out life itself. It's very highly distilled and concentrated—with a lot of artifice. I've spent a lot of time reading Virginia Woolf, and in general I like to think about various kinds of women who function as artists within their communities. Whether they're making ornamental cakes, or whether they're doing your hair, or whether they're writing a newspaper column—they're functioning as artists in a way that interests me. It's not product oriented like I think a male artist's approach is. It's much more organic.

DB: Have you always had this idea of the writer as being a part of his or her community? Was there some point where you went into this romantic phase of making the writer someone separate, better?

Smith: Well, I think I did go through that phase. Certainly for the last two years of college, maybe for the last three, I was very obnoxious. I went around taking myself very seriously. I wore a black turtleneck sweater, stayed up all night, and was just impossible to be around. Then later it happened that my first husband, James Seay, was in charge of the visiting writers who came to the various campuses where he taught, and I had to entertain these personages and I very soon realized how ridiculous a lot of this notion of a priestly vocation was when having to deal with writers, particularly poets. Poets are terrible. You know—the business of taking yourself very seriously while having little to do with what is really writing. I finally just got more interested in the work and much less in the personalities involved.

DB: Isn't the writer somehow special though? Don't you have the sense that they have one foot in and one foot out of the water?

Smith: Well, they do have to have one foot in and one foot out. They have to know enough about the community that they are writing about so they really are a part of it, and yet they have to have the necessary distance to write about it as well. They have to be involved, yet also distant. I was just reading about Faulkner on the plane—how though he lived in Oxford, Mississippi, all his life and was *of* that community, he wasn't really *in* it. I think all writers have to be separate from their community enough to see the community, enough to write about it. If you're completely enmeshed in something you can't see it. You have to have the distance.

DB: There has been some comment recently about women writers creating heroines that have harsher lives than the writers themselves. Do you think this is true of your writing, and do you feel this could potentially create or perpetuate a negative image of women?

Smith: Well, this is very difficult, and I have discussed this with several of my extremely political women friends. One of them came to me after I published the novel *Black Mountain Breakdown,* which I thought was very much a woman's statement, a feminist statement. It's a cautionary tale, if you will. It's a book about the dangers of being passive. At the end, the heroine is lying flat on her back being fed jello by other people. She is literally, completely, immobilized by her passivity, by her failure to act and take responsibility for her own life. So I thought I had made a really strong feminist statement. My friend came to me, furious, and said, "If you want to be a writer the most important thing you should do is be creating these women characters that are self-realized, functioning." But you know, that isn't the nature of fiction. The nature of fiction is people who can't cope as well as others. It's conflict. If everybody is just functioning great and they are all self-realized, it's not fiction. It's something else. I don't know what it is.

DB: It's like the Socialist Realism ideal that "great workers" should be the only subject of fiction.

Smith: And as a result, there's no story.

DB: So in regards to feminist literary criticism, at least radical criticism, there is a place where you part ways. Is it a matter of a differing concept of women as well as art?

Smith: I don't think so. No. I think it's just that you finally have to make a decision whether you want to voice a theme, whether you want to be didactic, or whether you want to tell a really good story, to meet the exigencies of storytelling. Whether you want the story to be good, or whether you want the message to be clear. I decided long ago that I wanted the story to be good—which means that the message is sometimes more ambivalent, more ambiguous, than it would be otherwise. Life is complicated and muddy, and so is good fiction. I don't believe that fiction serves a moral purpose. I think it's nice if people can learn something from fiction that is of value to them, but you should write an essay if you want to get something specific across. Or—at least in my own work—I feel I can't mix the two very well.

DB: Recently I've been reading John Gardner's *On Moral Fiction.* It's hard to pin him down on what he means by moral. The best I have been able to figure out is that moral literature enhances life. Is this definition enough for you?

Smith: That is good enough for me. And I think the highest calling of all is to write that kind of fiction. But referring back to the question you asked me earlier in the day—about Helen selling out at the end of my story "All the Days of Our Lives," how she refuses the promotion at her job and decides to let her next-door neighbor court her—actually my interpretation of the ending is even a little more cynical than yours. She is saying yes to life—but only to life such as she can conceive of it. Unfortunately, she can't conceive of being a self-realized person, and taking that job and doing this and that. Unfortunately, she's trapped, and when I wrote the story what I had in mind was that she is trapped forever—by these romantic ideas of love she has. That's why that rainbow is arcing over the lawn-sprinkler at the end. She is completely trapped by these notions of romance fed by the T.V. and the surrounding culture. So the ending's pretty cynical. She's saying yes, but she doesn't understand as much as maybe the reader does.

DB: She is trapped, but it's not necessarily because she's female. It's because as an individual she is satisfied with T.V. reality.

Smith: She doesn't know anything else. She hasn't had a chance.

DB: The protagonists in your stories do seem to exist on different wavelengths than the people surrounding them. Like Michael in "Not Pictured," they are always "staring away from the group." Are they misfits, or are they really each and every one of us seen from a fresh perspective?

Smith: I guess a story's main character is always the person who doesn't fit into the world of the story—for whatever reason. So each one, in his or her own way, is a kind of misfit. Sometimes at the end they will decide to just go on their way, and other times they will try to fit in—maybe like Helen is going to try to do. I am real interested in the idea that some people are just *separate.* I think from time to time we are all in a panic of what to do, how to be our own selves and yet function in society.

DB: I was very much taken with the point of view in your story "Cakewalk." Basically you have portrayed everything through the internal discourse of the proper older sister, everything is from her point of view. The sympathy, though, seems to shift to Florrie, the free-spirited younger sister.

Smith: I had so much fun writing that story. I loved Florrie. I had been to the North Carolina State Fair where they have a section for ornamental cakes, and there I saw all those cakes that are in the story. I saw Mount St. Helens before and after eruption. And I saw a woman that just started the whole story in my mind.

DB: And you recognized a fellow artist.

Smith: I thought so. Yeah, it seemed to me like that.

DB: I noticed that Michael in "Not Pictured" was the only instance in *Cakewalk* where you use a male persona. Was this conscious?

Smith: No, actually I have written a number of other stories where I have a male protagonist. It's just when you pick which stories are going to go in a book you try to pick the ones you think are better. Overall, I thought some of those stories with male protagonists didn't work as well for me. So it wasn't a conscious choice in that I was attempting to write a book specifically for women with all female protagonists.

DB: Why do you think the stories with male persona were less successful? What do you think of the current debate concerning the idea that males can't write about females and vice versa?

Smith: I don't know what to think about it. As a whole, I think it is sort of hogwash because I can think of a number of men who have written very well about women and vice versa. But I personally have trouble with the male protagonist. I really write much better from a female protagonist's point of view, but that's not true for numerous other writers.

DB: Last night you said that the story is always the teller's tale, that history—personal or social—is a subjective enterprise. In "Cakewalk" where the story belongs to the older sister, where she holds all the cards in her presentation of her younger sister, why is it that the reader comes away with a reading Stella did not intend?

Smith: I guess that's the convention of the unreliable narrator, of the unreliable narrative. If it is done right, the sort of "point man" can feel one thing and the reader can come away with the opposite. Certainly Stella's view of Florrie is very different from the view that I want the reader to take of Florrie and of Florrie's way of life.

DB: The old granny narrator in your novel *Oral History* says that she can't tell her own story, only that of others. Does this point out the situation of the novelist, turning attention away from his or her own life in order to better listen to the lives of others?

Smith: I think it does. What she goes on to say is that if I told my own story I would be all hemmed in by the facts. But to make a good story, you have to feel free to embroider, to do what you want. We were talking about the necessity for a little bit of distance in transforming autobiographical material into fiction. You can't do it while you're living there, while you're right in the middle of it. You have to get distance. And, of course, one of the oldest forms is making it be "about" somebody else. It's like when a student comes in your office and says I have a friend who. . . , and immediately you know that it is going to be them. But to tell it they have to have a "friend."

DB: So there is some sort of reticence involved in writing, that you don't necessarily want to divulge your own fragility, to disturb your own emotional privacy.

Smith: That's right. I think also that often it's because the writer doesn't really understand her own feelings. But if we write about it and have a character who is sort of bearing the freight, who is carrying the emotional baggage, then we can, in a way, deal with our own feelings and ideas without flat out having to take responsibility for them. It's kind of like cheating—and very interesting.

DB: Last night, there was indeed a shift between the way you talked while introducing excerpts from *Oral History* and when you were reading the text itself. Were you conscious while writing the book of tapping in on a voice distinctly different from your own? It might have been a voice you knew, grew up with?

Smith: No, I wasn't. But, no matter where you live or how you live your life, when it comes to writing there is something about the way you first heard language. How, when you are really into a story, this is the voice that often comes. I was just reading—again, because I was teaching it—Tillie Olsen's "Tell Me a Riddle." The voice is so good. It's almost like English in translation, which fits the fact that English is the woman protagonist's second language. It's so authentic. And who knows if when Tillie Olsen was writing it, she was or wasn't conscious of using those inversions and all those other particular ways of speaking. It's just that when you get deeply into those characters, that is how they speak, that is how they think.

DB: I've sometimes found that beginning writers have less trouble with dialogue than with the voice of the narrator. Is it because this narrational persona is hard to develop, because it is harder to listen to yourself than to others?

Smith: Well, I don't know. In my case, because early on I was a journalist as well as a writer of fiction, I made much more of a split between fiction and non-fiction than many other writers have done. In my own mind, I still feel I either write fiction which is not autobiographical in any traditional sense or I write non-fiction, which is often autobiographical. The two don't overlap with me. There is never a character that is thinly disguised as me. That is, there might be other people thinly disguised in my fiction, but I'm not there usually. However, Max Steele, whom I used to teach with at the University of North Carolina, has said that all fiction is finally autobiographical in certain senses that are not on a one-to-one relationship—"I am this character," or vice versa. I am also reminded of Anne Tyler's remark that she writes because she wants to have other lives. But I think a lot of what I do and what I have observed in my own students is that they will try on other hats in their fiction. They will write about somebody doing something that they would never do in their life, but are fascinated with. Or possibilities, things that might happen in a family that almost, but didn't, happen in theirs.

DB: Actually I had in mind something a little different. For instance, one student recently showed me a story that, for the most part, is composed of his grandfather telling various stories that I found out later the writer himself made up. That part of the story is absolutely wonderful. But when he quits the voice of the grandfather and shifts to being the narrator the level of the language drops drastically. I wonder if it might be a matter of him not treating his own presence there on the page as a character that needs to have its voice brought out as well as he has already created the voice of his grandfather.

Smith: I think so. I think we can't imagine our own characters as nearly as well as we can imagine others.

DB: In your stories, "The Seven Deadly Sins" and "Horses," I noticed a different aesthetic at work. They in some ways seem like prose-poems, and the landscape seems to be a bookish one—metaphor, cultural/scientific allusions, etc.—more language-based than narrational. Have you expanded on this type of writing since then? Or were they just glorious experiments?

Smith: Oh, every now and then I'll do something like that. I went through a phase in my twenties where I was particularly fascinated with Nabokov, Barthelme, Borges. I have always been really fascinated with language. Then, in the last ten years that fascination with language has been more centered in my culture, where I'm from. Taking those ideas and that close perception of language that I think you get when you read writers like Borges and putting it all back into your own past. So I did have an earlier phase, and those stories are from that early phase.

Thomas Clareson: One thing that comes through explicitly in the reactions to your earlier novels, but including *Oral History* too, is that you seem to have an affinity for fantasy.

Smith: I do, I guess. I grew up hearing ghost stories and also being real religious. People still believed in hauntings and weird stuff. They still do today. It does make life more interesting, not to mention fiction.

DB: There does seem to be a slight bit of magical realism in your story "Georgia Rose," where you have a juncture of Southern realism and the supernatural.

Smith: I love South American writers. I love magical realism, all that kind of thing. In both my novels *Oral History* and *Fair and Tender Ladies* there is a lot of that creeping through.

DB: Is Georgia Rose's problem then a supernatural one, or is it basically the result of her personality, a self-fulfilling prophecy? Is her interpretation of her fate her worst enemy?

Smith: Well, I don't know. I have to confess that I know somebody like that. Somebody who professes to be able to see the future and can never have very many successful relationships, because as soon as she embarks on one she sees how it's going to end and just abandons it.

DB: So—self-fulfilling prophecy or oracular insight?

Smith: I don't know, but I was just fascinated with the idea. In fact, I don't know her anymore; she was very difficult to be around. I guess you could say this was a psychological problem, but what if it really is true? That is where the starting point of the story is. What if this person really can see the future. Then what?

DB: In *Oral History* you had a chapter that would explain that the witch was not really a witch, but your editor talked you out of using it. Why is it that this sort of ambiguity is vital to the art of fiction?

Smith: The mystery?

DB: Right. The fact that she might be a witch and she might not.

Smith: It does make—and my editor said bluntly that it would make—a better book if you don't explain away the mystery. And that's always true, particularly when you think about what is good fiction and what is not. Good fiction allows a much larger space for the reader to live in, a much larger area of ambiguity, a much larger space to breathe. Bad fiction, like generic fiction, is tied up with a very pretty bow all the time, and there is no space for the reader to be a real participant in the story. So I think what you have to do is leave as large a space for the reader by telling as little as you can and still making the story coherent. The amount of that space is really the difference between good fiction and schlocky fiction: "Then when the rose bloomed I realized I loved him all the time."

DB: It sounds like you have a very fine editor. What is the publishing house?

Smith: It's Putnam's, which is not noted for terrific fiction. But on the other hand, what this editor has done, this Faith Sale, is really very, very good. Since you brought up the other kinds of fiction that I was interested in before, it is interesting to note she also edits Pynchon and Barthelme and Barth. It's real funny. It would be interesting to get inside her mind and see what in the world the kind of stuff I do has in common with these other people that she edits. Now she is editing Vonnegut. It's a strange thing.

DB: Did it take you a while to find her, to find an editor who liked your work enough to work with it?

Smith: Essentially I have had two completely separate careers. I was real lucky and started out publishing quite early—right after college. I was living in the Deep South, and just sort of sending these things to New York and they would sort of be published. I didn't pay much attention to it. Then there came this point where Harper & Row, who had published my first three novels, said—and this was at the point when publishing itself had changed a lot, and Harper & Row got into all this sort of bottom-line cost accounting— and they said, "Sorry, honey. You haven't sold any books. Too bad." And they turned down my fourth novel. My agent in New York, whom I didn't have a close relationship with either, said the same thing—"Oh well. Sorry, honey." So then I didn't have a publisher *or* an agent. It took a long, long time to find new ones. I found a new agent first. I decided this time I needed a close personal relationship, so I found this woman who liked the new novel, the fourth novel, a lot. But then she went to Tibet to find herself on her fortieth birthday and she never came back. So then I didn't know what to do, how long I was obligated to stay with her. So that lasted about a year. It took a long time, and during that period I had really decided to stop trying to write fiction, except just occasionally. Just go back to school and get another degree and teach special ed so I could make more money teaching. Just kind of forget the whole thing.

DB: A voice on the verge of being extinguished.

Smith: Absolutely, because I had written this novel and here I was sending it around myself. It had been to like fifteen publishers. Nobody was interested. Finally, a good friend of mine, Roy Blount, hooked me up with his agent who really liked the book, and she found Faith Sale. It was a real long time—six or seven years, I guess. At the time I thought I was just being self-indulgent, but I was writing some stories all along. And thank God for the *Carolina Quarterly,* because a couple of stories came out there and made me not quit altogether.

DB: Have you had other readers that have helped shape your texts?

Smith: Actually, Faith has been the most helpful. The agent that I have now, whose name is Liz Darhansoff, is also very active. She doesn't just say "yes I will do this or no I won't," but also suggests things. But those are the only two who have ever suggested substantive changes. I really think since I started working with them my writing has improved a whole lot.

DB: Having lived most of your adult life in a two-writer household, has that helped or hurt the creative process, or have both careers, both writing processes, been distinct from one another?

Smith: My first husband was a poet, and my second husband is a journalist. I think in both instances that it's been helpful. If I had been married to other people they might have expected me to keep house more, shall we say. I think it is very helpful indeed. Writing is like a plant that dies very easily when it feels like it is in hostile ground. I teach a lot of continuing education classes with women who want to write, but are made to feel like that is a very bizarre and indulgent thing for them to do. They feel a writer is somebody who is publishing, not somebody who is writing. If you are around other people who care about writing and reading and words, then you feel comfortable doing it. Obviously, if there is competition, then it becomes different. But to my mind, that just hasn't happened with me, because the genres involved are so different.

DB: So you haven't really shown each other your work much.

Smith: No. I just read my husband's column every week so I know what it is he is doing.

DB: Getting back to the idea of the writer and the community, does your sense of community extend through time as well? Do you feel yourself a part of the Appalachians in the time before you were born?

Smith: I suppose I do, really, because I have spent so much time with older people. I was an only child, and when I was growing up I spent an awful lot of time with my grandfather and great-uncles and so on. My grandfather was the County Treasurer for forty years and I used to go campaigning with him up in all the hollers. On Sunday afternoons we would eat Sunday dinner about six times because you would have to sit down with everybody and talk and eat all this chicken and dumplings. I really do have a sense of place that goes back beyond when I was born.

DB: Can you remember any of the first stirrings of this sensibility?

Smith: No, but I think I was a really weird child because I was always reading and mooning around, as my mother put it. I was always interested in old stuff. I remember one thing as a little child—I think maybe this is in one of those stories in *Cakewalk*—I remember I was looking at some old family pictures and being profoundly upset, at the age of seven or eight, at the pictures where I wasn't there. I kept saying, "But where am I?" because I felt like I should be there, even in the really old ones. Later, I remember realizing about death, but this fear of not being born was much greater than any fear of death afterwards. I felt like I should have been there somehow. So I did start out with that sort of feeling, and I don't know where it comes from. My father loves old men. He would just sit around with old men all the time. The courthouse is right across from my family's dimestore and they are always sitting over there chewing tobacco, and my daddy was always sitting there with them, and my Uncle Curt was always over there. It's the way I grew up.

Smith: Last night you said that "there is a heart of mystery in the past that we cannot put in a Museum of Appalachian Culture." Is it to get at this heart the major reason you write?

Smith: Yeah, I think so. I feel like this is true for all of us who are compelled to do the kind of thing I do. Appalachia is changing. In fifty years or a hundred years, everything will have changed drastically. Even now there are these dishes where people are getting T.V. reception in the most remote hollers and coves. So I do feel a sense of trying to catch it before it goes.

DB: Tom Clareson mentioned last night how your work remythologizes the South. I can see how it might be a different South than that of Faulkner or Tennessee Williams—

Smith (*laughing*): It bears almost no relationship whatsoever!

DB: But how is this a different mythology from female writers like Porter, McCullers, Welty, Shirley Ann Grau, and so on?

Smith: Well, I don't think it's different in the way they write about characters, perhaps. I think it is different in the culture that is dealt with, rather. Where I come from is a rougher culture. It really is. The country I am from is not full of well-educated people. We don't have Harvard-educated lawyers drinking bourbon on the veranda—we just don't have that. We don't have the wealthy, neurasthenic mother lying on the pillows and being fanned by the help. There are just lots of things that we don't have in terms of culture and centuries of breeding. Now, with Eudora Welty, I do feel more of a kinship with a lot of her characters because many of them are the simple people, Mississippi hill country rather than Delta, though with some of them you do get into the Delta. When I first read her work it was very important to me because it did seem to me suddenly, when I read her as a very young woman, that a lot of the people I knew could be in her stories. Not all of them, but some of them.

DB: Do you know Shirley Ann Grau's stories? Her swamp stories take place in the black communities along the Gulf Coast, especially in the *real* delta—where the river meets the sea and you can't tell the land from the water.

Smith: Yes, I have read several of her novels and I really like them, but again they seem very different. It seems to me like you could be asking her all these same questions and she would have her own kind of culture that she's working with.

DB: So this idea of your remythologizing the South needs to be tempered with the fact that there is no "South"?

Smith: No, I don't think there is *a* South. The South is several distinctly different things.

DB: Are you familiar with Jayne Anne Phillips' work? She seems to me to be writing out of the West Virginia side of the mountains. Do you feel any affinities?

Smith: I feel a whole lot of affinity. I know her and we have talked about this. I also feel a lot of affinity with Bobbie Ann Mason. I also felt a lot of affinity when I first read *The Dollmaker* by Harriette Arnow. It just knocked me out. I also feel a lot of affinity with Fred Chappell's work. I think Fred Chappell is really a genius. I love both his poetry and his fiction that comes out of Appalachia. This guy who killed himself—Breece D'J Pancake—I feel close to his stories. So there are people I have an affinity with, but they are specifically sort of Appalachian. Fred being the biggie, as far as I am concerned.

DB: When you want to reconstruct a given time, a landscape, do you approach the research of it in any specific way?

Smith: Yeah, I think what I do is try to saturate myself in it for a while. Even though I feel I don't need to, even though I think I know a whole lot of stuff—I know the language I am going to be using and so on—I will get several things to read that will be written in heavy dialect or will be about a certain time period. Just saturate myself in it. Get a whole bunch of books to look at. Pictures. I've got recordings of real old ballads and mountain songs. For instance, I was up in the mountains a couple of weeks ago and I went up to Hot Springs, North Carolina, which is like the end of the world. I wanted to find this house of this woman who as a child collected all these ballads. So I went over there and it turned out to be the wildest place. The house has been turned into an inn. There was this religion professor who got disaffected in the sixties and just left and moved into this remote house. He sort of runs it like an inn—but there is no sign, so most people who come there are on foot off the Appalachian Trail. He just cooks and whatever he cooks you can eat. His name is Elmer and he is real surly. If pressed, he will admit that yeah, he does rent out rooms. I'm going to go back there and stay. Once you happen upon it then you get to come, but otherwise you have to know somebody.

DB: Do you interview people with a tape recorder?

Smith: I do that all the time—whenever I'm home. It's just plain interesting. After you become an adult-child then you have to have something to do when you go see your parents. So what I do is just walk around and talk to people and write stuff down. Nobody seems to mind.

DB: They would probably prefer that you did it rather than someone from Schenectady, New York, coming down.

Smith: You know, my father is a very popular man in that county, and there is a high tolerance in Appalachia for deviant behavior. I've been kind of mooning around since I was born. Nobody expects anything different out of me. They don't mind, so it's all right.

DB: Yesterday on the way to the airport, Tom told the story of your going into a beauty shop for a shampoo to listen to the way they talk, their gestures, and so forth.

Smith: Actually, I worked there. I have a good friend who was a beautician in The Kroger Plaza Beauty Coiffure, and she gave me a job.

DB: Is it spelled with a K or a C?

Smith: No, it's spelled right, but it is named The Kroger Plaza Beauty Coiffure—that's its name. I was going to write this book, and I did have in mind a real tough beautician character, but I didn't know how to describe doing hair. I needed to get seeped in what somebody would be doing and thinking and seeing. So I asked this friend of mine who had been cutting my hair for years if I could come down and work at The Kroger Plaza. She said yes, so I worked there for three weeks. I had one of these things that says "Sharon"—it was great. But they would never let me do anything but shampoo. They wouldn't let me cut hair.

DB: Your mentioning last night that you were the aristocracy of your area was very interesting, how the townkids were privileged in some way.

Smith: It was because our fortunes didn't depend on whether the mines were working or not, the unions were striking, and so on. Our fathers just didn't get killed right and left, or lose their arms.

DB: So this was your distance, your one foot in and one foot out?

Smith: Yeah, it was. There was also the fact that, and I don't know why this happened, my father had notions that for some reason other people didn't have. My Uncle Vern went to the legislature and my father, when he was fourteen or fifteen drove him, and so during this time when he was in Richmond he got these ideas, I think. Then later he sent me off to St. Catherine's—although I didn't want to go away to high school. Nobody I had ever known had gone to prep school. But who knows where my father got the notions he did? People that he met, certain things that sort of appealed to him—God only knows. He went to William and Mary, actually for . . . well, actually only for football season. He played football and then took off. But he was different—at least a little bit. He had this book of one hundred poems and would go around and declaim all these poems he had memorized. He and my uncles would recite "The Road to Mandolay," and all this kind of stuff. So I grew up a little bit different because my household was a little bit different. My mother was from the eastern shore of Virginia, so she was called a foreigner. She's from Chincoteague Island, where the wild horses are. So even though my family is very heavily entrenched in the community, my growing up was different, even from my first cousins.

DB: In one of your stories from *Cakewalk,* this Paul goes away to college and his sister goes away to boarding school. The point of view is that of the common people who live in the company houses. Reading the story I had the feeling that living in the company houses was your upbringing, your point of view. But really *you* were the girl who went away to school.

Smith: Yeah, that would be more accurate. But I always felt sort of guilty about it because my cousins and best friends didn't. They stayed, so I felt a sort of split. I think all writers do. They feel that split between the community and themselves, or they wouldn't write—just to resolve that split.

DB: The stories in *Cakewalk* do seem to be a little more about townsfolk than in your novels. Is there a reason for this? Or does the setting seem to work better for you in a short story?

Smith: I think it's because the stories were written a little bit earlier. I think it took me a while to sort of go with my gut instinct. At the time I was also a reporter—as I mentioned before—and when I first started writing fiction I felt I needed to stick a little closer to the truth.

TC: So your house was in the town, and so you wrote from the town's perspective.

Smith: Right. I grew up in the town, but I still had all these deep mountain experiences, these talks with my older relatives. So then I started doing research, and decided I would just sort of make this leap and do it whether I had been there or not, just sort of assume I knew more than anyone else what it might be like or might have been like and just set some things back in time and in a different social situation. But, yes, I was a town girl, and there *is* a difference. Our house was down along the creek, in Grundy, and all the hollers run up from it. But I was always fascinated with the mountain kids, and went up with them and spent the night there. I had cousins that grew up in a company town and I would stay with them. But I was always the town girl, always writing, the one whose father was weirdly bookish, the one who was always sent away to school.

DB: Do the people you write about read your books?
Smith: Sure! Yeah!

DB: You said that in your father's store your books are on sale.
Smith: By the popcorn machine. That's where they are. And a lot of the time I'll send different people different books that have stuff they have told me in them. Nobody has ever objected. Well, maybe they do, but the fact is my father is a very popular man (*laughs*), so when he dies maybe I'll be sued by eighty-five people, but at the moment everyone seems to be pleased.

TC: But as you've said before, many of those eighty-five people would be related to you.

Smith: Right. I think maybe I told you that I always use real names of people, which always gets me in trouble to some extent. For instance, in *Oral History* I talk about the Cantrells—and there's a lot of Cantrells in that county.

DB: You were talking earlier about the goegraphical limitations of Appalachia, that many people haven't even left their own counties. Referring back to Helen in "All the Days of Our Lives," is this her problem, the fact that her only journeys are made on TV?

Smith: I write a whole lot about that kind of insular vision, being unable to imagine another life beyond. And I think it probably has to do with where I grew up. You can't imagine the way the mountains are there. My mother used to complain and complain because the sun didn't come up until eleven. It had to get really high before it hit your yard. So I could understand people who had this claustrophobic sense—whether it's cultural, biological or literally geographical. My dad was literally trying to propel me outside of that, and if he hadn't done this I don't know how I could have done any of the things I have.

DB: So could one of the distinctions between your South and all those other Souths be that where you come from the sun doesn't come up till eleven?

Smith: I think it is. I remember talking a lot about this with my first husband who was from Mississippi, from an equally poor kind of region. But he said the road there would go on as far as you could see, through the Delta, and you knew it went to New Orleans, and you knew it went all those places. It was just different. And even as a child he knew people who had been places and had come back. Also, there's such a lot of clannishness among the mountain people that's not amongst Deep South people. And a great deal of distrust.

DB: At least two characters in two different stories in *Cakewalk* hold back from further contact with people because they have already told too much about themselves. Do you think that goes back to that clannishness and distrust of others?

Smith: Absolutely. My cousin is a judge and has told me again and again that most murders up there are people killing other people in their own family, but if someone else kills someone in your own family, then you go kill him.

TC: The difference between domestic and foreign affairs?

Smith: That's right. We can take care of our own, thank you. Even if I hate my cousin, I get to kill him—not you. You can't touch him.

DB: You mentioned earlier about wanting to write a book about a raft ride down the Ohio and Mississippi you made with some women friends from Hollins College before your last year of school.

Smith: It's the idea of a voyage, I guess. We were all ready to graduate from college and were simple-minded in a way. Just sail down the Mississippi. And in the interim so many things have happened to us, so many things that have happened to other women our ages. I just think it would be interesting to read. Actually, it wasn't all women. There were two boys. Maybe some of the parents wouldn't let us go for whatever reasons without them. But when we built the raft it turned out too big. It was in the class of craft that the Mississippi River Commission says has to have a captain. So we were stuck. Here we were in Paducah. We had it built and were ready to go, but we couldn't because it takes years to get a captain's license. But it was wonderful. There was this old folks home there called the Irvin S. Cobb. And the doors of the Irvin S. Cobb opened—it had once been a hotel but now it was an old folks' home—and an incredible-looking ancient gentleman in a white three-piece suit emerged and said, "I will take them down the river." He was a retired pilot, and he took us. His name was Captain Gordon Cooper. He just sat there under an umbrella the whole way.

Lee Smith: An Interview

Pat Arnow / 1989

From *Now and Then*, 6 (Summer 1989), 24–27. Copyright © 1989. Reprinted by permission of Pat Arnow.

Q: One thing I've noticed in your books, you use a lot of folklore. For instance, one of your characters puts an axe under the bed to cut the pain of childbirth. I was wondering where you got this kind of thing.

A: Well, I grew up in Grundy, Va., which is in Buchanan County in Southwest Virginia, and I was an only child, which means that I spent less time with other children and more time listening to old people. Although I was an only child, I had a real big family there. They were all real talkers. We would all get together, I mean we had Sunday dinner at my grandmother's, and then we had all these family picnics at the Breaks Park, and I just heard a whole lot of that stuff.

I lived in town. My father ran the dime store, but there was just one school. And so you go spend the night with people up in hollers.

And my grandfather was in politics for 40 years. He was a treasurer, and my whole family—all of them were into politics in the Democratic party— and I used to love to go with them around politicking where you just go, and you eat on Sundays at about five different houses, convince them to vote for who you want.

And then later, in more recent years, I've gotten interested in reading anything I can get my hands on of recorded folklore, oral history, whatever. It's my big passion.

Q: How are people taking your books up there?

A: Well, I don't know. Nobody ever mentions them hardly. It's real nice.

My mother died last spring. My dad still lives in the house I was born in and grew up in, and since I am an only child, I go back all the time. And so, what I've done for years and years is just write down stuff that interests me when I'm there. There are lots of people I talk to regularly, who tell me stuff. They'll say, "Well, now I've got something else to tell you about, curing such-and-such." But my books don't seem to be an issue.

Q: Oh, so they're not reading them when they come out and getting on you about them?

A: No, no. Everybody's real nice. The English teacher had me come and talk at the high school. I'm going back in May for three days to do stuff in Richlands and Grundy, and around that whole area. Up in Abingdon. I try to be as faithful as I can to the region and to the people.

Q: Do people ever come up and say, "Well, that was my sister," or . . .

A: No. But what I do, either I make them all up or I put them in whole cloth and everybody knows who they are, but they don't object.

This one book, *Black Mountain Breakdown,* was the one where I did put in a few people, community figures. Everyone would probably know who they were, but they're very lovingly portrayed, which is the way I feel about them. Nobody's ever bothered me about it.

Q: How long have you been in Chapel Hill?

A: I've been in Chapel Hill a long time—16 years. And I've never set anything in Chapel Hill in terms of writing.

Q: Any plans to?

A: No. I don't know why. I mean, I know that a university town is full of stories, too, but they may not be ones I can tell. You can't choose your material so much as it chooses you.

I'm gonna try real hard. I did try real hard with one book, *Family Linen.* I got about as far out of the mountains as Martinsville. I got out to (Interstate) 81.

Q: Are you noticing as you keep coming back to Grundy that there is more homogenized culture?

A: Yeah. I think the first thing that I tried to write which was strictly Appalachian was *Oral History,* and that's because I had a closet full of materials and tapes and books that I found incredibly compelling. I think it was when all the fast food stuff came in on Route 460 around the bend in the river from my parents' house. Suddenly that, and then those big dishes that you see everywhere, and you know that everybody's got TV, and that means that very soon all the kids are going to sound like Dan Rather. All the stuff with the language is going to be lost.

I suddenly did see this enormous homogenization about, oh, 15 years ago, I guess—or 10 years ago. I had been writing ever since I was a child, but I began to feel like I wanted to record my perceptions of that area. And certain kinds of people because that was going to be a thing of the past.

Q: Would you say that a 12-year-old in Grundy today is going to have a different voice than yours?

A: Oh, absolutely. Yeah.

Q: Then it won't be much of a mountain voice?

A: Well, I don't think it will be as much of a one, no. My parents were storytelling parents. A lot of people my age who are still in the mountains, only a few of them are consciously into this kind of thing. We just don't sit around and talk like we used to.

Q: You mean that if you do it, it's because you choose to do it? You have to think about it. It doesn't come naturally?

A: Yeah, telling stories down from generation to generation is not any longer a way of life. It still happens in some families because some people care about it. We've all gotten so many of our icons on TV now. I mean the kids are much more likely to get their role models from a TV show than they are from their grandmothers.

Q: Is this a problem with your students? Are you finding it hard to get them to write about their personal experience?

A: Well, no, see, because the students I get, they're already interested in writing. They don't have to be in my class. They're the ones that are predisposed to think about their experience and their families. But the average undergraduate that I encounter when I travel around the country is predisposed to think about how to make money, and that's a whole different kind of thing. I do think there are a lot of elements in our culture that came in with the Reagan years that are anti-history, and anti- a sense of community the way we have known it. There is that materialistic tone and tenor that goes against all that.

I feel like the books that I've written, which are particularly Appalachian books, are the kind of documentation that goes on in Appalachian Studies. I just try to use things the way they were and put them in their context so that anybody that is interested can go there and find them.

Q: I noticed that in the books I was going through this morning.

A: Yeah, there's too much information really, because I'm just fascinated with the way things were and the processes that the people have used, like making soap, and it gets in the way of the narrative. But I just love it. I'm fascinated with all of that.

Q: Do you think of yourself as an Appalachian writer particularly?

A: Yeah.

Q: I've heard you called a Southern writer.

A: There's a huge difference between a Southern writer and the kind of writer I am. For one thing, so much of what I think of as the canon of Southern literature does have to do with race and racial guilt. I'm talking about Eudora Welty or William Faulkner. I mean, we just don't have that. Or at least when I was growing up, I just didn't have a sense of that. And also, I never had a sense of an aristocracy. You know, there was nobody with big columns on their house, with lots of money or black mammies.

I just don't think of myself as a Southern writer. I really don't, because the class system was so different, the money situation was so different, even. Well, just the whole social structure was quite different, I think, from the deep South. I have spent some time—I lived in Alabama and was married for a while to a man from Mississippi. I see it as very different.

The family roles are different. There's not much similarity between a novel that comes out of Appalachia and a novel that comes out of the South.

Q: So you're seeing this as a distinctive region.

A: I think so. People who are not from the South maybe find it harder to understand the delineation because it all sort of sounds the same to them, but it's not the same—even the language is different.

And it is quite different. I think of Fred Chappell as an Appalachian writer. I think of Bobbie Ann Mason.

Q: Though she's from Western Kentucky.

A: Yeah, but still it's the same kind of language. It's got the same sound. It's the same kind of people.

Q: Do you have any trouble gaining acceptance from the mainstream kind of publishing and audiences?

A: No. I've been lucky, though. I was lucky because I started writing at a time when it was a lot easier to get published than it is now. I have students who are having trouble getting what I think are wonderful novels or stories published, or having them come out and having them not receive attention. It's just the whole cultural situation. It's just much tougher now than it was almost 20 years ago when I started publishing.

Q: And Appalachia was a little more trendy then, too, wasn't it?

A: Actually, the first things I did were not specifically Appalachian. They were just sort of, oh, "young-person-finds-her-way-in-the-world." They were typical first-writer things. It was just that, I wish I could get the statistic exact,

but there's something like 70 percent less fiction, serious fiction, being published now than there was then.

Q: Even in magazines?

A: Oh, yeah. Especially in magazines. It's real hard to get serious fiction
published today because there's almost no place that will publish it. You
know, everything's gotten generic and tacky and non-fiction-filled. That's
why I'm so pleased to see the growth of regional presses, so that some of our
young writers will get published.

I have been real lucky. There are a lot of people who like to read about a
time that doesn't exist any more. You know, all these people in their New
York apartments are listening to Garrison Keillor, and sometimes they'll write
me a letter or two—people I would think would never read anything that I've
written. And they like it. I think that a lot of people are feeling put off by the
way they live, the place they live at and their dislocation. So I don't think
that being a regional writer automatically cuts you off from a mass market.

Q: You don't think publishers are feeling any kind of pressure?

A: Oh, hell no. They love regional stuff. They love Southern stuff. The
problem is that they just publish so few titles in serious fiction, period. It's
much easier, I think, to get a novel published if it's a good regional novel,
today, right now, in New York, than if it's a good novel about life in New
York.

Look at *Lonesome Dove*. Larry McMurtry's book. I mean, people do like
to read about small towns in regional states. I don't think that that's a drawback at all right now for the young writer.

Q: Are you continuing to write about the past now, or are you going to
work on some contemporary themes?

A: I seem to be writing some stories right now, so I suppose the next thing
that I would have out would be some kind of a collection of stories, and they
are more contemporary and less rooted in place than *Fair and Tender Ladies,*
which was my last novel. I do worry that I'll get stuck and not be able to
write anything else except from a first-person woman's voice of 50 years ago
in Buchanan County because that's what I'm most comfortable with. So I'm
trying real hard now to write some stories that are contemporary.

Q: I was talking about doing this interview, and one person said she was
not disturbed about the sameness of your times and places, but was bothered

that all the protagonists seem to be good-looking blonde or red-headed women. She said, "Ask her why they always have to be good-looking."

A: Well, that's interesting. I don't know. The writer is the last to know. I mean I have absolutely no idea. But tell her that I'll write a plain one immediately!

Q: A Jane Eyre type.

A: Right, exactly.

Q: O.K., I'll pass that along. So you're trying some different kinds of stories?

A: Yes. When you're writing a lot, which I do, you just don't stop to think what you're up to, because you're just compelled to do what you do. But several people have mentioned to me—friends, not critics particularly—that why don't I write about men more, that I seem to write entirely about women. I'm working on that. I'm going to consciously have at least half of them from the point of view of men. It's like these pretty red-headed women. I do think that you can fall into patterns. That's one of the big problems with American writers; we tend to write the same stories over and over. And I don't want to do that. So with the stories that I'm writing now, I'm gonna follow my face some. I just sent my agent one of them, and she called me yesterday and said, "What the hell is this!" Because I don't want to do the same thing. It's hard not to. Usually you get a thing that you know how to do, and you're tempted to keep doing variations on it. I mean, Hemingway wrote one book, right? Which is a problem in American writing, I think. More so than elsewhere.

Q: I read about *Fair and Tender Ladies* that it was inspired by picking up a packet of letters from a garage sale.

A: Yes. It was a flea market, actually, in Greensboro.

Q: I was wondering if you actually used any of those?

A: No, because they were not Appalachian, for one thing. And I had this whole body of stuff I wanted to use. And so I wanted to have my writer be set there. But I was struck. They were from a woman to her sister, and she was a woman who had not had any particular education. I was just struck how every now and then she'd have this real literary image, or striking turn of phrase or something. And I just got real interested in the idea of somebody's letters being a sort of work of art. You know, letters over their whole lifetime. Is it art because there's a critic somewhere who perceives it as art?

Or is it art because it just is? I don't know. It's just some sort of aesthetic thing that I've had in my mind for a while that interests me.

And I have felt that there are a lot of other interesting stories in issues having to do with women and our creativity in particular. I think there's less of an emphasis upon the end product in the artistic work that women do, so often the process is what's important rather than the product. It's why in that book I was trying to show that the writing of the letters was more important than the letters. It's like the knitting of a sweater, the making of the quilt, and that kind of thing, you know, that something is art even though it's not perceived as public art. It's the difference between monumental sculpture and needlepoint.

Q: One is considered fine art and one's like folk art.

A: Yeah. I read this wonderful book recently of art criticism by two women and they point out in it that we all use the term "old masters." Where are the "old mistresses?" (The book is *Old Mistresses: Women, Art and Ideology* by Rozsika Parker and Griselda Pollock.)

Q: Well, they were making quilts.

A: That's right. Or they were painting miniatures. You know, they were encouraged to do pastels, miniatures and portraits as opposed to big huge things. And (there's the issue of) where you do it. Do you do it in your studio with apprentices, or do you do it at home?

Another thing I had in mind with *Fair and Tender Ladies,* I had the enormous pleasure some years ago of coming upon Lou Crabtree in a class that I taught in Abingdon, and she had been at that time writing for 50 years. She read this thing in class, and it just knocked me out. I said, "Do you have any more stuff?" And she said, "Why, yeah," and she came in the next day with a suitcase full of this stuff that she'd been writing and writing and writing. I was just so stunned by the idea of writing not for publication, but writing as Flannery O'Connor has said as a "habit of being." Her book, *Sweet Holler: Stories,* was published by LSU (Lousiana State University Press) with a lot of those things in it.

Q: It was interesting in *Fair and Tender Ladies,* this woman got herself trapped and couldn't do anything else. The letters were her creative outlet maybe. If she had come out of it and gotten published, it would have seemed less true to me. Even though Lou Crabtree actually did. But it's true that someone that talented could get that trapped.

A: Well, I think it happens all the time. All the time.

Q: It probably happens to men as well.

A: Of course it does. But you do have to write about what you know about, and I know more about women and their psychology at different points in their lives than men.

Q: Do you call yourself a feminist?

A: Yeah. I do. Although I have not been as actively political as I would like to have been. Oh, yeah, definitely am.

Q: What kind of stories are you doing now?

A: Well, the ones I'm trying to do right now are not specifically Appalachian. I'm looking at one right now which is about a young couple in Raleigh. But it's not the academic environment, which I just cannot seem to deal with.

Q: Do you read work about academic environments?

A: I read pretty much everything I can get my hands on.

Q: But that's not something you'd care to write about?

A: There's things that I'd like to read about, but then when I get ready to write my characters seem to be not in academia. I have also been accused, in addition of not writing about men, of being anti-intellectual. I don't know. You just have to write about whatever compels you, I think, to do any kind of decent job at it. Otherwise, it's artificial.

Q: At Raleigh, do you just teach writing courses?

A: Well, I teach other stuff, too. Various kinds of literature, which I have no business doing. You know, I don't have a Ph.D. or anything. I'm going to be in Virginia next year, though, at Virginia Commonwealth University in Richmond just doing a visiting year.

Q: Any chance you might come back to the mountains at some point?

A: Yeah, I'd really like to do that.

Q: To teach, or to live?

A: Either or both.

On Regionalism, Women's Writing, and Writing as a Woman: A Conversation with Lee Smith

Virginia A. Smith / 1989

From *Southern Review*, 26 (1990), 784–95. Copyright © 1990. Reprinted by permission of Virginia A. Smith.

VS: Richmond's *Style Weekly* said that "if you're going to read just one book by Lee Smith, make it *Fair and Tender Ladies*." How would you account for the success of that novel?

LS: Well, I don't know. But I feel that for the first time since I started writing I didn't really write that book. I felt like it just started coming to me. And it was very weird because with the three novels before that I had "wangled" one way or another a semester off from teaching in order to write a first draft. But suddenly I just started writing *Fair and Tender Ladies* with no time off from teaching and it came so easily. I just sat down and it wasn't like writing a novel; it was like writing some letters, and it was coming so easily that I got really freaked out, and I never did take time off, because I just didn't want to monkey with whatever it was . . .

VS: Whatever the chemistry was that was allowing this combination?

LS: Yes, with whatever it was that was happening. I know one thing that has to do with it some is just that my mother was dying while I was writing that book, and we were having some problems with our teenagers and different things. One thing I've always done in my own writing (and I think I know a lot of people who do) is to write to create a role model for myself. With Ivy Rowe, I really needed to be making up somebody who could just take whatever "shit hit the fan." Sort of assimilate it and go on.

VS: You were writing a role model? A woman you needed to be?

LS: I think I was. I didn't know it at the time. I just was totally compelled to write the book. When you have people in hospitals, you can't go out of town, and you just spend a lot of time right there, and it is when you most desperately need an escape, too. Having a novel there to write is like an open door that you can just go into, in a way. So there were a whole lot of reasons why I was driven to write that book having nothing to do with the book. . . .

VS: But what about the enormous appeal that novel has for readers, and the fact that critics have decided this is your best fiction to date?

LS: I have no idea, because when I finished it I didn't have a clue whether it was any good or not, and I really didn't even care. The whole time I was writing it I just knew it was something I had to write, and I just didn't care if it was too regional, too personal. I knew it didn't have a plot—it was just some woman's life from the beginning to the end, and that's what I wanted to do. Later I realized why I was writing it. But, for the reader, I didn't have a clue.

I have gotten more mail about this book; I have gotten a whole lot of mail, which is really strange. And interestingly enough a lot of it has come from women who have some terrible long-term situation to deal with. So there is some sense of that as a strength-giving book, or Ivy as a figure that you can use for that. I really have had a number of letters from people who were in the middle of a terrible divorce or people who have a handicapped child or—something.

VS: Well it is a strength-giving book. I'd like to talk about Ivy as an empowering figure for women and about female voice. Harvard psychologist Carol Gilligan has noted that women's "different voices" (different from men's) involve "not only the silence of women but the difficulty in hearing what they say when they speak." Will you comment on your treatment of female silence and women's different voices?

LS: I know that one thing I was really really trying to do in writing *Fair and Tender Ladies,* and to some extent in creating some of the earlier women, was to validate my mother's life, to validate the lives of these women I had known who had spent their lives doing for others, essentially—kind of like Ivy does. This is a creature who is totally ignored . . .

VS: By our culture, in fiction, both—?

LS: Yes, both. Particularly ignored by our culture. I just wanted to include the major events of a traditional woman's life—like childbirth, love, divorce, death, children leaving home, children coming back, illness, whatever . . .

VS: The rites of passage for traditional women or for mountain women?

LS: Yes, for traditional women. I write it about a mountain woman because that is what I know; that is the voice that comes to me most easily. But I meant it to be about and for any woman. I have always been really interested in this notion of women's creativity as being quite different from men's. It is not public; it's so rarely public.

VS: But it is very ritualistic. . . .

LS: Right, it's very ritualistic. Ivy's writing of the letters to me corresponds with, say, this aunt that I have who has made quilts and afghans or someone who is a wonderful cook. This goes back, too, to my early fascination as a girl with Virginia Woolf, who talks a lot about women artists. You know, Mrs. Ramsay and the perfect dinner party. . . .

VS: And that *is* a form of art, of domestic art, which is really the theme that ties the stories of *Cakewalk* together. Right?

LS: I think it is. And I've been real interested in it for a long time—all through *Cakewalk* and all through everything. And so then *Fair and Tender Ladies* was, maybe, as far as I can go with that.

VS: Could be. There's something else that you do in your fiction that is also going on in academic criticism. Much of the archeological project of feminist criticism over the last decade has been to dig up, to recover, to give voice to all those lost or erased women's stories. Clearly your creation of Ivy Rowe was an extension of your interest in Appalachian history, texts, and voices. But to what degree was your creation of "an ordinary woman's ordinary life" also influenced by your desire to create a sustained and powerful female voice?

LS: Yes, well that is really what I wanted to do. I just get so *tired* of these books that are full of "events," because I just don't think that that much happens to most people; and yet their lives are not less valid.

VS: Can you give examples of those kinds of novels?

LS: I was just thinking about books that sell a lot, books that always have huge *plots*. . . .

VS: International intrigue?

LS: Yes. And in most of our lives just not all that much happens.

VS: But if we think of much canonized American literature and the sense of adventure in Melville, Hemingway, and Twain that we were taught to read as an embodiment of *the* important American myths. . . .

LS: Yes. But women don't go to sea, women don't go to war. . . .

VS: Women were erased from those books.

LS: That's right. But I have always still been interested in the notion of heroes and heroism, and I read a lot of Joseph Campbell. So I guess I wanted to create a woman [in Ivy Rowe] who would have a heroic journey. But you had to put that journey in Ivy's terms and on her turf.

VS: And Ivy's is very much of an epic journey.

LS: That's right. I'm not unaware of the significance of Ivy's getting to the top of the mountain and all that.

VS: So in *Fair and Tender Ladies* you wrote with that sense of mythic magnitude which *includes* a woman's rites and journey. . . .

LS: Well actually I had been thinking about all this for a long, long, long time, and I had done a lot of research. I had taped people, and so I knew there were a lot of things [on tape] that I liked and might use. This woman had told me about the first time she saw the electric lights come on across the other mountains. . . .

VS: Oh, and that's a great scene.

LS: Yeah, isn't that great? I loved that. And so she told me that and I knew there was a lot I wanted to put in. And then there was this thinking I had been doing for a long time about myth and journeys . . .

VS: And women's lives?

LS: Yes, and myth and women's lives, and about the different possibilities of heroism. But you never know until you start writing what you are going to write; I mean, you think you know. I try to write as much about it as I can before I write, but you are never really sure. So [with *Fair and Tender Ladies*] I was just lucky. I think a lot of it has to do with luck. I think writers might have a certain idea at certain times in their lives, but they might not be ready to write the book, and they lose the idea and never do.

VS: *Fair and Tender Ladies* had to be a book written by a mature woman. Is that what you are saying?

LS: Well, I think so, because it takes Ivy into old age, which is something I couldn't have envisioned very well even ten years ago or before I sat at these bedsides of various dying people.

VS: In a conversation we had last year you referred specifically to *Fair and Tender Ladies* as a "woman's book." Numerous contemporary women writers are less at ease than you are with the term "woman writer."

LS: I am very much at ease with it. There are some books that I think of particularly as men's books, like *The Sports Writer* by Richard Ford. It's excellent, but it's a men's book. But I could enjoy reading that, so men could enjoy reading *Fair and Tender Ladies.*

VS: But some women writers view the term "woman writer" as yet another way to ghettoize or trivialize female cultural production. Can you discuss the ways in which you feel that *Fair and Tender Ladies,* or much of your fiction, is women's fiction?

LS: Well, I am probably not going to say anything that is going to be global enough for you to quote. I just feel that everybody has to write out of their own experience.

VS: But what does the term "woman writer" mean for you?

LS: Well, everything I write is real close to the senses and it's real close to *my* senses—and I'm a woman. So therefore I, and my writing, are real bound up in the body, to a big extent. I have come to realize it more and more in working with these students who don't seem to have *any* senses at all. And so it makes me realize that my work is more like that than some. I am just really caught in with my body in terms of my writing and in terms of sensory images.

VS: In the same way that Ivy Rowe is really tied into her body. Her self-narrated "passages" are always rendered through the body.

LS: But some people see this insistence on the sensual body as a real failure of imagination—that is, as a failure in not being able to write better men or to imagine men more fully, and I think that's true. . . .

VS: Well, plenty of male writers haven't been able to write very good women, either. But until very recently they have rarely been accused of not being able to transcend their sex.

LS: My writing is just real physical to me, even to the extent that I write in longhand.

VS: Longhand? No word processors for you?

LS: No, never. Everything about it is just completely physical, and I think that has something to do with it. I try real hard in this new book of stories— particularly there's one man that I got really attached to. And I'm going to try real hard in this next novel that I write, because I think that it *is* a failure of imagination. But my writing time has always been shorter than I wanted it to be. Maybe I just need to take some more time and really work with it, to try and imagine men better.

VS: I don't think it is a failure of imagination as much as a choice about craft, focus, vision. And you have created a variety of real and compelling male characters—Richard Burlage in *Oral History,* Sean in *Family Linen,* Oakley in *Fair and Tender Ladies.*

LS: But I am linked in a physical sense to a woman's body and a woman's perceptions. And it's interesting because I have these really intellectual kids in graduate school; they've been in school now for, what, sixteen years? But I say to them, "What does it *smell* like in this story? What does stuff *look* like?" And they just don't have a clue; it's like they are cut off from their bodies in this funny kind of a way.

VS: For me, probably *the* distinguishing characteristic about Lee Smith as feminine writer is your use of the female body. Hélène Cixous said that "women must write through their bodies" in their invention of a new language. Many American feminists were very uncomfortable with this—it seemed essentialist and determined and biologically based in an era when cultural feminists were very much divided over whether they wanted to celebrate or downplay sexual differences. But I definitely see your writing evolving out of a woman writing her own body. You are, as well, involved in creating women characters who struggle to write and speak about their bodies. And you are always concerned about what that means.

LS: I'm delighted to hear you say that, Virginia, and I hope that that's true. But you don't know what you're doing when you are doing it. Recently I was at a writer's conference with Clyde Edgerton. When someone asked him some question about his work he said, "Well, I don't know. It's like when you are a duck and you are flying in a 'V,' you don't know you're in the 'V.' Somebody else has to be down on the ground to see that." There are questions which are real hard to answer; this is just the way I write. And after you have been doing it for fifteen or twenty years, it gets real hard to say why.

VS: But women and the body are dominating your fiction. It's there from the start in *The Last Day the Dogbushes Bloomed* and *Something in the Wind.* Women writing their own bodies and speaking about their own bodies begin to emerge somewhere around *Cakewalk* and *Oral History.* And some of that is real dark stuff about postpartum depression and railing against the body. But Ivy Rowe, it seems to me, finds a way to take charge of her body and to celebrate it. Right on through puberty, pregnancy, postpartum depression, her affair, her aging, the voice we hear seems to say, "There's a lot about this life in the body I don't like—but this is much of what I am about."

LS: Yes, yes, that is exactly what I was trying to do with her; that is exactly what I was trying to show. I saw her as victorious, finally. Despite all the hardships that she had to put up with, she was really in harmony, in tune with her body and also with her world. With the natural world. And I really liked her husband, Oakley; I thought Oakley was just fine.

VS: You did something really gutsy in *Fair and Tender Ladies* when Ivy's baby daughter dies. In Sue Miller's *The Good Mother,* where the daughter doesn't die but is removed from the mother in a custody decision . . .

LS: Well, that's the worst thing that can happen.

VS: Right. Not only for a mother, but also it has become a kind of codified punishment to women in literature. You allow Ivy to risk a moral and ethical credibility when she writes to Silvaney that even after Lu Ida's death, if she had the affair with Honey Breeding to do all over again, she would do it. You refused to let Ivy *feel* punished for her extramarital sexuality—that was such a gutsy risk to take in that novel.

LS: Actually, I know of somebody who had that kind of thing happen. And she is just fine now.

VS: But you let Ivy remember and affirm the affair even as she is mourning the death of her baby—a death linked to Ivy's absence from home. You could have lost some readers there.

LS: Oh I did, I did! That really put a lot of people off. I have given readings where people have told me that at that point they quit reading the book. In fact, one woman came up to me before the reading and said, "I just want you to know I read *Fair and Tender Ladies* until I got to that point, and I put the book down and I never finished it." And this is the weirdest thing— she said: "And I just want you to know that I am not going to stay for this reading, either."

VS: You allowed Ivy to become the ultimate bad woman.

LS: I know: the "bad mother."

VS: You establish the connections in the novel between Ivy's passion, negligence, the child's death. I hung in there with Ivy, but I have to admit to a gnawing judgment of her. I've heard this from other readers, too. Not idealizing or censoring her was a gutsy step to take in writing a first-person woman's narrative.

So many of your female characters go mad—suffer breakdowns, are hospitalized, have visions, hear voices. What are you doing with that? It's a frightening thread in your work.

LS: I grew up to some degree feeling that if you didn't fit right in, if you didn't conform, you would go crazy. My mother, see, came from eastern Virginia and she was always trying to be a lady, and there was this notion that if you fit right in, if you were a lady and went to a nice school and married a doctor and so on, that that was somehow comforting and would somehow keep you from going crazy. But the idea of being artistic was being outside of norms in a certain way, and it was sort of dangerous. In fact, one of the women I knew who was sort of arty, one of my mother's friends, was mad as a hatter.

And also there is a lot of mental illness in my family. Once when I was a girl, both my mother and my father were in separate psychiatric hospitals at the same time. My father was overworked and had a nervous breakdown; my mother was always anxious and had colitis and every now and then would get into a "state." I was fourteen; I was staying with my aunt when my mother was in Charlottesville in the hospital. I remember going down there to see her with my aunt. Her doctor was absolutely wonderful. He took me out to lunch and—nobody ever said this to me before—he said to me, "I guess you're wondering if you're going to go crazy, huh?" And of course I was just *dying* to talk about that, but I wouldn't say a word. And he said, "Well, chances are, no." And then he went on, blah, blah, blah, and I was thinking, "Whew."

VS: So you carried around a firsthand experience of the southern Gothic?

LS: Oh, absolutely, yes, yes, absolutely! That was always in my family, on both sides. And there is something scary, too, about deciding to become a writer or a painter, because you are not within comfortable boundaries. You think, "Oh, God, what if I push too far at this stuff—will I go crazy?"

VS: Did it happen?

LS: No, it hasn't happened.

VS: Because you could be writing your madness away?

LS: That was what I was going to say. Probably for me, writing has been totally therapeutic, because anything that I am really worried about I just write about. So I never have to act it out in my life. In my actual life I have been oddly sane. I was very lucky, I guess, to stumble early on to this means of dealing with things.

VS: Do you think that women's voices are effectively infiltrating the contemporary canon?

LS: Oh yes, I do think so.

VS: Can you talk about that—where you see it, how you see it happening?

LS: The whole notion of this inviolate male canon is really crumbling. I see it with the graduate students that I have. So many of them are very interested in South American literature or Third World writing and all sorts and forms of women's writing. All these people used to be so revered—for instance, Hemingway. Now the interest is just in Hemingway among many others.

VS: Do you think that kind of thinking is going to change the notion of establishing a canon at all? Do you think that we are approaching a way of thinking about and teaching literature that is anti- or at least non-canonical?

LS: I think that we already are. But I think that a lot of people are very threatened by that. Threatened by people like Jane Tompkins, or by the fact that at Duke people are studying Louis L'Amour. There's always that sort of excessiveness or overcorrection. But that sort of thing needs to be done. . . .

VS: You mean cultural studies, the academe taking popular culture seriously as a discipline, as part of the curriculum?

LS: That's right. All of that is really important. Of course I have benefitted from it a lot, because the notion now is that regionalism is no longer a pejorative term. It is just giving voice to an undervalued segment of culture. That's good. But twenty years ago the term "local color" would have applied to me.

VS: So do you think that the status and identity of the southern writer has changed because of the new value placed on "regional writing" or "alternative traditions"?

LS: I think so, partially. Now, people want to have a specific voice which is separate from other voices. I think that that is prized now rather than looked down upon.

VS: So historically the regional writer has never been accorded universal status, has always been considered a "local colorist?"

LS: Well, except for Faulkner, rarely. He's the great exception. Although now a lot of these writers, like Ellen Glasgow, for instance, are being reevaluated.

VS: You participated this past summer in a workshop which had as its subject the southern writer and southern literature, isn't that right?

LS: That's right. The Chapel Hill Conference on Southern Writers.

VS: What does "southern writing" now mean?

LS: To me, it doesn't mean anything much in terms of theme. It just means the particulars of the novel; it really means setting and it has something to do often with voice, with colloquial voice, with conversational tone, with old-style storytelling, with things told at some length, not just straight to the point, so it has to do with narrative strategy, I guess.

VS: And Louis Rubin has said that, too.

LS: Yes. But as far as theme, I don't think that there is any delineation whatsoever. Any writing that is worth its salt is about the same stuff.

VS: Yes and no. Racial issues appear to be absent from your fiction, as they are also from the fiction of other contemporary southern women writers—from Bobbie Ann Mason's work, for instance, and from that of Gail Godwin, until her most recent novel, *A Southern Family.* Can you explain that? Why, for instance has race dominated the work of Faulkner and Styron, yet appeared less central now?

LS: Well, that's because there were no black people in the county where I grew up. I never saw any black people, I was never aware of them, and they don't in any way shape—particularly with the Appalachian things I've written—I mean, I think in *Fair and Tender Ladies,* because I wanted to have a company town I put in some black people in the company town. But I never really saw any. I remember being taken by my parents to Richmond when I was a little girl and they said, "Now you are going to see some Negroes; don't point."

VS: Richard Burlage says the same thing to Dory in *Oral History* when he's telling her about the train ride to Richmond.

LS: That's where that came from; that's why I put that in. And so there is a big difference to my mind—if we are saying, for instance, that there is such a thing as southern fiction—between what I think of as Appalachian and Deep South. For the Appalachian writer, there is an absence of racial guilt. For us—the people I think of as Appalachian writers, like Bobbie Ann Mason and me and Jayne Anne Phillips and Fred Chappell—we don't deal with that racial guilt. We don't come from a society that has a real upper class and a servant class. We just didn't have it—everybody was poor.

VS: So that the notion of class and race which dominate in Faulkner . . .

LS: Dominate.

VS: And which are both fundamental to Styron's work . . .

LS: Absolutely. And he's from a little bit south of here.

VS: So you are distinguishing between Appalachian, Deep South, and East Tidewater fiction, and you are using as a major mark of that distinction the degree to which racial guilt and class structure permeate the fiction?

LS: Right. We have none of either one.

VS: You certainly don't see either of those issues get played out in Mason's fiction.

LS: Of course not. Everybody is the same. The only difference is which church did you go to, Presbyterian or Baptist.

VS: You and Bobbie Ann Mason have been designated as New South writers. What do you think about that label?

LS: That is partially because a lot of people who have studied her work don't understand the delineation between parts of the South. It's not New South so much as it is Appalachian South. They don't know what else to call it, so they call it New South. But that's not really true, because if you were to write about contemporary life in Tupelo you would still have to deal with blacks and black issues, but Bobbie doesn't because she is dealing with Kentucky. So New South to me is maybe a misnomer. I think what it means is contemporary life in the South, and with Bobbie it is more contemporary Appalachian rather than New South.

VS: Although in Mason's work that part of Kentucky is a metaphor for contemporary American mobility and social change.

LS: Oh sure, that is true, but that is also not particularly southern. I think that the big split between people and culture doesn't come between North and South but between urban and rural. And she is talking about people who are losing their rural identities, and they can't grasp on to anything to fill that void.

VS: Any sustaining rituals . . .

LS: Yes. So I think those changes are very American and not particularly southern; it is just what is happening. I met this butcher when I was just up in Grundy when my father got sick. Here's the butcher in this food store who has his own church that he started—and this is somebody I went to school with. And I said, "Well, what's the name of your church?" and he said with a completely straight face, "It's the Church of What's Happening Now." Don't you love it?

VS: So what do they study there?

LS: Whatever he wants them to. He just preaches. And they all just talk about what is happening to them now.

VS: So it's sort of a cross between Unitarianism and therapy?

LS: I know! It's really funny. I said to him, "So do you all read the Bible?" and he says, "No, we just talk about stuff. And sometimes we go to the movies."

VS: You are quoted as saying that "the short story is a young writer's form, the novel form is a necessary tribute to life over time." Certainly your three most recent novels—*Oral History, Family Linen,* and *Fair and Tender Ladies*—are tributes to memory, to the recovering and creating of family and cultural history. Yet in several months your second volume of short stories will be released. Will you discuss the ways in which this collection shares and diverges from the concerns of *Cakewalk,* the collection of short stories published almost a decade ago? Have you incorporated your interest in representing the more mythic "long haul" of time and process?

LS: Well, yes; three of those stories are fifty- or sixty-page stories. And those that are short are very brief—a couple of pages. See, it has become increasingly hard for me to confine things to fit the stylistic needs of the short story. Either I'll do something that is just like a window onto somebody's life, or I'll just get into it all too much. It's real hard for me to hit the right balance for a short story. There are maybe three of them in that upcoming collection that are what they really ought to be. And the others are—well, in the *National Enquirer* it is always saying somebody is a "somebody-wanna-be"—the other stories are "novel-wanna-be's." In this collection I have three "novel-wanna-be's," and a couple of real short ones and only about three honest-to-God, decent, short stories.

VS: What is this new collection going to be titled?

LS: *Me and My Baby View the Eclipse.*

VS: That is the title story as well?

LS: Yes. It was the only one that seemed to have a title that we thought fit the whole collection. These people keep having eclipses of various kinds—throughout the collection. Various kinds of eclipses seem to come to them or to somebody that they love. And there is a whole lot of—you never really know why you do this shit—sun, moon, stars imagery going on in those stories.

VS: I'm tempted here to hum the *Twilight Zone* theme.

LS: Right—"nearnearnearnear, nearnearnearnear." Yes, and the sun-moon-stars stuff includes UFOs. I have this ex-sister-in-law who used to be in this UFO club in Iuka, Mississippi. And it's in there. So there's all this . . .

VS: Funny cosmic stuff and serious cosmic stuff?

LS: Kind of. Or—who can tell which? (Laughter.)

Lee Smith

Irv Broughton / 1990

From *The Writer's Mind: Interviews with American Authors, Vol. 3* (Fayetteville: U of Arkansas P, 1990), 277–97. Copyright © 1990. Reprinted by permission of Irv Broughton.

Irv Broughton: The *New York Times* calls your work "seemingly effortless."

Lee Smith: Well, no, but it is true that when I really get into something I do really write like rip. I don't write as much as other writers—I don't write every day. Sometimes I don't write every year. But when something hits me, it's like a compulsion. It's not an effort at all. So I don't know how it reads, but in terms of the writing, that much is true.

IB: Compulsion?

LS: Yes, I'm real compulsive. I don't think of it as work. I mean, I think of my teaching as my job.

IB: What's the longest you've gone without writing?

LS: Three years, four years maybe.

IB: And you didn't miss it?

LS: I don't know. It's like when I have something to write, I'll die if I don't do it.

IB: You grew up in Grundy, Virginia. Did Grundy shape you?

LS: Yeah, it did as I think wherever you grew up always shapes you. In my case, it particularly had to do with the way you first hear language—the kind of ear you develop or sense of self you see. In my case, when I was growing up there, Grundy was one of the most remote areas in the world— Appalachia is—because of being divided off from the rest of Virginia, from the rest of the South, from everything. It is a very special place. But, when I was growing up there, I hated it. Like any teenager, I just wanted to take off. But in later years I've realized more and more the very unique culture that was there then.

IB: It was a mining area?

LS: It was a mountain culture. Mining was the only industry in that county.

My dad didn't work in the mines, but lots of my family did, lots of the people that we knew did. In fact, in my *Fair and Tender Ladies,* there's a section that takes place in a company town. When I was growing up, my cousins lived in the company town so I played there a lot. I went up there a lot, but my father has a dime store on the main street of Grundy that he still has—he's eighty.

IB: Did you ever feel isolated from your friends whose families worked underground?

LS: Yeah, I did. I felt very isolated. I felt kind of like a little princess in a sense. One thing people don't understand about Appalachia that makes Appalachian writing very different from Southern literature: there is no upper class. There was nobody wealthy. I felt sort of embarrassed to live in town, and I had friends whose lunch would be buttermilk and cornbread in a mason jar. But I lived in town, and my mother was from the Eastern shore and had pretensions. When I was really little, I think I was like a princess because I didn't go back up in the "hollers" after school. It was very funny; when I grew up and went away to school, I realized I had had the most middle class of childhoods. But given the circumstances, those of us who lived in town— the neighborhood we lived in was called Cow Town—there was a bottom along the river and those of us who lived right in town, we really thought that we had something.

IB: How did this manifest itself, Princess?

LS: Our lives were different just because our family lived in town. People were always getting killed in the mines—I remember so well when I was growing up—or being disabled. And our families weren't disabled, who had stores in town.

IB: Did you feel guilt?

LS: Yes, very definitely. I still feel a lot of guilt because this really is where I grew up, and this is something I know a whole lot about, but I still feel a lot of guilt because I didn't grow up in the "hollers." I didn't have a father who went down in the mine every day. So you say, you haven't any right to write about people who never ventured more than nine miles from the place they were born in. But I do think if you're from somewhere and you've hung around there all your life and you have family there, you feel legitimately qualified. And I've done a lot of research.

IB: Do you refurbish when you go back?

LS: Oh yes, absolutely. Maybe it's because I know so much about everybody. We know all the families going back for years. To me, it's still the most interesting place in the world.

IB: A dime store is a magical place—the old-time ones.

LS: It was wonderful. I remember one of the favorite things was before Easter. In the days when I was little, the Easter baskets didn't come pre-packaged. We'd have two or three nights when everyone who worked in the store would come and stay real late, and we'd make the Easter baskets. There would be these huge boxes full of straw, much larger than I was, and I would get in them and go to sleep. It was just great.

IB: You wrote about the Easter baskets in one of your books.

LS: I think I mentioned it in one of them. At Christmas, I would always get to pick out fun things and sort of spruce up the dolls. I felt real special growing up because my father owned the dime store.

IB: Were your parents funny?

LS: Yeah, they were funny, but it was also kind of tragic. I was an only child. My parents were real old when I was born, and I don't think they expected to have children, so they completely spoiled me and indulged me in a way. I think I wouldn't have started writing except their attitude was, "Well, you don't have to marry a doctor. Just what are you interested in?" They always encouraged me to be interested in things and do what I wanted to do.

IB: If you hadn't escaped the mountains, what would you be doing?

LS: I don't know. I would probably be running a restaurant in Grundy, if I was still in Grundy. Maybe I'd have escaped as far as Abingdon—a lot of people have moved over to Abingdon. But you know, I'm still very drawn to my family that lived there. I really like them. I don't have brothers and sisters but I have lots of cousins. Maybe I'd be teaching English at the high school. I've always wanted to run a restaurant in Grundy.

IB: What would your main dish be there in Grundy?

LS: *(Laughs.)* I can't imagine.

IB: The "I-Can't-Imagine Omelet."

LS: I can't imagine doing it. But I've always wanted to do it. There's just no restaurant there.

IB: What were you like in college?

LS: Wild. I was among a group of girls there at Hollins who were pretty much just like I was. We were just all on fire with reading and writing. I'd been that way for a long while, but I'd sort of hidden it because I was at St. Catherine's. My father had sent me off to St. Catherine's to turn me into a lady, and it wasn't okay to be that way. But when I got to Hollins there was this whole bunch of girls that were recklessly deadset on the same path I was. It was wonderful. Anne Jones, Cindy MacKethan, Annie Dillard, Roseanne Coggeshall, Margaret Gibson—a lot of them have gone on to write.

IB: Did you adhere strictly to all the rules?

LS: I got in trouble. In fact, I was kicked out for a semester. I lived in a boardinghouse and worked on a newspaper in Richmond, which was very good for me. I was on Hollins abroad in France when I was kicked out, and I broke some of their rules. I can't remember even what they were. I loved Hollins, but when I got there it was like I went, "Wow," sort of. I was writing all the time, and I was excited about everything, and I somehow just couldn't seem to notice the rules. I don't think it was so much a rebellion as an exploding in all directions.

IB: Outside of English classes, were you attracted more to politics, sociology, or history?

LS: I didn't do anything. I don't know how I graduated. *(Laughs.)* I had one of the lowest averages in the world. I didn't try to do anything. I was literally just crazed with the stuff I was interested in.

IB: Did you write *The Last Day the Dogbushes Bloomed* in college?

LS: I wrote a series of short stories from the point-of-view of a child, and it was a voice—when I was maybe nineteen or twenty—that just came easy to me. I wrote several stories, maybe five or six that sounded more or less alike. Then I decided I would make it into a novel, and I did. I was writing the whole time I was out of school. I was out quite a bit actually. I was out that semester in France, and I was out for a semester, working in Virginia. Anyway, I was writing all the time, and by the time I went back as a senior at Hollins I did have these similar stories. So I went to Louis Rubin with them, and he said, "Go ahead." That it would be an independent study and I would get three hours credit. So I did.

IB: Was it hard adapting the stories?

LS: I think the main task was what it always is with a child narrator—not being too cute, because it was a very serious book. There's a kind of cute voice that you can listen to for the space of story but that you just can't stand for the length of a novel. It was really hard for me. I had to change the voice to make it suitable for the novel. I didn't really change it enough. By the time it was done it was a novel that was suitable for three hours credit, but it wasn't suitable for publication because it was still too cute. So I revised it and sent it to an editor who had been at Hollins a few years before, Shannon Ravenel. She was with Houghton Mifflin. She did not publish it, but she wrote me a very detailed letter about what was wrong with the narrative voice.

IB: What did she say?

LS: She just said it was too cute, it was too coy, it was pretentious, it was tongue-in-cheek in places, and it was too clever. So I worked on it really hard and then a publisher did accept it.

IB: Little Arthur was a kind of evil force in that. Where did you dredge him up from?

LS: From this boy in my neighborhood.

IB: What was that boy like?

LS: Just like Little Arthur.

IB: Just *exactly* like Little Arthur?

LS: No, he was just bad. We had a club, and he just came and wanted us to do all this. He came to visit his grandmother, but he wasn't a made-up figure, he was just a bad boy.

IB: How do you approach a novel in terms of plotting and characters?

LS: Well, I think this is fairly new for me, because the first several novels that I wrote were a kind of compilation of short stories. I would be writing short stories and they would be all related. All of a sudden I'd realize that if I did this and this and this, it could be a novel. That was true of my second, and that was very true of my third novel too, because I was living in Alabama and writing a bunch of Alabama stories.

IB: That was *Fancy Strut.*

IB: Yes, and it's only been recently that I have thought of the novel as a novel. I wish I'd done this before, because it somehow makes it much more fun to write. I mean, I love that kind of rush you get when you write a story. It makes it less of a job to write a novel—and more of a rush if you can think of it as a whole.

IB: Which comes first, the plot or the characters?

LS: The characters. I have a lot of trouble thinking of anything for them to do. Sometimes I just lift the plot from newspapers or something.

IB: Newspapers?

LS: Yes, the *National Enquirer. (Laughs.)*

IB: Do you write fast and work long hours?

LS: Well, again I think there are a whole lot of people who write every day. When I'm really writing, I'll take as much time as I can get. I may write for a six-hour stretch, and I'll write thirty pages or something.

IB: Do you have to revise that thirty pages a lot?

LS: Sometimes, yes, and sometimes, no. It just depends on the nature of it.

IB: You've just finished thirty pages. Can you say to yourself, "Oh, this looks good. I think this is going to be able to be set in concrete."

LS: No, I never am able to have any judgment on anything I write. Sometimes the stuff I feel compelled to write is really not very good. I have characters very set in my head before I start. I do often get very frustrated at what they're going to do. If I'm going to have a character in a novel, I will fill up a yellow pad with stuff about them—stuff that I'll never use in the novel. What they watch on TV. Where they buy their clothes. Everything. I spend a long time in what a friend calls "prewriting" so when I actually write it, I rip. But I spend a lot of time before I write doodling and staring out windows and driving through stop signs.

IB: How have your children affected your writing?

LS: They have affected my writing enormously because they have expanded the subject matter. I think one thing that children do is they shut you out of any tendency toward insularity that you might ever have because they expose you to whole other worlds and people and activities and just all kinds of things. I do write a whole lot about family.

IB: You'd do a lot of that writing anyway, wouldn't you?

LS: I'd do a lot of that anyway because the culture I grew up in was very family-oriented. It was not mobile. Nobody ever moved out of Grundy. *(Laughs.)* They just married their cousins and lived next door. I probably would have written that anyway, but the fact is I have had these children.

IB: You seem to write a lot about family secrets. You got any family secrets we ought to know about?

LS: I've got a lot, but none I could tell. *(Laughs.)*

IB: This obviously interests you—family secrets. Do you think the South has more than its share of family secrets?

LS: No, it just seems to me the whole idea of secrets is just fascinating. I think everybody has them and every family has them and many families simply revolve around them. But I don't think the South has more than its share. I do think that you have to know somebody an awful long time—you have to know a family an awful long time—to know exactly what their secrets are. I do think, as I say, in some of these small towns like the one where I grew up, the static quality—the people who live there have *always* lived there—means that you know what the secrets are. You know that this family had a son that was killed in a car wreck when he was eighteen and they've all never gotten over it. You just know that—you've known it for years. I think you may find that quality more in Southern writing because of the static nature of the culture.

IB: How'd you look at secrets as a little girl?

LS: I loved them. I had lots and lots and lots of secrets. In fact, I went through this wonderful stage that so many little girls go through where what you're going to be is a girl detective. My cousin Randy and I had a detective agency for years where we tracked people all over town, looked in their windows, and just did all kinds of bizarre things. We would imagine that we found clues, and we did this whole, huge construct. There was this one woman who worked in the drugstore that we were sure was a killer. It was all very comical. So, sure, I was always very interested in secrets.

IB: You have this real eye for behavior—as a detective, of course.

LS: *(Laughs.)* I think one of my great failings is an inability to be interested in ideas because I am so fascinated with people. I always have been, and I think if I hadn't become a writer, I would be maybe . . .

IB: . . . Working in Grundy.

LS: *(Laughs.)* . . . a psychologist or something like that. But if I were in Grundy, I would be running a restaurant. I don't know. I've always been absolutely fascinated with people. I suppose it's because some people in my family were such gossips and that was all they'd talk about. You'd come in from school and they'd say, "What'd ya hear today?" The kind of stories you listen for and the kind of stories that really interest me involved people first and principles and themes second. I guess another thing is . . . My husband says—he's from Nova Scotia—the thing he doesn't understand about the South is that the people down here will tell a long, long anecdote about something that he wouldn't consider worth mentioning and make it a big story—men as well as women. I don't know. When you don't have too much to talk about, you sort of learn to make a story out of the fact that you saw somebody go out of the house with her apron on; it's a big deal.

IB: What do you think she was hiding under the apron?

LS: And what was the matter with her, or what's going on? *(Laughs.)* Big deal.

IB: What are your favorite jokes?

LS: I guess the kind I really like are not jokes but long anecdotes. I love the kind of thing that Garrison Keillor does. I love humorous stories more than jokes. I went through a phase in my twenties of being very fascinated by puns, and I was reading Nabokov a lot—writers like that—and somehow I got tired of them.

IB: Talk about the murder in *Family Linen*. Where'd that idea come from?

LS: There are a lot of people who read it and still don't know who did it. It's a real murder. It happened in Raeford, North Carolina. There's really a woman who went to the psychiatrist because she had migraines. Under hypnosis she remembered seeing her mother kill her father, chop him up with an axe, and put him in the outhouse, not the well. In real life what she did was call the FBI and then call her mother. Her mother drove her white Cadillac out into the middle of her tobacco field and shot herself, because it was true. All these years she had been a pillar of the community. So I didn't put that part in there.

IB: Is there any problem with using things like that?

LS: I'm sure there is, but I don't know. My feeling is that nobody ever reads fiction. *(Laughs.)*

IB: How do the poets feel?

LS: *(Laughs.)* I know she would sue me because if you would turn your own family in to the FBI, you would sue me, right? If it ever got made into a movie or something, then she would be aware that I used the story.

IB: What about confrontation? Are you good at it?

LS: I think that's one problem in real life: I avoid confrontation. I think that, when you write fiction, you put characters in situations where they're really face-to-face with their devils, in a way, and I'm much braver about doing that when I'm writing than I am in my real life.

IB: Which of your characters is most like Lee Smith?

LS: I don't know. I think all the time when you write your characters, they are aspects of yourself. Each one is like an exaggerated aspect. I'm not very interested in autobiographical fiction; in fact, I don't write it. But I think your characters particularly embody certain psychological aspects of myself. I think that the woman in the most recent book, Ivy in *Fair and Tender Ladies,* is definitely most like me, except you wouldn't be able to tell that because the circumstances of her life are so different.

IB: It took you a while to write about Grundy, didn't it? Why do you think so?

LS: Oh, for one thing, I think you do have to achieve enough distance from any material in order to be able to manipulate it, switch it around, and make it into fiction. It just simply took me a while to get that distance.

IB: How many years did it take you?

LS: I think around the time I was thirty, which was about thirteen years ago, I began to get very, very interested in Grundy and Buchanan County. I don't think I got interested in it as a subject for fiction so much as I first began to get really panicked that it was getting modern and all those special things about it were blending into contemporary America. And I began to tape my relatives.

IB: So you sort of did an oral history?

LS: Not in any systematic way. It's just that what I did when I went home was to write things down when I was there. Once you ask folks things like that, they really like to tell you. And they'll tell somebody else. And he'll say, "You really ought to go up there to have Uncle So-and-so tell you about the time that they hanged John Hardin downtown," or whatever it happens to be. So you just kind of go around doing that. I got real interested and had a lot of stuff that I had written down and collected. I finally just decided to write a book that would incorporate as much of this material as I could, which was *Oral History.* I began to use some of the history earlier, too, in *Black Mountain Breakdown.*

IB: Was it hard?

LS: It was wonderful. It was so easy it felt like cheating. It still feels like cheating. I read about somebody who would go up a hollow where there's a moonshine still, and the woman comes out and shrieks three times and throws her apron over her head. Then I wrote a scene around just such an incident.

IB: Then we learn what's under the apron?

LS: Exactly, that's what she had under the apron. (*Laughs.*)

IB: You didn't run into anyone up there in the mountains who was a little proprietary with their information?

LS: They just tell you what they want you to know. They don't necessarily tell you the truth. They make up stuff—some people are like Little Luther in *Oral History.* They're sort of putting on everybody up there who's doing an oral history on them. They'll make something up and sort of die laughing when the next one comes along because the first one wrote it all down. I try to use accurate detail, particularly when I'm writing about the mountains because it interests me so much the way things were done—like the way logs were roped together and sent down the river to Kentucky or how to make soap or if I'm writing about a beauty contest that I was really in, what it was really like. But I think if you're going to be a writer you have everything in the world to write about and you never have to write about anything real or any real person in such a way that it would hurt their feelings. I mean, why bother? You can always make up some other better person.

IB: What's the hardest thing about combining the research information and the imagination?

LS: It is real hard in a sense, because if you're like me, you have a tendency to want to throw in so much information that it sort of stops the narrative dead.

IB: But you work beyond that—your books really move.

LS: Well, part of it has to do with editing. I have a wonderful editor. There are several parts, particularly in the Appalachian books like *Oral History,* and the latest, where I got so fascinated with the material that it stopped it dead. She came in and said, "This might be a good place for a three-paragraph cut. Nobody really wants to know how to shear a sheep." It's also very difficult to know when to stop researching and when to start writing—as well as how much detail makes something accurate before it gets boring, I guess.

IB: What Southern writer do you owe the biggest debt to?

LS: That's kind of hard to say. Probably Eudora Welty, originally. Then, of course, I've read Faulkner always. I loved *The Dollmaker* when I first read it because of the Appalachian material. I love to read Fred Chappell, I love to read Bobbie Ann Mason—some of these writers I like to think of as being Appalachian writers. One of the writers I love right now is Anne Tyler because she writes about secrets and magic.

IB: What did you get from Miss Eudora?

LS: Mainly I got an idea that it was okay to write about the kind of people that I would ultimately write about. Before that I thought that literature had to happen on some sort of high plane. Literally! I thought I had to write about glamorous people, stewardesses or something. Rich people, or people that I didn't know anything about. For one thing, I grew up reading voraciously, but I wasn't ever around anybody who was a writer or a serious sort of literary type, so although I read constantly—I read everything in the library—a lot of it was real schlock. It wasn't schlock even—it would be stuff like all the novels of John O'Hara, all those large religious novels by Taylor Caldwell. I didn't have any idea really what was good or what was schlocky. I remember when I was quite young reading *Raintree County,* and it knocked me out. I read every *Reader's Digest* condensed book ever published for ten years. It was a long time, maybe a year or so after I was in college, that I realized that you didn't have to have huge Biblical plots. It was all right to write about people like Miss Welty wrote about, people that may have even lived in Grundy.

IB: What else do you like about Eudora Welty?

LS: The mythical elements. It's like there's a whole other reality that's kind of shimmering around the edges.

IB: I visited Eudora Welty once, and I saw these note pads stationed all over her house with tiny little writing on them. There was one right where the upstairs leveled off, one on another table, another by a lamp. It looked like she went around the house making little tiny literary notes.

LS: That's great. I write a lot of stuff down and sort of tape it to the wall.

IB: You use the scotch tape literary method.

LS: (*Laughs.*) Yes. When I start a book—a novel—I'll write the last line first and scotch tape it to the wall and sort of shoot for it. (*Laughs.*) Here's the last line from *Fair and Tender Ladies,* "when I walked in my body like a queen."

IB: What did you have to learn or unlearn from working for newspapers?

LS: The best thing about working for newspapers is that it's like an open door into other people's lives. You have your pad and pencil, so you can ask them all these personal questions and they don't even mind. They love it—it's amazing. It's a wonderful entrée for the young would-be novelist. I had a hard time sticking to the facts, though. I was always fighting a tendency to fictionalize the news. I also had a movie review column—my married name then was Seay—and the name of the column was "Seay Saw." Isn't this embarrassing? I was a terrible critic. I got them all wrong. I remember when I saw *Harold and Maude*. I said it was trivial, ridiculous. And it's a long-term cult classic.

IB: What was the challenge to writing *Fair and Tender Ladies?*

LS: It's been a real difficult time in my life the last two years. What the book is about is a woman who writes letters as a way of making sense of her life, or documenting her life, or holding herself together. She's unable to put too much faith in religion, but the act of writing is a kind of salvation to her. That's what's happening in the book and paradoxically that's what was sort of happening to me when I was writing the book. All the inescapable trage-dies of middle age began to pop up, and somehow writing the book became something very important to get me through this little period, just as the woman in the novel writing her letters got through. It's quite different from anything else I've written. It's not a cast of thousands—it's very intense, it's just one woman's letters to other people her whole life long. It's *about* writ-ing in a sense. It's about writing as a way to make it through the night—or save your life, whatever.

IB: Had you looked upon writing as that before this?

LS: No, I hadn't until the last couple of weeks when I began to realize that's what I was doing.

IB: Do you sometimes have a hard time getting the point of view?

LS: Yes, most of the time, the stories that I abandon, it's because I cannot get the point of view straight.

IB: Do you abandon many?

LS: I realize that the things I end up writing are the things I've thought about for years. But sometimes I'll have some bright little quick idea and write it, and it never seems real. It seems sort of a made-up kind of thing, contrived, and I abandon a lot of those.

IB: Herb Gardner said in *A Thousand Clowns* something about how laugh-ers are really rare.

LS: I think that life is fairly tragic. It's real hard, but you've got two choices: either you can go in a closet and be real depressed or you can laugh—you get what you can get out of things.

IB: Do you ever laugh while you're writing?
LS: Oh, yes.

IB: Outrageously?
LS: (*Laughs.*) Oh sometimes, yes.

IB: Does it ever stop you for five minutes?
LS: Yes. But I don't think my work is really, really funny, not like, say, Clyde Edgerton. When I read *Raney,* I remember I thought it was just so funny when the guy got the fish hook in his nose. (*Laughs.*)

IB: If you could be in the *Guinness Book of Records?*
LS: Nothin' having to do with writing.

IB: You used a lot of voices in *Oral History,* which was really sort of masterful.
LS: When I first began writing that book, I wasn't going to have voices at all. In fact, I wrote maybe eighty pages that I had to scrap. It was going to be told in plain old omniscient American English, and there was going to be a section of these different people saying some thoughts. What I was really trying to do—in those early sections—was to use all these wonderful turns of phrase, real mountain vocabulary. But it sounded like *Hee Haw* when the narrative part was written in plain old Norton Anthology English, and the people would pop up and speak in idiom—the dialect. It made them seem really dumb. So finally I realized I would have them tell their story each one in turn—if I wanted to use that language and I really did. I had written down these great things. I had notebooks full. That was one of the purposes of writing the book, to try to use the language as it might have actually been used. Who knows? But as it might have been.

IB: Do you have relatives you uncovered in your oral history work—any horse thieves, turncoats?
LS: There's all kind of stuff I can't tell you. For instance, my great grand-father was murdered, apparently for good reason, but he was shot while he was riding his horse.

IB: Do you know what the good reason was?
LS: Sure. But I won't say.

IB: What moves you to write?

LS: I don't know. I always did it, even while I was a child. I would write poems like, "I'm a flower in God's garden," things like that. I was an only child and I read all the time, and I'd write these dumb little stories in school and at home. One of my teachers at Hollins told me, "You write very well, my dear, but you have very little to say." Even now twenty years later I can see the accuracy of that. It's something I have to be very, very careful about. So I'm not so interested right now in writing *more*. I want to read a whole lot more and think a lot more before I write anything else. Writers who are too prolific tend to repeat themselves.

IB: If someone goes through your work and sets things straight, "that cow couldn't have died from dew poison . . . it had to be nightshade." How do you respond?

LS: Well, who cares? Not me. They do this all the time because it's true that sometimes if I can't find the right kind of folklore fact, I'll just make one up. I've done this. And it drives them nuts. With maps, for instance—I take a great leeway with geography and maps, and I use all these place names in Buchanan County, but I put them where I want to. This summer along came two graduate students who are doing something on *Oral History* and they got hopelessly lost. They were trying to follow the map in the front of the book, but nobody can follow the map because it's not real.

Interview with Lee Smith

Elisabeth Herion-Sarafidis / 1991

From *Southern Quarterly*, 32:2 (Winter 1994), 7–18. Copyright ©
1994. Reprinted by permission of *Southern Quarterly*.

EHS: You have published both novels and collections of stories. Do you have
a favorite among your own books or do you simply feel closest to the last
thing you have written?

LS: The last book published was a short story collection, *Me and My Baby
View the Eclipse,* but the one I prefer is *Fair and Tender Ladies* and I imagine
I always will prefer it. It is a very emotional book and writing it was a very
emotional act. I cannot even read the end of it; in fact I have never read the
end of it since I wrote it in longhand. It just did me in to finish it.

EHS: To see Ivy all the way to the end.

LS: Yes, yes. Anything that I know is in that book. I don't know anything
that is not in that book. So anything else I write will not be as close to me,
psychologically.

EHS: Is that because of Ivy?

LS: I don't know. I don't understand how this stuff works. But Ivy is not
in any sense an autobiographical character. She is a much stronger person
than I am and she is a much less lucky person in the sense of not getting an
education and not "getting to be a writer." But somehow there is really
something that is me in her voice. It was really like living her life. And, you
know, I did not revise that book, because as soon as it started, all I had to do
was to sit down and it would be like automatic and all I had to do was to
make sure I had time to sit down, to be there. It was really strange. And, also,
the writing of it came at the time when my own life . . . when my own mother
was dying. It was a long protracted illness from emphysema, and I had a son
who was very sick at the time. All these things were going on and it was
wonderful for me to write this book. Every time I sat down to write it was
like a total escape from these illnesses and from what was going on in my
family. So for that reason I think it is for me all very tied up emotionally.
And I think, Ivy, when I was writing, was sort of like a role model for myself.
Because she was very tough and I kept hitting her with these awful things

and she would be real tough. There was a lot going on when I was writing that book.

EHS: You really needed to write it.

LS: Yes. It was an escape, but also a source of strength. Every time I sat down to write it I would come back a lot stronger and calmer. And all of it went on for a long time. Interesting, you know. I have found in my teaching, when I teach fiction writing, that a lot of times people write things to try them out. I mean, things that they may contemplate doing or trying out personalities that they are really not but would like to explore. Several times I have had a woman write about leaving her husband and then leave her husband. Sometimes people also act things out on paper so they will not have to act them out in real life. Anne Tyler, who is one of my favorite writers, when asked why she writes, said that "I write because I want to have more than one life." She can have all these lives, be all these other people and therefore she does not have to go out and do it. But writing is an extension of your life, an expansion of the personality. So in Ivy, I think that I was trying to create a role model for myself without knowing it at the time.

EHS: Ivy says several times that she needs to sit down and think about things, to mull them over and see the connections.

LS: That is right. And me too. At the time I wrote the book I had been thinking a whole lot about writing, the act of writing. So it was writing about writing too, thoughts that had built up over the years.

EHS: How did the idea of this novel, *Fair and Tender Ladies,* come to you? Did you start out with Ivy's first letter?

LS: I always do a lot of "free writing," which is just a lot of jotting down of notes. Before I start a novel I might have five pads of paper full of notes, extensive notes to myself about each character, notations about what is actually going to happen. Then I will go back and work in the most important things, make those into scenes. The other things I just want to make sure to mention. I never stick to it, but somehow it helps me to realize I might finish the book if I have done all this much work before I start. And that is the part that takes the longest. So when I start to write a novel I may spend two or three months dreaming through the novel. It is a process of making it up and discarding certain things and saying no, she would not do that. It is like another world, in my head, before I actually start to write.

EHS: In a sense it is getting to know . . .

LS: Getting to know, that is right. I am astonished at these writers who say they sit down to write a novel with not an idea in their head. I just don't know how they can do that.

EHS: They are taken over by their own character, which certainly sounds intriguing.

LS: Much more romantic, that is for sure. My way sounds so . . . methodic. I plan it all and outline it and that sounds, well, methodic. But it is what I do.

EHS: That outlining in itself is certainly a creative process, in the sense that there is a dialogue between you and the character, as she materializes and becomes someone in her own right.

LS: Sometimes, when I do that it just does not happen and I realize it is not going to be a novel. And I will not write it. But I will spend enough time with it, usually, to where if it is just really taking off and becoming real in my mind I realize it is a novel I am going to write. Other times I realize, now, that is a story. Or, no, in fact that is not something I want to write. So a lot of the times I say that I am writing I am just sitting around twiddling my thumbs, making a few little notes but not pounding away.

EHS: You have written both stories and novels, seemingly with equal ease. Many writers have great difficulty with this: what started out as a story always becomes a novel.

LS: Oh, you can see it. Having taught for so long, I have had many of these born novelists in class. They cannot write a story even though they write really well. The form I prefer is the one form which is impossible to sell, which is the really long story. In *Me and My Baby View the Eclipse,* there are a couple: one is "Intensive Care" and one is "Tongues of Fire." This was never published, although it is my favorite story. But it is an impossible length, a forty-five or fifty page story. I love that length. You know, the older I get I find it hard to stick to the kind of short story that is like a window into a life and then it closes. I find that I want to write short stories that are more like collapsed novels, and I do find it harder to stick to the shorter form. But I love stories, I like stories better than novels. You just get very worn out, finally, before you finish a novel.

EHS: Your two later novels, *Oral History* and *Fair and Tender Ladies,* are to some extent, maybe not collections of stories, but perhaps short story cycles.

LS: The book I am writing now [*The Devil's Dream*] is like that. It is more like a short story cycle. I think that this attracts me because I started out with stories and I still really like them, but I cannot seem to leave them alone. I always want to add another and another and have a whole community or family. That is what I am doing with the book I am doing now, which is a country-music book covering several generations. The whole thing is going to be like an album. I am writing all the songs, strange but fun. There are lots of voices, in the first person narrative most of them. In this respect it is like *Oral History*. It is set in southwest Virginia, in a poor valley where the Carter Family is from, which is real close to where I am from. I used to go over there and hear them play music on Saturday night when I was a child. And I am spanning a period of pre-Civil War up to the 1970s. I am trying to show the roots of country music, thematic and actual, using it as a structure of the book. I am terrified, really. In *Oral History* I wrote Little Luther's songs and I have always written songs, all my life.

EHS: I heard you read from this new work, and the voice of the female character that you were giving us reminded me sometimes of Agnes in *Black Mountain Breakdown* and sometimes of Ora Mae in *Oral History*.

LS: Yes, that is true: the jealous sister. She is the only voice like that so far in this book—the jealous sister, the onlooker. The genesis of that is probably one of my favorite stories. It knocked me out many, many years ago when I first read it. It is the Eudora Welty story, "Why I Live at the P.O."

EHS: A marvelous story—but difficult for many students these days.

LS: It is a very subtle story and my students also have problems with it. The ones that are really tuned into language get it, but the average freshman class at NC State, where I get so many brilliant kids in technology, they just don't get it. There are many things like that they don't get. I remember one of my favorite stories, "Araby" by James Joyce. They simply don't understand what it is about.

EHS: It helps, I think, to hear it read.

LS: Yes, that Welty story is very much an oral story, a spoken story. That interests me too, writing that is supposed to be spoken and the different varieties of the first person speaker, whether it is a spoken story or whether it is written. In that sense *Fair and Tender Ladies* is written.

EHS: It seems to me that in many ways that is what *Oral History* is about, the immediacy of all those voices.

LS: Yes, it is. And another thing that fascinates me about the notion of oral history is that I think it is an oxymoron: if it is spoken it is not history; if it is spoken it is automatically the storyteller's tale. I have gone around collecting oral history, listening to people's stories for so long and that aspect interests me. You can ask a whole bunch of people the same thing and get six different descriptions. I did this in Grundy, Virginia. One of the last men hanged in the county was hanged in front of the courthouse in Grundy, where I am from. I asked all these old people who had seen it, what John Hardin looked like. They said he was tall, they said he was short, they said he sang a song right before he died, they said he prayed, they said all these different things.

EHS: You used that story in *Oral History.* And beginning with *Black Mountain Breakdown* you place your stories in this region. How come you did not start out using the mountains, tales and oral history in your fiction?

LS: That is because when I started out I thought the idea was to be sophisticated. To be a good writer, I thought, the idea would be to learn elegant language, write fancy sentences about an upper-class person. I read like crazy when I was a child, indiscriminately I read everything, lots and lots of English novels and I really did not happen upon anybody like Eudora Welty until I took courses at college. But I did not happen upon anybody who would be writing out of the same smalltown experience. So it never occurred to me that would be a subject to use in fiction. I was a little too close to the mountains, too. I think I needed to have a certain distance. But now I return, all the time. I would really like to live there now. I think I could now, but when I grew up there I felt very claustrophobic.

Going back I have talked to and taped people I knew as a child, including my family. I know who I want to talk to and about what, not like many young oral historians who are going into Kentucky or West Virginia and, you know, they are from New Jersey. I love to do it and I think one reason has been to preserve certain aspects of that culture, because they are all going, Elisabeth. And this is as backwards a county as you will find, but there are all these fast-food stores, and television is a great leveler. People don't sit down on their porches and talk anymore. They are all watching TV. And the kids all sound like TV. In this county where I am from, the economy is so bad that all the young people are just leaving. You have only children and old people there. It is just not a place where you can make a living very easily because the coal business is so bad. So I have wanted to interview people and set it down while I can get hold of it as close to the source as possible. Because when I was growing up my grandparents and aunts and uncles, they all spoke in this heavy dialect and that is the way which I heard, growing up. I can still do it. I can write it because I heard it first. And when I did go back I got really interested and also went back and read accounts of people from outside who had come into that region. I did all kinds of research and it got even more interesting. But with this book I am working on now, I have probably exhausted that, at least in my mind.

EHS: This recapturing, setting down in words of ways of life, ways of speech is, it seems to me, a very important aspect of your work, especially of *Oral History.*

LS: That is exactly what I was trying to do, and with *Oral History* I set out at first . . . I had a closetful of tapes and notes I had taken, people's diaries and all kinds of stuff, and I just wanted to write a book that would use as much of this material as possible. And at first I did not think it would be a novel. I thought I would make a scrapbook and it would still be published, under "Appalachian Lore," but I really don't know how to do that. What I know how to do is write fiction, so then I just tried to think about the plot that would allow me to use the most, cover the most ground.

EHS: In both *Oral History* and *Fair and Tender Ladies* you are spanning a long period of time, this whole country, picturing changes that have come to these mountains.

LS: In *Oral History* I was particularly concerned with land, what happened to the land. People from outside came in and first they took the lumber and then bought up the mineral rights and stripped it for coal. Right before I started writing *Oral History* there was another one of those horrible floods that they have all the time, which completely wiped out my father's house and his business for the third time. I was really angry, I think, about that. It is a more thematic book. The land was really raped. And not for the benefit of the people who lived there. Everything was taken away from them, like when in *Fair and Tender Ladies,* Ivy finds out about the mineral rights. So *Oral History* really is a lament, or even more of a wail over what has happened to the land and even more what has happened to the people. It is very sad. If you would go there with me tomorrow you would be really saddened by this particular town and this county, because you see mainly a lot of old people, a lot of people who look not quite right. They are leftovers, don't even think they can work now. It is a community which is pretty much devastated at this point. I think it is going to be a ghost town in a hundred years. And there are a number of ghost towns around those mountains. That is why I feel so strongly about having a record of all that has been.

EHS: There is a strong presence in your books, a kind of echo from one story to the other of what you have just been describing. And clearly your interest in lore and myth has then served as an inspiration for you as a writer of fiction. Moving on somewhat, I would like to take up the aspect of characterization in your novels. Your stories are always centered in a consciousness—and sometimes more than one—of someone whose life is rather ordinary, in the sense that it is neither very easy nor happy.

LS: Well, that is really what I am trying to do. I hate these books that are so popular, the sort of commercial fiction, the glossy ones you see in the drugstore with BIG plots where all these things happen to people. That is just not true.

EHS: The lives you portray are certainly not glamorous, and the things that happen to your characters are both harsh and sad. Still, your books have often been described, quite rightly I think, as being, in the final analysis, life affirming. You certainly have a great sympathy for the people you create and write about and usually give some kind of psychological explanation of why a character acts the way she does, which actually detracts from the malevolence of "evil" of a certain act. There is not a villain to be seen. . . .

LS: I know. I am going to have one though. But I don't think I have one in the book I am writing now. I will, though. I decided the other day that in the next thing I write I am going to write something about evil. I don't ever deal with that. That is true. It is not evil, just sort of the hard knocks we all get by just the way life is.

EHS: The only character you portray as truly evil from the beginning, even when he is still a child, is Ivy's brother, Garnett, the evangelist. He seems to me to be a villain.

LS: Well, he acts like a villain, but I think he is a fool. People like him come off as villains sometimes in the way they treat other people, but I think I need to write about someone really evil.

EHS: He certainly lacks empathy. It is interesting, I think, that from the minute you get him into the story the reader senses that there is something wrong with him, beady eyes and all, that he will cause suffering.

LS: It is very interesting to me, having watched my own children grow up, how much you can see in children of what they will be. I mean lots of things can happen, but there is a basic kind of character in us all which is there right from the start.

EHS: You have Ivy say something to that effect, in a letter to Jolie, her granddaughter, talking about the time she met the bee-man Honey Breeding and, in a sense, followed him to the end of the world. She says that she did not know she was going to act like that, but that the seeds of what we become are probably always in us.

LS: And we can either act on them or not. But I have got to have an evil person in the end of the book I am writing now. It is not too late. You will see him and you will know where he came from.

EHS: That will really be something to look forward to. But to continue looking at your different characters, it is clear that you seem to feel more at home speaking through the voice of a woman. And looking at your novels, there are some fascinating parallels as far as characters go: Ora Mae of *Oral History* and Agnes of *Black Mountain Breakdown,* the ugly ones on the outside looking in; Beulah of *Fair and Tender Ladies* and Pearl of *Oral History,* driven and lost, without ever understanding of what the emptiness in their hearts consists. But Crystal in *Black Mountain Breakdown* is different.

LS: The character she would be closest to is maybe Dory in *Oral History.* She is damaged, too passive, the world is too much for her. You know, that is the one book where I did not get so involved in the characters at first, where I really had a theme. It was because I was at a point . . . where friends and all these people that I had known, who in their twenties had tried to act a certain way to please other people, were changing. A lot of Americans, in particular southern women, do try to please, I think. And then it just sort of exploded and I was really interested in seeing this in myself and all the women I had gone to school with. So I was trying to write a book about the dangers of being passive, of letting other people define what your life is going to be like. I think there are a lot of problems with Crystal and maybe she does not ever seem quite real. She is more of an embodiment of a certain attitude. You do try to make your characters as real as you can, but I think that is a flaw with that book, a flaw in her and in the book.

EHS: Crystal is different, I believe, from other characters you have created in the sense that whereas they may be lost or miserable and not understand what it is that has hit them, *she* does. At the end she realizes this quite clearly, and then she does something rather unusual in your fiction—she opts out. She actually chooses suicide in that she wills herself to become paralyzed, but it is a strangely passive act, a negative one. She chooses not to act forcefully, but to simply withdraw from life.

LS: I was never quite like Crystal, but as a girl and a woman in my early twenties, like so many young southern women, I did try really hard to fit into certain notions, certain roles. And at the time I was writing that, I was trying to get out of this and could identify, really empathize with Crystal.

EHS: I believe that many women can understand this. They don't have to be either American or southern to be able to know what this dilemma is all about. In looking for herself Crystal is never real to herself; she is only real as she is mirrored, as crystal, in how others see her and treat her.

LS: Which is a scary way to be. And there is still a lot of it.

EHS: But what about the ending of *Black Mountain Breakdown?* The picture of Crystal curled up on the bed, having to be fed and turned every three hours is a very distressing one. And then on the last page, you somehow turn it around and end on a positive note. . . .

LS: Well, I don't think it is a positive note. There is a horrible sense in that that is what Crystal always wanted. She does refuse to be saved. She has done these things that have damned her and I think there is a sense in which it is suicide and that is what that positive note is about. It is fulfillment. All of it has somehow to do with her father and the amount of time that he spent closed up in that front room. This is somehow a way of getting to him, getting back to him. I have, I think, written a lot around the whole issue of depression and mental illness. My own father suffered from depression and had several different bouts of literally lying in bed until he was taken to the hospital. This kind of thing can affect the children who grow up in that kind of situation.

One notion that I got from books I have read on family therapy was that sometimes in really cohesive families, which I was trying to write about in *Black Mountain Breakdown,* something like a phobia affecting the grandmother will be transmitted to a child and become a real neurosis. And if it continues in the family it might be transmitted down as a psychosis, getting worse and worse. In *Black Mountain Breakdown* it is that same strain of not wanting to go out, not wanting to do anything. So there is a sense in which the ending to that book is a culmination. When things become too much for her, Crystal just closes up. At that time, a friend who was a psychiatrist took me out to a mental hospital and showed me one group of adult patients who were lying in big cribs, having been depressed for so long that they were catatonic. It is a rare state, but it occurs. And Crystal was such a passive character.

You know, that book was almost not published. It went through something like eighteen publishers. My first three books had not sold well and when I wrote *Black Mountain Breakdown* the publishers turned it down for two reasons, I think. First, because they were then publishing fewer books by writers who did not sell and instead going more for nonfiction, but also because it is such a depressing book. And it went around to all these different houses and I lost my agent, too. I was about ready to quit writing fiction. I was teaching, but I had applied to go back to school, to the school of special education, because I had decided there was no future in writing. And then finally it sold.

EHS: And it was the same book? You did not make any drastic revisions?

LS: No, it was the same. The problem was that everybody got so exasperated with Crystal because she is so passive. You do want to just kick her. The only major revision I made when it was published was because my editor felt that it would be good if there was maybe *some* possibility of hope. So then I added the part about Crystal taking the job as teacher. Before that, it was just one unrelieved sinking into passivity, which was just too much. It still is too much.

EHS: It is just that she differs from your other characters in that they learn—and go on—but she cannot bear what she finally understands. Someone like Ivy is the opposite, someone who embraces life the way it happens to her, pain, dreariness and all.

LS: Yes, they are at opposite ends. But I could never have thought of a character like Ivy until I was this old. You don't even know what is out there, for one thing, to be afraid of. But *Black Mountain Breakdown* was a very serious book, deadly serious. You know, I have gotten a number of letters from readers who suggest that I have Jubal come and heal Crystal and get her up again. They are really worried about her, wanting me to write a follow-up. And I have never understood these people that can go back and resurrect all the characters in a book. My friend Clyde Edgerton has just done it in his new book, but for me it is really hard. John Barth has done that somewhat. I don't see how they can do it because I think each novel is an aesthetic whole and you end it when you have to. And this is a statement about being passive and you cannot go back and say, well, I did not really mean it.

EHS: You would undo all that you strove for in that book. But maybe people are just looking for "the happy ending," Hollywood fashion.

LS: I have a favorite aunt, my Aunt Milly who lives in Florida, and she just does not understand any of the books and she says, "Why don't you have a happy ending?" I guess it is comforting to have a story end like that. But those of us who are serious about writing don't want it for comfort, we want it for insight. But I think they want it for comfort, to be out of their lives but into lives that are less painful. I went down to see my Aunt Milly and she lives with retired people in an apartment complex and they have a little club-house by the pool where they have a bookcase, where they offer the books they like the best to share, and they are all romance novels and historical fiction and things where you have a happy ending. With the young kids, their whole notion of narrative derives from TV: they want the happy ending and they want it in thirty minutes which is the length of a sitcom.

EHS: Having recently read Kaye Gibbons's work, I find that there are a great many interesting women writers in the Southeast, Josephine Humphreys and Jayne Anne Phillips, to name a few. In Kaye Gibbons's short novels I find a number of parallels to your work, though your "voice" is different, in its poetic quality, and you have a manifest interest in lore and myth. But the similarities have to do with the kind of people both of you write about, the focus on the here and now, the physical reality of the characters, instead of abstractions.

LS: Kaye's latest book [*A Cure for Dreams*] interests me a lot. We are friends and she called up after she had finished *A Virtuous Woman* and said, "What do you do after you are just written out?" Having been written out many times myself, I said, well, go to the library and read something. Read the WPA tapes—which is really where this [*A Cure for Dreams*] is from. Then she came to my class, she was wonderful to the class I was teaching at Duke, and brought in hundreds of pages of notes of nifty little stories and anecdotes and brands of cereal and different things from the war years. And she had everybody look at them and she showed them how she sank into that time period, and then she read from the book. And it was great for my students because they could see how you can use research to write fiction. You do it all and it soaks in and then a voice has got to emerge to tell the story, because you cannot be writing history.

EHS: We mentioned before the way you have structured your novels, that they are not novels in the traditional sense, rather "story" novels or letter novels. This is another way in which Gibbons's work resembles yours. They are both written in the same rather episodic fashion. Phillips's *Machine Dreams* is another example of that kind of structure.

LS: That is very interesting. I wonder if it is more common today in women's writing?

EHS: *Love Medicine* is another one.

LS: Yes, it really is. It is true of Amy Tan, too. Maybe you are onto a trend. Why that is I don't know. Women creating a mythology?

Belles Lettres Interview

Renee Hausmann Shea / 1993

From *Belles Lettres* (Spring 1993), 32–34. Copyright © 1993. Reprinted by permission of *Belles Lettres*.

Reading The Devil's Dream, *I felt that you must have had fun writing it—that you love country music. True?*

Oh, I had a great time writing *The Devil's Dream!* I felt so much energy. I think we all have a soundtrack from our childhood, and mine was country music. When we got up in the morning, my mother would turn on the radio in the kitchen to a country music station—in Grundy, Virginia, it was WNRG—and we'd listen to whatever was popular, like "Ring of Fire." I remember loving Johnny Cash and Tennessee Ernie Ford singing "I Sold My Soul to the Company Store."

We'd just listen to it all day, and then I would go play with my best friend down the river, Martha Sue Owens, whose father was a country music singer. He played the fiddle and the guitar—traditional music. He would often sit outside on a lawn chair looking out onto the river, just playing and singing to himself. All the children were sort of in love with him because he had what we understood at the time to be a "romantic heart," and he didn't work much. Actually, he had had rheumatic fever as a child, but we thought it was "romantic fever." He was a little bit pale, real good-looking with a droopy black mustache. He cut quite a figure in my childhood and in my memory.

He often played "The Devil's Dream"—a Scottish air, a pre-Civil War tune. If you play it fast, it's good dancing music—a party song—but if you play it slowly, it's kind of mournful and beautiful.

So I think for all of these reasons, I was drawn to country music and never quite got over it.

You dedicate The Devil's Dream *to "all the real country artists, living and dead, whose music I have loved for so long." Who are some of your favorites?*

I'm crazy about Nanci Griffith and my friend Marshall Chapman and Lyle Lovett and Guy Clark, who I think is a genius. These are some of the newest. I also like the traditional singers. Some of my very good friends here in town are Tommy Thompson and the Red Clay Ramblers.

You're a fan who knows a lot about country music, but it seems as though
you did a great deal of research to write this book.

I did. And I talked to so many people. Jean Ritchie for one. I admire her
so much and, in fact, not only do I admire her, but she has written the best
book that I think has ever been written on traditional country music and its
place in the home. It's called *The Singing Family of the Cumberlands,* and it
was reissued recently by the University of Kentucky Press. It's a beautifully
written book. So I thought of the Ritchie family as my model for the family
in *The Devil's Dream,* as well as the Carter family from Virginia, the Stone-
man family from Virginia, and the White family from Tennessee.

I talked to a great many women while I was writing. The first story in the
book—about the girl from the fiddling family who marries the preacher's
son—is an actual story I ran across up in Madison County, North Carolina,
where I was visiting a group of storytellers and traditional ballad singers. In
particular, I was being helped by a young woman named Sheila Barnhill,
who is a seventh-generation ballad singer. (Her granny, Dale Norton, is quite
famous.) They're all from Sodom, North Carolina, which is where the first
ballads were recorded. Then, in the course of my talking to Sheila and the
women in her family, Sheila decided she would write her own book. She
knew great stories—there were more than I could ever use.

*One reviewer wrote that "Each chapter [of*The Devil's Dream*] is the equiv-*
alent of a country song, combining the tragic, the hokey, the joyous, and the
ironically inevitable." Was that your intent?

I thought about this book as an album: Each section of it would be somebody's song, and together the songs would make up an album.

Now my friends Clyde Edgerton and his wife, Susan Ketchin, have made
an album called *The Devil's Dream.* They were real interested in this book
when I started writing it and suggested several sources. We were all having
so much fun writing songs for the book: in fact, two of the song titles were
contributed by Susan, who then wanted to write the whole song. So she did,
and it's a fabulous song. (One title is from Annie Dillard: "Two Lefts Don't
Make a Right.") Then they started coming and singing when I would give a
reading. We started giving concerts that were half reading, half show. Finally,
we made a tape called *The Devil's Dream,* which has traditional tunes and
some original music.

I love country music because the songs are stories, and it seems there's a
renaissance in storytelling today. Do you think people in the '90s are drawn
to stories?

I think in the '80s a lot of us revolted against the Yuppie values we were hearing and seeing everywhere—"I'll get mine, you'll get yours." These people live with no connection to other people. We've become very interested in our roots and traditional ways of life because I think we're in danger of turning into people who live alike, and sound alike, have condominiums, and don't know our grandmothers. I think people are very interested in Native American, Appalachian, and African American writers, for instance—because their writing connects us with something beyond ourselves.

And many of the storytellers are women—which is true in The Devil's Dream.

To hear our mothers' stories and our grandmothers' stories can connect us back to something that can give us a firm footing, which contemporary life hasn't given us with its nomadic quality, high divorce rate, and so forth.

I think a lot of us have gone back to feel more secure. The stories are the way back. And much more often than not, it's the women who tell them, who keep alive what's important from the past.

I grew up in a family of talkers, but the women were the ones who told the family stories. The men told jokes, and they were always in politics and went around telling tales.

You've talked before about your interest in "domestic art," women's creativity that is often overlooked and is certainly different from men's creativity. But in this novel, men and women alike express their creativity in music. Is this a departure?

Well, I think the writer is always the last to know! It's true that I've always been most interested in women and women's creativity, but in this book I was also trying to do a kind of history of country music. It has been, as I say, largely a male business, and there is the doomed alcoholic rockabilly figure and other great characters to write about. In the research I kept coming across fabulous types that I knew I wanted to embody in my own characters some way, so it became not as much a woman's book as I had thought at the beginning. But I liked the way it turned out. It's more an accurate history, I hope.

Yet aren't women central to this novel?

Yes, of course. In thinking about how women's horizons have expanded in Appalachia and in the South, it seemed to me that country music was almost too obvious a metaphor for finding one's voice as a woman. At the beginning, you know, when country music started, it was all men. Then came Patsy Montana's first big hit, "I Want to Be a Cowboy's Sweetheart," which was not "I Want to be a Cowgirl." It was linked with men. It wasn't until Kitty Wells sang "Honky Tonk Angel" in 1952 that a woman had a major hit in terms of selling records. Then Loretta Lynn sang songs like "Don't Come Home a Drinkin' with Lovin' on Your Mind," which she had written herself—Kitty Wells had not. Lynn is an important figure because she wrote songs and sang them. Now, of course, we have women who are actually in charge of big production companies, such as Dolly Parton. So I think singing your own song and being in charge of how it's actually produced, recorded, and distributed is a certain metaphor for women getting in control of their lives.

Songs seem to give women a way to think about themselves. One character in The Devil's Dream *sings a song that she doesn't even realize she's going to sing.*

That's Katie, and the first time she has a chance to sing what she wants to sing and to sing by herself—in other words, to find her voice—what she finds herself singing is a traditional family tune that goes way, way back. She doesn't plan to sing it. It's just there.

A couple of women in the novel seem negative. What about Dawn, the singer who buys some of Katie's music but then refuses to give Katie her agent's name?

She has become commercialized, which is a danger. Actually Katie is very successful and becomes a really autonomous person, but it's a mixed blessing because our final image of Katie is encapsulated in a tour bus. She's cut off from family and friends as she goes hurtling across America—she doesn't even know her own little twin sons.

That's the great thing about country music. It always embodies the opposites—the dream of the road, plus the dream of home, which are incompatible. So are songs about raising hell and getting saved and being a good woman and a honky tonk woman. All these opposites are right there, which makes it great stuff to write about!

Miss Covington, the traveling nurse, seems so different from the others. Why is she there?

I just wanted an outside view. I think one danger of having people tell their own stories is that the reader at some point will say, "Hey, wait a minute, what *is* the case? what is true?" I wanted an outsider to come in, to have a little part of the book that was from a more distant perspective.

Several of your novels seem perfect for movies. Is anything on the horizon?

There's been some interest. The person that produced *Coal Miner's Daughter* and *Sweet Dreams* is interested in doing something with *The Devil's Dream,* but he called and talked and talked and never has called back. So I take a dim view of all this film stuff because I've had several things that would get to the point of even scouting out locations and then they fell through. So I never really believe it's going to happen.

Are you working on another novel now?

Not really. I've been working on a book with Shelby Lee Adams, who is from eastern Kentucky, real close to Grundy. For over 20 years, he has been making photographs that represent his vision of the outcasts among us, the people in America disenfranchised through poverty and illness and so on. He has done a powerful book of photographs, and he has asked me to write an introduction. Instead of writing a straight introduction trying to explain the photographs, however, I wrote a series of voices trying to illuminate them from within.

In Dorothy Hill's book about your work she says that you do most of your "pre-writing" in your head, but that once you begin, you write the last sentence first, tape it up on the kitchen wall, and write toward that ending. Did you do that for The Devil's Dream?

I do that with everything. In a way it helps me know that I will be able to finish writing the book because there's a point when you're right in the middle of writing a novel, when you say, "Well, I'm crazy! I'll never finish. What am I doing?" If you have a notion of where you're going, it's like the pot at the end of the rainbow. I just sit down and head vaguely toward that.

So what was on the kitchen wall this time?

Tampa telling her old stories one more time. That's where I wanted it to end because that's what it was all about.

Unshackling the Patriarchy: An
Interview with Lee Smith
Claudia Loewenstein / 1993

From *Southwest Review,* 78 (Fall 1993), 486–505. Copyright © 1993.
Reprinted by permission of *Southwest Review.*

Loewenstein: You recount an anecdote in your review, "Shopping for Body
Parts" in this year's *New York Times:* where, on a return trip from Elizabeth
Spencer's reading of *Cousins,* one of your students bursts into tears and rue-
fully wails, "I'll never be a Southern writer. I don't even know my cousins."
Smith: Right.

Loewenstein: My understanding is she has no sense of family and therefore feels she could not become a Southern writer. I thought we could begin
today with defining what you feel is a Southern writer.
Smith: Okay. Although I have to say I think even as we define it, it's
already changed, which was one of the points I was making in that review. It
was a review of Patricia Sears's very fine book of stories. I think, traditionally, the Southern writer has had a very strong sense of family, possibly an
even stronger sense of the importance of place, of ritual, of tradition, of
simply knowing everybody in town and what their father did. There has been
also, whether a person was religious or not, a sense of the importance of
religion in the community, and just a sense of community. I mean, people
have their fixed levels in society and if they move from one to another there's
a story. There's a whole lot that is sort of fixed, I think, in the traditional
world of Southern fiction, but I have to say that it seems to me people are
writing about things from about ten or twenty years back anyway, because it
takes you that long to get a perspective and to begin to write—so already
what I'm writing about, for instance, hardly exists. What that student will be
writing about we don't know. It's really interesting. We're getting some sense
of that from some people who are writing now.

Loewenstein: Is a sense of "roots" no longer a requisite, do you think?
Smith: I think it's going to change because I think we have become such
a mobile society that so many people do not live in the town that their parents
lived in, do not have any sense of their own roots. They were in families that

moved and moved and moved, so they may be writing stories set in the South in which roots will have no part. The divorce rate alone completely destroys the kind of configuration that produces Southern writing because you don't have these families that are totally coherent and stay together over generation and generation. You have people moving; you have splits. And all the ills that beset contemporary society, beset the South too—such as the divorce rate, the break-up of the family, the loss of ideals in general, the failure of education to address what's happening with the kids—all these things are Southern too. What we think of as Southern writing is already in a sense passé. Even those of us who are doing it, unless we set things back in time, those of us who use those underpinnings as the basis for our fiction—we'll be lying. You know we're lying anyway—we'll be lying even more!

Loewenstein: Would you say that there's such a thing as the New Southern versus the Old Southern writer?

Smith: Yes. I would. And I would say that there are some writers who are definitely writing about the New South. One of my favorites is Bobbie Ann Mason who I think is just wonderful; but she's writing about a society in which the fixed points no longer hold, and she's doing it really well. There are lots of writers who like to write about a South that is essentially a New South: Barry Hannah, Padgett Powell, Kaye Gibbons—Patricia Sears in that book I was reviewing.

Loewenstein: You mentioned in your article that these particular writers call attention to themselves because they're obsessed with the language.

Smith: Yes, I think so. Because you have to claim your territory as a writer—you have to make it your own—and if it has become cliché-ridden (and the Old South *has*) you have to do something new. For many of us who are my age and Ellen Gilchrist's age, maybe we do it with *style*. The younger ones coming alone will do it with characters who are interacting with their world in an entirely different way. We don't know what they'll do.

Loewenstein: The departure from the Old South cliché, then, is what you refer to as the "idiosyncratic style" of newer Southern authors?

Smith: Yeah, yeah. Those of us who have come along right after the great Southern writers, we have to do something but we feel our experience of the South is much like that of the great Southern writers, such as Eudora Welty. My experience of a small town and small-town life and people who live there is not much different from Welty's, I would say, or Peter Taylor's, but I have to write about it completely differently or everything I write would be completely derivative.

Loewenstein: It's intersting you should say that you feel you have to "claim your territory" because in *Harper's* magazine, Frances Taliaferro categorizes your writing regionally as "a portrait of a corner of America I've come to think of as Lee Smith Country."

Smith: Well, see, I'm lucky because really Appalachia has no resemblance to the rest of the South. I grew up in the mountains, so a lot of my experience is very different from the great writers we talk about who were Deep South writers. A lot of my experience is real different and that has given me a wonderful source for my fiction. Very little about Appalachia is like the Deep South—I mean we never had any black people, we never had any racial guilt, we never had any *money,* we never had any people in the upper class, so there are lots of differences.

Loewenstein: Your reaction to a narrowly defined regional designation for your work is positive, then?

Smith: Yes, well I want to be as regional as possible, I would say. That's true.

Loewenstein: In the context of language, in an interview with NPR, you voiced a concern that Appalachian children are growing up to speak like Dan Rather.

Smith: Well, they are. And that's one reason I have wanted to set my books back in time to try to reproduce Appalachian speech as it was because it is just so, it's like Black English, or any other, or Gullah—it's just so rich, and so wonderful, and it's dying out.

Loewenstein: Gullah?

Smith: Gullah is something that black people off the coast of South Carolina speak.

Loewenstein: My impression is that you feel language in itself can ensure the survival of a culture of a heritage. Do you take this as a personal crusade?

Smith: Yes, well I do. When I first started writing about the mountains, I remember specifically it was like a crusade. When the first fast foods started to go into Grundy, where I'm from—suddenly there's this Wendy's and this Captain D's seafood, whatever it is, on the road of the river bend right up from my dad's house, and satellite dishes then began to dot the hillside. I realized this was all changing; it's changing in my lifetime, and I really began to consciously interview the older people I know and write down what they said and the way they expressed themselves and search out people who could tell me a lot about the way things were and had been. But it *was* a crusade, and I didn't know what I was going to do with it at first. I had a closet full of this kind of material and I was thinking that I might write some kind of nonfiction book, but there are so many really good nonfiction books that have been written with Appalachian material and I only know how to write fiction, anyway, really, so I changed my mind.

Loewenstein: When you were growing up did you speak English just as you are speaking to me now?

Smith: Yes. My mother was a schoolteacher. In fact, she graduated from what is now James Madison University; it used to be Madison Teachers' College. She went to Grundy and taught school for years and years, so she was an educated woman, which made her a rarity. My dad was a mountain man whose family had lived there for generations and generations, and he went off to school for one semester and that was it.

Loewenstein: Were you considered an outsider?

Smith: No, I wasn't, because I grew up and lived there forever, but my mother was considered an outsider though she lived there for sixty years. I remember at her funeral another old lady came up and said to me (my mother was called Gig—her name was Virginia but she was called Gig) and a lady came up to me and said, "Well, you know, Gig was mighty nice for a foreigner." And you know she'd been there for sixty years. Isn't that amazing?

Loewenstein: Yes, it is, after so many years—a foreigner—that is remote.

Smith: You can't imagine the isolation of this little pocket in the mountains at the time that I grew up—even at the time I was married. But it all changed with the coming of the roads. There's a song about the coming of the roads. It all changed with the coming of the roads, and the coming of the satellite dishes, and the coming of McDonald's, and then I began to panic and decided it was time to capture it on paper because that's the only place where it was going to be captured.

Loewenstein: Did you have to work hard to cultivate the different regional voices?

Smith: No, not at all, because I think the first language we hear is really our heart's language, and for me that is the real heavy Appalachian dialect I grew up hearing. And so that comes so much more natural to me than, say, the speech of somebody in an English department, which is how I've been making a living, teaching for twenty years. I'm really interested in language, too. I think if I'd gone on to school I would have been a linguist rather than having had an interest in literature.

Loewenstein: Language is an aspect of your writing that fascinates me.

Smith: Oh, I love it. And I really like to show the ways in which it's changed; and one thing I noticed with all the older people in my family, a lot of them, started out speaking pretty heavy dialect and then they'd get some education, or make some money, or both, and begin to speak in a less country way; but when they got old, they would go back to those double negatives and back to those expressions. My dad did it too. It just fascinated me so I tried to have Ivy Rowe do that in *Fair and Tender Ladies.*

Loewenstein: There are some critics of your regional voices, and I'm thinking of Roz Kaveney who would say you have trouble finding a context for aural realism and that your possession and ear for language can actually work against you in that your characters get "thoroughly on your nerves." How would you defend his comments?

Smith: Oh, I think it's absolutely true.

Loewenstein: So your characters get on your nerves?

Smith: Well, sometimes, yes. When I start writing I do a lot of homework first, and the process of writing for me is that I just sit down and go crazy, frankly. I just lose myself completely in the characters and they write their own stuff. And, yes, sometimes they really do get on your nerves. If you have a character that you love, that's fine, but other times—it's just like if you have a next-door neighbor that keeps coming over and won't shut up—it drives you crazy. And that has happened to me at different times in my books—well, it's true; I mean, it's absolutely true, and the way I write, it's just to plan as much as I can and then release them, let them go. I do have a horrible time with plot. A lot of times I can't get one at all and I just appropriate it from some source, like in *Family Linen,* which I agree is terribly plotted. I had all these characters walking around in my head wanting to talk, and so finally I borrowed a plot from a crime that had just happened in North Carolina. But it was a very imperfect marriage—they didn't fit.

Loewenstein: I would imagine that your novels, because they're regional, are appreciated differently in the South as compared to say the West Coast?

Smith: Yes. I think this is interesting because I do go around and do readings and so on—my husband, by the way, is fascinated that Southerners read Southern novels so much and he can't quite figure it out because you don't have people in California wanting to read about people in California, you know—or Midwesterners wanting to read all about the Midwest. It's a Southern phenomenon and I think it has to do with a kind of self-canonization that Southerners are into anyway. They love to recognize themselves in their work. They love to get *Southern Living* magazine and see other people like themselves out there having hors d'oeuvres in their green pants on their patio. They love to see themselves depicted. John Shelton Reed has called them South-Americans, like Polish Americans, or Italian Americans, a real ethnic sub-group. One of the things is they have institutions that perpetuate their myth. Okay? And one of those is lots of books in which they can see themselves. I can remember going to see one of Clyde's plays—

Loewenstein: Clyde Edgerton?

Smith: Yes, it was *Raney,* made into a play written by John Justice, and it was down in Fayetteville. I was sitting with a whole bunch of people from Fayetteville, and they kept saying things like, "That's just like Susie—ooh, I love to eat Vienna sausages," and they were totally recognizing themselves in the work. I don't know why Southerners like to do that, but they really do.

Loewenstein: And, I guess, isn't it more Southern to trace one's ancestry?

Smith: Oh, sure.

Loewenstein: Except for the Mormons, I can think of no other group as obsessed with tracing their roots.

Smith: I'm always much more interested, frankly, in the reaction of somebody who is not Southern, because I think outsiders are a lot more likely to not just pick up on what they recognize of themselves or their experience, but get more at what I hope it might be about.

Loewenstein: What kind of responses are you getting from New Yorkers?

Smith: Nice responses when they actually read me. But I think a lot of people in the Northeast and elsewhere in this country just simply don't want to read Southern writing because so much of it is cliché and is about the same, you know, "dead mules" and "Mommy"—and so they have a notion that it's not something they read. I mean it's very interesting, Claudia, for instance, the difference in the way Eudora Welty is viewed in all Southern universities and then you go to, say, Toronto and nobody's heard of Eudora

Welty. Southern writing is still kind of a regional phenomenon and these books are just not treated nearly as seriously, I think, outside the South. I think there is a feeling and I think it's probably accurate that a lot of Southern writing does trade on what I think of as oral skills, as storytelling, and there are a lot of people in this country who are readers who do not like that kind of thing. They like a more intellectual book. They would rather read a wonderful book such as Norman Rush's book, *Mating,* for instance, or books that are in a sense more intellectually rigorous, that are not so much storytelling as that other kind of novel writing. You see what I'm saying?

Loewenstein: Yes, in fact with regard to storytellers, I went to the Dallas Art Museum a few weeks ago and saw a painting by Odilon Redon, *Initiation to Study—Two Young Ladies.* In fact, I've got a copy for you. . . .

Smith: How great! Oh, how wonderful.

Loewenstein: I was struck by how much this painting made me think of your novels. Something clicked for me about the way older women in your novels, often storytellers, seem to initiate the younger women, and I was wondering if that is a true perception.

Smith: I think it is.

Loewenstein: Is it a feminine tradition?

Smith: Well, it's a tradition where I grew up. Because we do have in the mountains the older women who are really revered and people turn to them for advice, more than they turn to the older men. I mean, there's a tradition in the mountains of the Granny woman who was the one who was wise and who was turned to and who has, in a sense, lived beyond sex. Younger women fall into, I think, categories or phases of life where they're functioning in certain ways but older women can sit back and understand things and tell you things that are helpful. I was lucky enough to grow up with a number of older women, in my own family, who were real helpful to me in lots of ways.

Loewenstein: Is there a storyteller in your own life?

Smith: Well, there are a lot of them. There was my mother, there was my Aunt Kate, there is Ava McClanahan who kept house for my mother for forty-six years. You just sit around and the way people transmit information is through a story. It's never "this is what you ought to do"—it is never abstract, it's always with a story. Now look at this picture. This is Lou Crabtree—she's probably been more influential to me than any other single woman. I ran into her in an adult education class that I was teaching through the auspices of the University of Virginia, and she's a mountain woman. It turned out she'd been writing her whole life long, and she was in her seventies then. She came into class with these fuzzy bedroom shoes on, just looking like hell. She has palsy and her head shakes and she said, "I'm Lou Crabtree and I just love to write," and I thought, "Oh, no," and then we went around—everybody was supposed to read the first line of something they had written and I'll never forget the first line of her story was "I had thirteen miscarriages and named every one of them," and I just went "AAAAAHHH," and it was this wonderful story and I said, "Have you got any more stuff, Lou?" and she came in and she brought a trunk, literally, and so the upshot was I made some selections and typed it. LSU published it and now she writes a column for her local paper.

Loewenstein: What's the title of these stories?

Smith: *Stories from Sweet Holler.* It sold four printings. She's sort of become famous now in her town. Here, I've got a great copy of a newspaper story about her. It was just recently done. If Ivy Rowe is based on anybody real, it would be Lou—because she's so strong. At one point, she had five children under six and didn't even have running water, and I mean, she's really something. She used to teach in a one-room school out from Abingdon. She taught me a lot and so she's been real important to me.

Loewenstein: Are we losing this tradition of storytellers?

Smith: I actually don't think so. But the kind of information that's being transmitted is obviously different. I mean nobody has to tell a young wife how to make soap or something. But it seems to me, here in Chapel Hill, my women friends that I have, women, in particular, are talking a whole lot more about themselves and their lives, and their possibilities, and their feelings about things. We are, in somewhat a different context, telling our stories more than ever, it seems to me, to each other and to younger women.

Loewenstein: Do your storytellers and other characters arise from a mythical past?

Smith: Well, they do and they don't. You see I was a reporter first, while I was writing fiction, sort of by training, so a lot of what an urban reader or a non-Southern reader might think of as mythical is really real. I mean I just took my mother-in-law to Grundy; my mother-in-law is a smart woman, a schoolteacher from Boston who grew up in the Northeast, and she kept saying, "But I thought you made all these things up!"

Loewenstein: Perhaps what I may have thought to arise from a mythic past might—

Smith: Is actually fairly accurate in terms of people that I have known. Yes, that's true. I really take a lot of notes all the time on real people and real situations and I'm glad it comes off as mythic, but some of it may not be.

Loewenstein: Red-headed Emmy?

Smith: That was really based very closely on a witch tale that I heard in the mountains. That's a very traditional witch tale. The witches were red-headed where I'm from and I heard again and again the story of the witch who tries to pass herself off as a regular girl and traps a boy, and then rides him at night. While it's mythic, people will tell you, "Yes, she used to live right up there," or something, so it is and it's not mythic. It's like the first story in *The Devil's Dream* that was so horrifying, about the girl whose husband wouldn't let her play the fiddle, and she goes mad. Well, I was told that. I found it later in a book, too, but I was told that as if it really had happened, about this particular cabin up above Hot Springs, North Carolina, where I was running around doing the research. So it's mythic, but it's also factual a lot of the time.

Loewenstein: Do you make a distinction then between mythic and legendary?

Smith: I might let you make that decision. I mean if I write in such a way these stories appear to be mythic, I'm delighted, but they are always based on actual fact. Everything I write, particularly all the mountain stuff, is really in this attempt that you said earlier is me as the crusader, to set down things I've heard about—the way it was. Not nearly as much is made up as you might suppose. Almost nothing is made up.

Loewenstein: The name Arthur keeps coming up over and over.

Smith: I hadn't even thought about it. Really?

Loewenstein: Little Arthur in *The Last Day the Dogbushes Bloomed,* John Arthur in *Fair and Tender Ladies,* Arthur in *Family Linen* . . .

Smith: My God, I never thought of that.

Loewenstein: I assumed they were from Arthurian legends.

Smith: No-o-o-o-o!

Loewenstein: I was going to ask you what it was about the Arthurian legends that fascinates you.

Smith: Nothing! It comes up because one of my favorite uncles—he was either, I think now, partially retarded or maybe a kind of schizophrenic who lived always with my grandmother—was named Arthur. He raised dogs and I always was crazy about him. I just like to put his name in. That's it, that's it. I do. That's true.

Loewenstein: I'm glad I got that straight! In all your books, for me, there is a strong searching and spirituality.
Smith: Yes, yes.

Loewenstein: Two *grandes lignes* of spiritual transformation seem to recur: those characters who go out and actively seek signs from God, often in vain, and those who are sought by God in a Joan of Arc way, as is Ezekiel when he comes home stumbling drunk and God finds him even though he doesn't want to be found.
Smith: That's really true. Everything I write is really personal, and this is one of the central concerns of my life that I have never worked out. "Tongues of Fire" is autobiographical, not in terms of the family but in terms of the little girl who hears the voice of God at camp—that's me.

Loewenstein: Tell me more about that.
Smith: Well, when I was a child, we were a very religious family who went to church every time they cracked the door, the Methodist church, but I wanted to be Pentecostal, I wanted to be Holiness, I mean that was me. That little child, that personality was exactly me.

Loewenstein: How old were you then?
Smith: Well, from 7, 8, 9, 10, 11, 12, I really was a very religious child and I started going off to the Holiness church with one of my friends.

Loewenstein: This is exactly like your book!
Smith: It's *exactly* like the book!—and got saved and kept getting saved. And then later I had a boyfriend who was in the Church of Christ and I would go to his church and get saved, and my mother finally put her foot down and sent me off to camp so I would quit getting saved. While I was at camp, I either had a fit or I heard God, who knows which—

Loewenstein: You literally heard the voice of God?
Smith: Yes, absolutely. I heard this voice saying, "Lee, Lee," and it was a Sunday morning at an Episcopal camp, and everyone else was up at the church service and I had bronchitis or something so I was in my tent and—

these were kind of big tents, not little pup tents or anything and I heard this voice. And I remember, it seems really funny now that they took me to the infirmary because I kept saying, "No, it's not a fit. No, I heard God speaking to me," and they said, "Well, what did He say?" and I said, "Well, He just called my name. He said Lee," and they said "Well, how do you know it was God?" and I said, "because there are no men at Camp Allegheny," which in retrospect I think is hysterical. And then, I would also go around—I was real religious, you know—I would go around and testify in the MYF and at the Methodist revivals. Anyway, I had this very intense spiritual life that was either an intense spiritual life or a mental illness. I really did hear things, and prayer had this enormous intensity. I've been interested recently in reading *The Spiritual Life of Children* by Robert Coles. Have you heard of him?

Loewenstein: I am still rather astounded by this childhood experience of yours—but yes, I've heard of this book.

Smith: Well, it's very interesting. He believes that a lot of what is interpreted as pathology is really a child's actual experience of God. Children do have this impulse and I really had it but then I went off to St. Catherine's School and then I discovered boys and got more interested in boys, just as the girl in "Tongues of Fire" does. At St. Catherine's School in Richmond, which was an Episcopal school where everything was suddenly ritualized to the point of total boredom, during Holy Week you had to do all this shit. I mean, you had to kneel and chant and carry on, and that sort of thing. It sort of did me in, or else growing up did me in, and I really turned away from religion with a vengeance. I just didn't want to have anything to do with it. I saw it as scary and I wanted to put it behind me. I guess I liked the ritual end of it. Ritual kept at bay those forces that were real emotional and real scary to me, and so ever since, it's like I keep searching for that kind of religious feeling that I had, and for that sense of intensity that I associated with God. I search for it in my books. But I'm real scared to go to the kind of churches where I know I might find it.

Loewenstein: Because of the intensity?

Smith: Yeah. I loved the church that I made up at the end of *The Devil's Dream,* but if I went there I just know that I'd be one of those women stroking people and having fits, and so I don't know. At some point I'm going to have to reconcile it. I've never talked about this before, by the way, but it's true.

Loewenstein: In *Black Mountain Breakdown* when Crystal is raped by her uncle, I find this so interesting because as she's getting raped she says she felt as if nails were being driven into her head, you seem to sacrifice her in a Christ-like way. What was the connection between the biblical allegory and rape?

Smith: I don't know. I mean, I just absolutely don't know. I do know that in my mind there has always been some link between religious intensity and sexual passion, and I mean in my growing up it was a direct link. I mean the only thing to do on a date was to go to the revival. But what you're talking about would have been totally subconscious for me when I was writing that.

Loewenstein: Did you keep sexual passion bound up in religious intensity throughout your growing up?

Smith: I did somehow pull away from my earlier child-like sense of religion, when I found boys. I mean it was like . . .

Loewenstein: Puberty!

Smith: Yeah, you know, a big intensity transferred from one object to another. I'm sure that shows up in my writing.

Loewenstein: Roland Barthes—and I am aware that you poke fun at literary criticism—in *Le Plaisir du Texte* talks about "codes antipathiques" where the pleasure for the reader comes from a rupture of the expected, and where for example, there is a collision of the noble and the trivial. It strikes me that this is true of your writing . . .

Smith: It strikes me that it is, too.

Loewenstein: I say this because you champion the seemingly trivialized, stereotypical females: hairdressers and pageant contestants.

Smith: They don't strike me as just trivial—they strike me as really interesting.

Loewenstein: They hold wisdom that far surpasses what people typically might expect of them.

Smith: Well, yes, which is always true in life. I mean, again, it's what I really believe. I choose these characters because they're people like people I know, or have known, who were in those roles.

Loewenstein: You spend time in their circles?

Smith: Oh yeah, I still do. Right now I'm feeling very weird because my dad died and so I have sold his house in Grundy and later this week I'm going up to arrange the details for the sale. In a way I always depended on being there a lot of the time. My sense of myself as a person is linked to that town because my parents have always been there, and his house is the house I was born in. So I'm wondering what will happen when—as you say, "do you move in those circles"—yeah I do, this is my family, these are the people I know. So I never had to leave, in a funny kind of way, and I will now because once I close that house and sell it, then my original home is gone. And that's going to be real interesting to me to see how that affects everything.

Loewenstein: And why are you selling this house?

Smith: It's in Grundy, Virginia, and we live here. I can't afford to keep it. I have to sell it.

Loewenstein: That's really tough.

Smith: Yes, it is. And I'm an only child, which makes everything a little more concentrated.

Loewenstein: When you write about these people such as those you know in Grundy, is it a socio-political statement?

Smith: No. I don't mind if anybody else says that; but no, because I just tell a story, and I tell a story that I feel drawn to tell. But I firmly believe that there is nothing you write that is not political.

Loewenstein: I guess I'm trying to separate out Home and Hearth Smarts from the collective wisdom of political movements, the women's movements in particular. Maybe the two are inseparable.

Smith: I mean, there's nothing that doesn't derive from the situation, the circumstance surrounding the story, so everything is political to my mind. You can't go out and pick your material; your material has already chosen you, by the circumstances of your birth.

Loewenstein: I've been reading your work now for a long time, since I was in my twenties.

Smith: Well, you have! I'm sort of embarrassed . . .

Loewenstein: I'm now in my early forties, and it seems to me that your women characters are getting wiser and wiser. For me personally, a culminating moment is in *The Devil's Dream* where Katie Cocker stops defining herself through her men.

Smith: I hope they are! I hope they're finally getting some sense. You see, I've been writing since I was in my twenties, and now in my late forties I think I've written fiction the way other people might write in their journals.

I'm not much of an analyst of my own work but I can see that in the earlier books a lot of the women were like Crystal, who is a prime example of women who felt completely imprisoned by their lives. Now that you mention it, Crystal also defined herself in terms of men, always changing her personality to fit whoever she was with.

Loewenstein: She ends up catatonic.

Smith: I hope we've gone from that to Ivy Rowe or Katie Cocker, who are able to write their own story or sing their own song, or whatever it might be. But it's taken me a long time to see that that's possible myself. It took me a long time to get to Katie Cocker.

Loewenstein: I'm glad Katie rids herself of the patriarchal shackles. I couldn't help but want to cheer.

Smith: There's a price to pay, though, because I think the final image of her is certainly problematic. Breaking the shackles is great, and that's one thing, but the price of autonomy often is a certain kind of isolation from what nourished you. I think this is one reason I was so drawn to writing about country music. It is so full of interesting contradictions—between home and the road, for instance—really it's the *dream* of home, because home was pretty much shit! Poverty and all that kind of stuff is idealized in all the songs, and so they want to sing about it but you can't ever go back to it.

Loewenstein: How about when you go back home, are you treated as a famous person now?

Smith: I'm not. Are you kidding? My daddy ran his dime store there for forty-six years and, I couldn't write this, but what happened to him was he finally decided after forty-six years to go out of business because the whole town was becoming a ghost town, economically. It's one of those coalfields that's just mined out, and it's horrible, and there's this migration, and there's nobody downtown. So he decided to close the dime store—which I was very much against because I couldn't figure out what he'd do with himself. He was eighty-five and went to the dime store every day of his life. The last day of the Going Out of Business sale, he went home and had a stroke, and fell and broke a bunch of ribs and was put in the hospital there. I went up to see him and as soon as I got there, he had this massive hemorrhage and died.

Loewenstein: That's extraordinary. Here it is once again, another of your stories—mythic? or truth?

Smith: It's symbolic—I mean you couldn't write it because you couldn't get away with it. Everyone would say "Oh, that's too symbolic—that's too obvious." Well, it's true. You know, it's true, I mean, it's just really true.

Loewenstein: Sex is a touchy subject in many ways and you seem to write about two extremes: there's the repressed, puritanical mind, such as in "Tongues of Fire," that refers to sexuality as "down there."
Smith: Right. Yes.

Loewenstein: Or Sybil, who refers to her internal female anatomy as "dark and murky." It's often the mothers who are the repressed characters. In contrast with females you write about who are unafraid of their sexuality.
Smith: Well, in my mind, there was this split, and it did have a lot to do with my mother who was a lady and a teacher and so on, and my very ladylike Aunt Gaygay who's the one that all the great quotes in "Tongues of Fire" come from.

Loewenstein: For example?
Smith: "Let's have a drink, honey, it's dark underneath the house," "down there," all that. I did grow up with this strong sense of "nice girls," this real sense of dichotomy. It was only as I got older that I realized there need not be such a dichotomy.

Loewenstein: In pop psychology—what are they calling it—the Madonna-Whore Complex?
Smith: Yes, right.

Loewenstein: In your novels, women who have affairs often become stronger and the affairs even resuscitate their own floundering marriages. That doesn't sound like your Christian approach to sexuality. . . .
Smith: But again, see, I don't make that much stuff up and it's not that it's happened to me, but I've had a couple of friends to whom that happened, so I just think that's true, and this makes it worth writing about.

Loewenstein: Can you tell me more about why a woman might feel compelled to have an affair in order to revive her life?
Smith: I think it's possible for a person to go for long periods in her life where she has got so much she has to do, or she is so overwhelmed by certain things that she just loses touch with her body. I mean, this happened to Ivy Rowe in *Fair and Tender Ladies* with having all those babies and then there are the endless needs of the children and just responding, responding, responding. Her affair with Honey Breeding gave her back a part of her life

that was gone, so she was a much fuller person afterward, she could respond to her husband. It gave her back her self, in a sense. I know that's an unorthodox view—it's not anything that I'm endorsing, but I think sometimes it happens.

Loewenstein: So that's the connection between women restituting their bodies—that is to say, the connection between experiencing their own sexuality and self-revelation?

Smith: I think part of the experience of Southern women for years and years—to become a lady would divorce you from your body. You read about ladies undressing in the closet, they might have eleven children but their husbands would never have seen them naked, and all this kind of thing. . . . I do think that girls were brought up to feel that any bodily function was dirty. I certainly was, and most members of my generation who had "nice mothers" were. So it's something most of us have had to work through if we wanted to own our bodies in any significant way.

Loewenstein: You're speaking of domestic life. On the one hand, there seems to be a common theme in your work that domestic life is dangerous. Mamaw talks about being attacked by a domestic cat and—
Smith: That's funny, yes.

Loewenstein: Then, on the other hand, you seem to have a protective quality in female relationships.
Smith: What do you mean, "protective quality"? You mean females taking care of other females?

Loewenstein: Yes, exactly. Do you think domestic life is dangerous?
Smith: Yes, I do.

Loewenstein: Tell me something about that.
Smith: Well, I think particularly for women, who are the ones who are supposed to take care of things, taking care of people, could be completely taken over. I think it's very dangerous to become domestic in a certain way. But I'm also the kind of woman who gets a lot of pleasure from setting the table and cooking, and so on, so it's like religion—another area of great conflict for me. I'm real domestic in a way and I'm terrified of it in another way. It's just like I'm real religious in a way and terrified of it in another way. So I suppose that the things you can never work out turn out to be what you write about. It's something I'm always struggling with.

Loewenstein: It seems you've created a new breed of man—the Melungeon man?

Smith: Oh, no, no, no! The Melungeons are real.

Loewenstein: The Melungeons are real!

Smith: Oh, sure! When I was a little girl growing up, my Daddy used to tell me to be good or he would give me to the Melungeons, which was a great threat. We knew some Melungeons. There's a whole racial group, they live in East Tennessee on a ridge named Newman's Ridge, overlooking the Clinch River.

Loewenstein: Am I the only one who doesn't know of the existence of the Melungeons?

Smith: Well, that's what I mean about writing about things that people take as mythic but are not. They're real and they're just fascinating and there are many, many theories as to where the Melungeons came from. Some people think they were the lost tribe of Roanoke Island; other people think they were Portuguese who were shipwrecked and intermarried with black Americans and Native Americans. There are endless theories about them, but they're absolutely real.

Loewenstein: I just learned something new. I thought you created it.

Smith: Oh, no. In fact, I read that section out loud once in Tennessee, I think in Knoxville, and there were three or four Melungeons in the audience who were just amazed to find themselves in print.

Loewenstein: Vital Spark pills for male weakness?

Smith: Oh, those are real.

Loewenstein: Made from amazingly virile Oriental turtles?

Smith: Yes. Isn't that great? No, I did a lot of research for *The Devil's Dream* and there is a person here on the faculty at UNC, Glen Hinson, who is considered a world authority on medicine shows, and I used his wonderful tapes and notes. Nothing in there is made up. I mean, it's true, it's true.

Loewenstein: I've seen a transformation in your male characters. They seem to be more gentle—I'm thinking back on the violence in *Cakewalk* or the brutality in the *Last Day the Dogbushes Bloomed,* compared to the men in *The Devil's Dream.*

Smith: I teach people now who are the age I was when I started writing, and they see *everything* in such extremes! You know, you do think in stereo-

type, and you think in black and white when you're young: you're all turned
on by one thing and appalled by something else. One of the main things to
me about getting older is realizing that everything is so much infinitely more
complicated than we ever knew when we were young, when everything
seemed good or bad. Well, no absolutes exist as far as I can tell any more.
So I think that that obviously would come through in the writing.

Loewenstein: In *The Devil's Dream* many of your men characters who
are perhaps less appealing are defined more in terms of their frailties, rather
than what they did wrong.

Smith: Right. Exactly. There's lots of reasons why Wayne behaved the
way he did, I guess. That's true. They do mistreat the women, but out of
desperate needs of their own. I've always been interested in that aspect of it
and also because, again, I did so much research and learned that so many of
the women, country music stars, had histories of abusive relationships. So I
was looking into that and trying to figure out why and how that happens.
And then I have a really good friend here who works for the Coalition for
Battered Women and I did some oral history work out there too, listening to
everybody's stories.

Loewenstein: It seems impossible that I could have a conversation with
you about your writing without talking about The Nervous Breakdown. I
wonder if you'd talk more about it.

Smith: Because I've written about that a lot?

Loewenstein: Yes. I've almost come to expect it.

Smith: That's interesting. Well, it's just because it was such a fact of my
youth. Both my parents were institutionalized many times. And the nervous
breakdown was something that happened a whole lot in my childhood, so
naturally it found its way into the writing.

Loewenstein: Have you ever had a nervous breakdown?

Smith: No. But I think a lot of nervous breakdowns in the older generation
that I grew up among really did have to deal with the rigidly prescribed
modes of behavior for both men and women.

Loewenstein: You teach writing. Is there a marked change, do you think,
in young writers?

Smith: Yes. I do think a general change has to do with television, actually,
Claudia. I think my students tend to write what I would think of as cinemati-

cally now. There are very few young writers capable of writing long passages of narration. There are very few of them capable of writing a transition from one scene to another. It's like scene and then white space and then scene and then white space.

Loewenstein: Like sound bites?

Smith: Yes, and it's up to the reader to make the kinds of connections that Henry James or Peter Taylor or more recent writers like Alice Munro (who's one of my favorite writers) make, with these long discursive narrative passages. You don't see any narrative passages.

Loewenstein: A lot of people are saying that the trends in literary criticism are really unintelligible and you obviously mock them in *The Devil's Dream.*

Smith: Sure.

Loewenstein: Tell me what you teach your students, and do you think that literary criticism is unintelligible?

Smith: I do think it's the writer's business to be as divorced from criticism as possible. I also, however, love to teach and I'm very interested theoretically in what is happening in criticism.

Loewenstein: What about literary criticism in reference to your own work?

Smith: I did have one hysterical time once when Anne Jones and I decided we were going to give this program together. I read something from *Oral History,* then she read a paper she had written on the part I had just read. It was just hysterical!

Loewenstein: How's that?

Smith: I just thought it was full of shit! She read her paper and I was staring at this whole room of people and was asked, "What did you think of that?" and I said, "Well, I just think it was one of the strangest things I've heard. It's just totally ridiculous." And then Anne said, "It doesn't matter what Lee thinks," which is so funny.

Loewenstein: Are you working on something at the moment?

Smith: Nothing. I'm not writing anything. I'm just so involved right now, as I say, in this business of having my father die, and selling the house, and sort of losing my identity as a person without any legitimate claim to life in that particular mountain town, which has nourished my fiction. Luckily we have a cabin up in the mountains in North Carolina because otherwise I think

I would feel completely adrift at this moment. As far as being a person in academic life, I've felt I'm just kind of passing through. It's what I have to do to make a living, but my sense of identity has derived from the mountains.

Loewenstein: It will be interesting to see where you go with your writing in the face of this loss.

Smith: Yes. I mean it's affecting me profoundly and so obviously will affect whatever I write. Just having a home to go to. What do you do when you don't have a home to go to?

Lee Smith: God Not Only Speaks but Sings

Susan Ketchin / 1994

From *The Christ-Haunted Landscape: Faith and Doubt in Southern Fiction* (Jackson: UP of Mississippi, 1994), 44–55. Copyright © 1994. Reprinted by permission of the University Press of Mississippi.

When Lee Smith was a little girl, she gave God a tea party. Perhaps remembering that, she told me she was relieved when she learned that I would be interviewing Harry Crews; until then, she said, she'd been concerned that her interview would be the most "heathen" one in the book. Such good-humored worry about piety and heathenism is emblematic of Lee Smith's utterly engaging personality, how she greets and is greeted by the world. Of medium height and build, with blond hair and light blue eyes, a radiant smile, and Scots-Irish fair skin, Smith is noted for her generosity of spirit, quick wit, and completely unaffected, easy manner. A native of the small mining town of Grundy, Virginia, she speaks in a clear, mountain accent, telling stories with an ironic twist, a self-deprecating joke, or a pinprick at pretentiousness. In describing her genuine struggles with religious belief and morality, she says, "I'm so much *not* New Age."

An extraordinary number of friends from every part of the country and from all periods of her life still come to see her. On vacation at a friend's summer house in Maine, she sits at the kitchen table, looking out over the lake and mountains beyond, and writes funny post cards (one card that pictures a moose grazing in the foreground, a little apart from the herd, gets the caption: "Married moose dreaming of the single life").

Recently, Lee Smith teamed up with the Tarwater Band (a folk trio who named themselves after the backwoods prophet in Flannery O'Connor's *The Violent Bear It Away*) for a combined reading/concert in which she read from her latest novel, *The Devil's Dream,* and the band sang original and traditional mountain tunes from the book, such as "The Riddle Song" and "Shady Grove." Introducing a passage, she confessed, "I always wanted to write a story in which God speaks; in this one, He not only speaks, but sings."

Lee Smith claims that she cannot sing (or even keep rhythm), but all who know her know that she sings beautifully through her work and her life, with

129

a feeling, a clarity—and a wallop—that is as extraordinary and as comforting as corn whiskey and wild honey. Throughout my interview with her, she talked with a lively sense of humor about her life and work. A keen listener, observer, and storyteller, Smith spoke openly and poignantly about her impassioned religious sensibility as a child, how in her beloved mountains God and nature were one, so that her "whole childhood was really full of God and wonders."

On a warm June day we sat drinking coffee on a chintz sofa in Lee's downstairs den. Bookshelves lined the entirety of one long wall; her writing desk sat in a corner between the bookshelves and the gray brick fireplace on the wall opposite us. Sliding glass doors provided a pleasant view out over thickly wooded land. The day was balmy, clear, and breezy, like many June days in these parts; the tulip poplars and oak trees were budding with new green leaves, providing rest for our eyes as we talked.

Let me begin by asking you about your religious sensibility and its origins. Flannery O'Connor once wrote that she always admired believers who came to the faith as adults because she would find it difficult to believe in some of the more mystical tenets of her faith without having been "brung up to it." How were you "brung up" to your religion as a child in Grundy? Do these experiences show up in any of your fiction? One way to approach this might be to talk about Karen, in "Tongues of Fire."

"Tongues of Fire" in a way is truly one of the most autobiographical stories I have ever written. The family is all made up, but the character of Karen is absolutely the way I was as a child, including the obsessive reading and the obsessive religion. I was raised in a little church, the Grundy Methodist Church, that was very straight-laced, but I had a friend whose mother spoke in tongues. I was just wild for this family. I would have gone to live with them if they'd let me. My parents were older, and they were so overprotective. I just loved the "letting go" that happened when I would go to church with my friend.

And then later, I got a boyfriend who was a member of another church. This was a *wild* church. And I would go to the revival with him and be saved—constantly. So religion and sex—you know, excitement, passion—were all together. I couldn't differentiate between sexual passion and religious passion. This was what we all did on dates, was go to the revival. It was a turn-on.

Things were done very literally. One thing they did at that church that I'll never forget, was that they had a big ply-board thing, in the front of the church, full of light bulbs. This was at regular church. If you were present, you and your family, you'd go up and screw in your light bulb. And it would turn on. And over the top of the whole thing, it said, "Let Your Little Light Shine." And if you weren't there, it would be so obvious to everyone else in the congregation because your little light would not be shining. Something about that, I don't know—it was the only thing that was happening for me in terms of excitement.

You were saved several times?

Yes, I was just given to rededicating my life and being saved. All this was an embarrassment to my mother. I was a Methodist, and I had been sprinkled as a baby. I was perfectly saved as far as she was concerned and she wished I would quit going to these other churches and "acting up." You know, it was a "low-class" thing to do, in my mother's eyes. But even in the Methodist Church, which I went to, and MYF, and church camp every summer, and retreats, I was—more so even than Karen in the story—a very religious child. A *very* religious child. I was such a religious child that I used to think that I heard God speaking to me. In fact, I still think I may have. I mean I'm not putting that down. Because I was an only child, and I was by myself a lot of the time, and I did a whole lot of nonstop praying, reading the Bible, thinking, and so on. I loved Joan of Arc, and I loved those inspirational stories like Karen does.

Nature particularly inspired me. For instance when I was at camp, several times I was absolutely sure that I heard God, or saw a vision, or whatever. I'm sure there could be a psychiatric word for the kind of little child I was.

I was also given to rituals. Like before I went to bed at night, I had about twelve things I had to do. The door had to be cracked a certain way because there was a witch in the closet. The light had to be a certain way, this and that. I was always prone to imaginings.

Did this passion last throughout your girlhood?

Yes, up through high school—all the time I lived in Grundy. I would go to youth revivals. I would speak at youth revivals—up until the time I went away to school to St. Catherine's [a preparatory school for girls in Richmond]. St. Catherine's was Episcopal. I'm telling you, all that stuff, that institutionalized ritual, just knocked it out of me. It deadened all the passion. Somehow, in the town I grew up in, I associated religion with a kind of a life force. Then all of a sudden at St. Catherine's, since it was an Episcopal school and it had all these rules, I began to associate religion with a death force. I guess it's fair to say I outgrew it; I got interested in other things. It was one of those things of childhood.

Do you feel sometimes that you miss it? Or was it somehow a relief to go beyond it?

I was sort of glad to outgrow it because it was wearing me out. It was becoming clear to me that I was getting to be at an age that I would have to do a lot more with it, or just give it up. Because with me, I've always been, unfortunately, an all-or-nothing kind of person. I still feel that way now. I feel like, okay, if I want to start really going to church again, I'm going to have to really go.

I've heard you mention that before—that you'd have to be involved completely if you should ever think about becoming involved again. It is as if there aren't any restraining forces, that you must go whole hog.

Yes, anything I'm in, I get completely into, and for that reason, I think I have held back. I think it is because I was that kind of a child. I was so completely wrapped up in it. You know, I associated it with nature, and I was a real tom-boy. We played in the mountains, all the time. And it was like the whole world of my childhood was really full of God and wonders. But as you get older that sort of thing scares you because there are not any boundaries. It was terrifying. So I think in a funny way, I was glad to hit St. Catherine's, and all those rules, and all that mumbo-jumbo.

The ritual did seem to kill any joy; it's a "kill-joy." Though you felt that need for ritual in your daily emotional life as a child, the institution managed to overdo it. Was it a matter of overkill?

It was for me in terms of religion. After that I pulled back. I still have the sense of it, and probably some day I will have to find that again. I have a feeling that it's out there. I associate it with the mountains. At some point I'll have to move back to the mountains, I think. At some point I'll have to throw myself into it all again.

Have you ever been to any black church services? The times I've been able to throw myself into things and even be transported have been at black revivals.

Yes, as a matter of fact I just heard Jesse Jackson in Atlanta, last Saturday. Just the way the crowd is! Yes, being transported is something that I have always both desired and feared. More than anything else. It's what used to happen to me as a child, but it's what's scariest to happen as an adult, because as an adult, you have to be responsible. You know, I can't be transported. I have to go to the grocery store.

Yes, and I have to be back by three to pick up the kids.

I can't have a religious experience; I have to be back by three. All these people are depending on me. I did feel a sense of being lifted up at Jesse Jackson's sermon; everybody was holding hands, swaying. That was a wonderful time.

You know, I think it's significant that your sense of being carried away as a child was so sensuous, so concrete. You felt closest to the spiritual in the mountains, in nature. Everything was all of one piece rather than the spiritual being divorced from the physical and confined to an institution, a church, a separate place. In the usual idea of what it means to be religious, church is where you go and are asked to renounce the physical world as being the source of temptation and sin. You're asked to separate the physical from the spiritual, at least the sensual from the spiritual.

I surely did have that sense at the Episcopal Church. I did associate that renunciation with all the rules at St. Catherine's. When I went there, we had so many, many social rules.

It's as if some churches fear the physical so much that they feel they have to build a containment vessel for it, like they do for a nuclear reactor.

And strangely enough, I married somebody who had a similar experience. Jim Seay had been the most religious boy in the world, in Mississippi. In fact, he had gone to a Bible college, Mercer College, and even when he was as old as twenty-one, he was going to be a youth minister, and he went to Ridgecrest every summer. But he had stopped all that by the time he got to Ole Miss, fairly late, in his twenties. When I married him, he, too, was threatened by the consuming power of his religion, didn't want to fall back into it. He did not go to church, did not want to go to church, did not want anybody else to go to church. Maybe if I'd married somebody who was a church-goer, I would have learned how to maintain a balance. Or seen how I could be religious and not have it take over my life. But as it was, for a long time, I didn't have anything to do with the church.

Yet, oddly enough, I was writing about it all the time. Except in my work, I didn't want anything to do with it. [Laughter] But I was always thinking about it.

Except in one of the most important areas in your life, your creative work.
Right, exactly. But I mean in my daily life, I just shied away from it.

I understand that so well. I had a similar experience growing up. And here I thought I was the only one. Have you ever read The Spiritual Life of Children *by Robert Coles?*
No, I have not. But I want to.

It presents with such respect accounts of the spiritual lives of these young-sters who talk quite openly and lucidly about their own spiritual lives and what we've been talking about. It's very moving to read.
And it's all real.

I think one reason it's so real is because for these children, religion involves their whole body, along with the whole mind and spirit. They do not have the capacity or the desire to compartmentalize the experience. And, as you said, you still feel a mixture of desire and fear, you still feel you have to "contain" yourself. Ironically, this only demonstrates that you are an intensely spiritual person.
Well, I have never gotten away from this ideal, this notion—I take it seri-ously. I'm always worried about what's the right thing to do. It's so hard to figure out in the real world what is the right thing to do. What is good? I struggle with it all the time. I spend a lot of time thinking about it. It's just old-fashioned morality, I guess.

It's making a genuine effort to know, to understand, to do what's right.
Yeah, I think we all have to make the effort.

There are some people who don't do that.
Yes, they just don't think it's anything to worry about. And you know, my whole notion of morality runs counter to the "Do your own thing, follow your bliss" idea. I'm so much *not* New Age.

What do you think of Joseph Campbell?
I love Joseph Campbell's ideas on religion and culture. I love to think in terms of comparative religions. I think Joseph Campbell is very much a mor-alist. But a casual reading or a casual interpretation of his theories does lead to a very hedonistic, New Age kind of thinking that a lot of people are follow-ing that I don't think he ever intended.

Some people might find a way to make any statement self-serving and hedo-nistic, in any case.

What they're looking for is more of a justification of what they're going to do anyway.

This intensity, and passion, and your need to achieve a balance—
Yes! I'm still working on it. I believe in God, I've just never been able to find a way to act on that without having it take me over. I'm scared I'll be taken over. I need to find a church somewhere, some way to be able to act on it more without feeling I'll be engulfed.

Caught up in the whirlwind.
Yes, I see it as a whirlwind, I really do. Also, as I get older, more and more, I see the importance of the church in the community. I was against the institution of the church for two reasons for a while—the Episcopal church was so deadening with its rituals, and the primitive church that had turned me on so much as a girl, well, they put down women. Therefore, as an adult, I still need to find a church that doesn't put down or stamp out things that I believe are basically good. It's something I struggle with all the time. Maybe I'll just die struggling with it and never get it reconciled. But it's real important to me.

It's a very painful thing, isn't it?
It's very real.

You mentioned something about it being something you've needed to pull away from, except in your writing. How do you think this struggle is played out in your writing?
I don't know. I'm not very articulate in talking about my writing. I'll say one thing, I'm one of those kinds of writers who writes a lot. I have written a lot ever since I was a girl. I write fiction the way a lot of people write in their journals. It's only several years later that you go back, read through your journal, and see what's going on. I go back and read my fiction, and see what's going on. *Fair and Tender Ladies* is so much about the struggle we've been talking about. And Ivy is like me; she is unable to find a religion that suits her—an organized religion. She makes up her own. Writing for her is sort of like it has been for me—a sort of a saving thing. Almost a religion of its own.

Writing is a kind of salvation?
Yes, as a way to get in touch with that intensity, a way of getting in touch with and staying true to me. I do feel, when I'm writing at a fever pitch, that

intensity that you feel when you get saved. There's nothing else that makes
you feel like that. There's getting saved, sex, and writing. Those are the only
things I know of. [Laughter]

*That pretty much says it all. Except, of course, chocolate pecan pie, which
some people say is better than sex.*

It might be! But anyway, Ivy struggles with those things, with the only
religion she is exposed to, her mountain church, in the same way that I struggle. And she dies without finding God in the traditional sense. And I might
too.

*For Ivy's people, her community, religion is a serious matter. It evokes ex-
treme behaviors. From early childhood, it was a norm for you to think about
good and evil, and when you'll be saved, will you go to heaven or hell. That
is one reason I loved Karen, and Tammy's mother in "Tongues of Fire." The
book I'm doing is a book about southern religion as it's treated in southern
fiction. There may be some fascinating connection between being southern
and being compelled to come to terms with religion.*

You do have to, if you grew up in a southern community. You can't evade
it. Now you can grow up in some place like Chapel Hill, as my own children
have, unfortunately, and not really be exposed to religion and not be called
into account for not knowing anything. There are plenty of children who are
not regular churchgoers, these days, whose families are not, and it's no social
stigma, or anything. But in Grundy where I grew up, when some family was
mentioned, somebody'd say, well, they're Methodist, or they're Presbyterian,
or they go to So-and-So's church, or whatever. In the South, if you grew up
at the time when we did in a small community, you were exposed to it intensely as a part of daily life. It is still true in small towns; it's only not true
in university towns and in towns as big as Atlanta and Charlotte.

*You know, when Karen got saved, over at Tammy's church, as she was stand-
ing there dripping wet, Tammy suddenly looked at her differently, as if a wall
had gone up between them. What was that all about?*

I think that Tammy herself didn't take all that "religion stuff" as seriously
as Karen. It was just a part of the way her mother was to Tammy. Tammy
could take it or leave it; but for Karen, it was a big deal. Karen was on a
spiritual quest. Tammy wasn't. To Tammy, it was just something that embarrassed her.

*When Karen was spending the night with Tammy, she saw Tammy's mother
reading her Bible at five o'clock in the afternoon, during "gin-and-tonic*

time," as Karen says. This was a striking difference between the two families and cultures that she had never thought about before. That contrast in turn came to be a wall between the two girls. When I read the story, it struck me how very sad this story is. It is a story about loneliness and difference, the alienation, of many of the characters. It's one of the saddest stories I've ever read.

It's a real sad story. It's really sad what's happening to the father there. It's dealt with in a sort of ironic tone, but it's just terribly sad, what's happening.

Here we've got a brother well on his way to alcoholism, in a coma, almost dead, a mother who has no earthly notion of how to handle anything, yet she's "got her hands full," a father who is slowly having a nervous break-down, a sister who is promiscuous, and thirteen-year-old Karen whose wonderful gifts and seriousness about life are going by unseen.

She's invisible, as she says.

Like the "Camp Spirit." Did you become invisible in your family?

I didn't because I was an only child and I couldn't. I think I wanted to. I was entirely *too* visible. Which was why I was glad to leave home. So the story wasn't autobiographical in that sense. Everything I did when I was growing up was remarked upon.

Every breath you drew. Especially in a small town, I bet.

Oh yes.

Who are some other characters in your fiction who are trying to work out their religious ambivalences?

I think Crystal in *Black Mountain Breakdown* is. And in *Oral History,* what Richard Burlage goes to the mountains for is to become less "Episcopalian," to loosen up. To listen. In a way he's sort of an autobiographical character. It's the notion that if you loosen up too much, if you become too spiritual, you go nuts.

You said that writing has enabled you to make some kind of resolution of your own ambivalences?

I continue to feel deep conflicts. But the link for me between my own religious feelings and creativity is that with writing, you go out of yourself— but you know you can come back. You won't stay stuck in the craziness.

Several writers I've interviewed have talked about a deep conflict between their own creativity and the church, both its norms and teachings.

Yes, for me there is a great conflict between the church and my own creativity, all the time. I knew from the beginning I couldn't write about sex or
violence, not and expect to go back home. For instance, when the play *Fair
and Tender Ladies* was performed in my hometown at the high school auditorium, people came up to Barbara Smith [the actress playing Ivy Rowe] afterwards and talked to her as if there were no difference between the character
she played and herself, the real person. And for them, there isn't. There is no
difference between the characters and the writer who created them, either.
Some church-going people were upset with the sex in the play. You shouldn't
write about it, you shouldn't act it out.

But I must be honest when I write, or else why write? So I've got to write
about *some* sex, *some* violence. And about religion. I mean, Jesus has actually
spoken to me. It happened to me. When I was young, about thirteen. I heard
a voice and it said, "Lee." I think that's why I must write about it, we all
must write about it.

*Do you think that will remain true for writers and artists here in the South
as it becomes, in Walker Percy's phrase, more "Los Angeles-ized"?*

Oh, yes, more so. I think religion is not dying out, but becoming more
influential. You see more and more churches, more little churches everywhere. As a teacher, I see it more in my students.

*Doris Betts describes herself as someone who consciously deals with Chris-
tian themes and images in her fiction. She says she tries not to hit you over
the head with her beliefs, but instead to speak in a whisper, as one does in
trying to get the attention of small children. Reynolds Price, too, has spoken
openly about this dimension of his life and his writing.*

Yes, and Doris and Reynolds Price are both great writers that way. I don't
consciously think about those things. I do consciously go through rituals
when I'm getting ready to write my novels. I read the Bible all the way
through when I was writing *Fair and Tender Ladies*. Ivy did that, too. She
hates a good part of the Bible. But she loves Ecclesiastes, where there is the
passage about a time for everything. And, in fact, Ecclesiastes became the
structure of the last chapter of that novel and of the whole thing. I mean Ivy
thinks the Bible has some "pretty good stories." But Ivy can't accept religion
as being available to her—religion as it was taught to her in her mountain
church was so anti-women. Also, those early primitive churches in the mountains taught salvation by grace alone—and that's a problem for me. It just
seems like another way of justifying frontier hedonism—for men only, that

is, not for women. It seems like much of that kind of religion was instituted by men and conspired to hamper women.

You deal with some of that in The Devil's Dream, *don't you?*

Yes, very much so. There was always this split in the mentality of the culture, in its members. In the early days, some bands I write about even had two names, the gospel name for Sunday mornings and the honky-tonk name for Saturday nights. There was always a pull between the honky-tonk life and the church and home life. There were these huge polarities. One big conflict was how to be a star and keep Jesus. Often in these early days, when you got saved, you were given your "gift song," the song you sang when you accepted Jesus as your savior and renounced your old life. All your music had to then be sacred music, dedicated to God from then on.

There is an old story I read about in the Southern Historical Collection [at the University of North Carolina], and I wrote about it in the new book. It's about a mountain girl who sang and played a fiddle. One day her father forbade her to sing any longer, saying it was "of the Devil." Grief-stricken, she goes mad and plays the fiddle on her front porch until she dies. It's a true story.

The Storyteller's Tale

Peter Guralnick / 1995

From *Los Angeles Times Magazine* (May 21, 1995), 15–17, 27–28.

On Writing—I didn't have an image of a writer [as a child]. I didn't know any writers. I grew up in the midst of people just talking and talking and talking and telling these stories. My Uncle Vern, who was in the Legislature, was a famous storyteller, as were others, including my dad. It was very local. I mean, my mother could make a story out of anything; she'd go to the grocery store and come home with a story. And I was a reader. I read everything I could get my hands on. I didn't know anybody [else] that was reading; I didn't have anybody that I shared this with. I was just always reading. I mean, nothing else affords me the kind of intense pleasure that reading does. So it just seemed like writing was the next step.

It was never a question whether I would do it or not. I don't think it mattered whether I got published. It [was] just really necessary to me. I mean, it's my work, but it's also my deepest joy, just to do it every day a little bit—and do it a lot other days. I think it's my religion. It's my religion—it's what I do.

I guess my favorite thing is before you even start writing, when you're sitting down every day just thinking about [it], and it's all completely fluid in your head and there're all these people running around, and there's infinite possibilities of what they might or might not do in the course of the novel. And I'm always thinking about this for several months before I actually start. And I love it. Everything is all intensely alive, and it's just total possibility, [but] as you write it, in a certain way you're nailing them down. I mean, it's very exciting, but it's also—you're nailing them down. And when you finish, when you put the book in a little box to send to New York—and a writer I admire, John Ehle, used this image—it's like putting it in a little coffin. That's how I feel—you know, it's just the process of it.

You would have to hear Lee Smith's voice to fully absorb its range of expression and moods. Of course, anyone who has read one or more of Lee Smith's seven previously published novels and two collections of short stories—her

new novel, *Saving Grace,* is just out this week—will have gotten a good
sense of the accent, the passionate and puzzled humanity and fine appreciation of the absurd, but for further insight into its variousness, its unpredict-
able, almost desperate humor ("I mean, it's a wild world out there"), the true
beauty of its Appalachian song, you would almost have to attend a reading,
as I did recently at the Cameron Village Regional Library in the Raleigh-
Durham-Chapel Hill area of North Carolina, where Lee Smith has lived for
the last 21 years.

There, a roomful of listeners with no apparent common denominator was
transported, without hesitation or exception, to the world of Smith's latest
novel, transfixed by the voice and tale of Florida Grace Shepherd, the daughter of a serpent-handling preacher, and her struggle for salvation. I had read
the book carefully, I thought, but Smith's reading added new dimensions of
humor, and of gravity, to it as well. There was a lilt to the language, and an
attitude to the words, that almost demanded the author's voice (imagine Mark
Twain reading *Huckleberry Finn* to us, without the intervention of an imper-
sonator or the passage of the years). There was, as always, a fine and unbut-
toned declaration of individuality (think of Zora Neale Hurston transported
to the mountains of Appalachia), a celebration of the striking uniqueness of
her characters and their world.

"Lee Smith taught us to be proud of who we are," is the way one admirer
put it ("If she can get that stuff published, we know we must be OK," was
the way the quote went on), but the author could just as easily turn the expression around. It was her embrace of her own past and the particularity of her
own experience that made her proud of who *she* was, and she could well be
seen at the center of a movement, loosely defined as New Southern Regionalism and incorporating everyone from Bobbie Ann Mason, Jayne Anne Phillips and Cormac McCarthy to Jill McCorkle, Kaye Gibbons, James Wilcox
and Larry Brown, which has found new inspiration in this simultaneous embrace of past and present, this insistent chronicling of the small, heroic battles
of the human spirit, a recognition of the dignity and absurdity of the commonplace.

Regionalism alone, of course, could not account for the diverse appeal of
all this work, and in many ways the label has served as a barrier to its broader
acceptance, as critic Louis Rubin, Lee's teacher at Hollins College and, later,
founder of Algonquin Books, the publishing house that has been a corner-
stone of Southern regional expression since 1983, points out. "If Lee's a
regional writer, so is Thomas Hardy; I think the relationship of the literature

to the society is very intense, no question about it, but to see that as a limiting factor. . . . I mean, Eudora Welty is an American writer *because* she's a Southern writer, not in spite of the fact." Or, as Lee's friend, humorist Roy Blount, Jr., said a little less reverentially (but no less appreciatively) of one of her books, "The closest thing to reading this would be reading *Madame Bovary* while listening to Loretta Lynn and watching *Guiding Light.*"

Grundy Girl—Lee Smith was born in Grundy, Va., in the coal-mining country in the far western corner of the state, in 1944. She was a "town girl." Her father, Ernest, operated the local five-and-dime; her grandfather was county treasurer for 50 years; various uncles owned and operated the local movie house, the Piggly Wiggly and the Ford dealership in town. Her mother, Gig, was a "foreigner" from Chincoteague Island on Virginia's eastern shore who'd "come to do good, she'd come to teach." Still, it would be wrong to get too much of a sense of privilege in a town like Grundy. There was, says Lee, no real class system—everyone in town went to the same school. If you look at a picture of the neat little house on Main Street that she grew up in, you will see the Dismal River right behind it and, rising in the background, just across the river, the slag heap that the coal company left behind.

"Grundy, Virginia," wrote Dennis Covington in his recently published *Salvation on Sand Mountain: Snake Handling and Redemption in Southern Appalachia,* "[is] a mining town on the lip of a widening river between mountains so steep and irrational, they must have blocked most of the sun most of the day. It is difficult to imagine how children can grow up in such a place without carrying narrowed horizons into the rest of their lives." "Which I just loved," cackles Lee. "When I finally met Dennis, he said, 'I'm sorry what I said about Grundy.' " But you *know* she takes it as a compliment.

What set Lee apart was neither geography nor class but her own situation and imagination. She grew up as what she might herself describe as "deeply weird," consumed with reading on the one hand ("Oh, I was always having nightmares and little nervous breakdowns and every kind of thing—*Raintree County* put me to bed") and social success on the other ("I was Miss Grundy High—I *was.* I got a set of Samsonite luggage and a steam iron"). She was an only child, born to parents in their late 30s who were themselves not like everyone else, even if her father was "the most loved man in the community" and her mother was elected queen of the Junior Prom every year by the girls in her Home Ec classes. For both parents were what would now be called manic depressive, her father alternating workaholic activity with periods of complete shutdown, her mother suffering similar bouts of crippling depression.

"They were the sweetest people—I mean, they were just wonderful, but it was almost like they were too sweet to live. I mean, they were not tough. And it was interesting, because when one of them was having a hard time, the other would be the strong one, except one time when I was 13 and they were both in the hospital at the same time."

It did not, Lee insists, stigmatize her in any way. To the town, the Smiths were just "kindly nervous"; if they had to go away from time to time, "things would go on running, my dad's dime store would go on, I might live with my cousins for a while, but you know, in a town like Grundy there was a high tolerance of any kind of abnormality or unusual behavior. In fact, eccentricity was not only tolerated but prized. It was just—I did have a sense that the world was kind of precarious, and there was stuff you couldn't understand, and there were sad things, and there were complications."

Perhaps the reading was a retreat, then, and one that threatened to get out of hand. The librarian, Mrs. Lillian Elgin, a friend of her mother, probably said nothing when Lee read *Jane Eyre, Little Women, Johnny Tremain* and all of Mark Twain over and over again, "but every now and then they would try to exercise some control, because I was reading things like *The View from Pompey's Head* and *Forever Amber*. But nobody else had read the books, so they didn't know what to tell me to read or not, so I just read everything." With other neighborhood kids she put out a magazine called *The Small Review* and wrote plays that they would put on in the breezeway of her friend Martha Sue Owens's house. Her first story, written at the age of 8 and printed out on her mother's stationery, was about Adlai Stevenson and Jane Russell, who went West and became Mormons, the very themes, she says, she is still writing about today. "You know, religion and flight, staying in one place or not staying, containment or flight—and religion."

She went to the movies every Saturday night, worshiped Grace Kelly and tried to look like Sandra Dee, and wept for days at the tragic, *unfair* denouement of *Imitation of Life*. She frequently visited A. P. Carter's store in Maces Spring and heard various members of the Carter family sing and play, and she saw the Stanley Brothers when they performed at her uncle's drive-in on Saturday night before the movie went on. She lived a worldly life, yet was saved again and again in spectacularly demonstrative fashion—to her mother's acute Methodist embarrassment. One time at summer camp she heard God speak to her, and "I told everybody about it, and they put me in the infirmary and called my parents—this is really true." At 16, she went off to boarding school in Richmond ("My father was worried that I would marry my high school boyfriend. Which I probably would have"), where she worked her way through a considerably more extensive library. Then, in the fall of 1963, she arrived at Hollins College outside Roanoke, Va.

Finding a Voice—It's hard to tell why a kid's a writer. Sometimes it takes a writer a long time to get going, and then there are the ones who are extremely good as undergraduates but for some reason or other never go beyond that. But then you get the occasional writer like Lee, who you just knew from the very beginning was going to write. I mean, Lee's a real writer. She writes all the time. She writes when she's down. She writes when she's up—that's just her way of dealing with the world. And you could tell that from the very beginning.—Louis Rubin

She felt a sense of release when she got to college. It was the old Jane Russell-Adlai Stevenson story: containment or flight. "I think I had just felt so circumscribed and pigeonholed. By the geography *and* by the sense that your life is totally determined by who your family is. It's like, you have to go home with the one that brung you. Don't get above your raisin'. All this sense of determinism. So I had this kind of breakout period. I just went kind of wild."

At the same time, Hollins, Class of 1967, was exuberant enough *en masse* to promote a sense of wildness in almost anyone with the capacity to dream. "This group came in the fall of '63, and they cut a wide swath," says Louis Rubin, who had begun his teaching career six years earlier. "There were seven or eight of them who kind of grouped together. I think three have Ph.D.s; one of them became a good newspaperwoman; Lee, of course, writes fiction, and Annie Dillard writes various things. Remarkable group of kids— they were there for four years, and they just took the place apart."

For Lee the experience offered not just liberation but reinforcement. "What I fell into at Hollins was like a womb. It was like the warmest, most nourishing possible surroundings for a writer, or a would-be writer. I was with other girls who wanted to be writers. We had a creative writing program that was totally nourishing—I mean, they read a work like it *deserved* to be read. Which it did. And it was just wonderful. I mean, a women's college was really important for me. Because I was raised as a Southern girl, where you're not supposed to put yourself forward, you're not supposed to be too

smart; if you're weird, you try to hide it. And I can just see myself never
having written—or written with the enthusiasm, or come out into the open as
somebody who was passionately interested in this, if I had gone to a co-ed
school. I really think that's true."

She read passionately, and all over the place, both for her classes and for
herself, working her way, alphabetically, through the school library: Mark
Twain and Virginia Woolf (she and Annie Dillard were go-go dancers for an
all-girl rock band made up of English majors called the Virginia Wolves),
Harriette Arnow and Marcel Proust. There was a strong commitment to work
but an equal commitment to exploring the broad "terrain of the imagination,"
wherever that voyage might go.

The summer after junior year, Lee and a half dozen other girls decided to
emulate *Huckleberry Finn* and take a raft down the Mississippi. They suc-
ceeded in constructing it in Paducah, Ky., then ran into bureaucratic red tape,
which required them to have a licensed captain. "So we were all on TV
crying, right? And Captain Gordon Cooper—he was a riverboat pilot who
had retired into the Irvin S. Cobb Retirement Home and never expected to go
on the river again—he saw us on TV and emerged from the door of the Irvin
S. Cobb in his white outfit and said, 'I will take these girls down the river.'
And he loved it—I mean, he just had the best time. He was a real storyteller,
and he never shut up." The story of that journey, how a free-spirited voyage
of exploration was transformed into a media field day ("Well, you know, we
had imagined just floating along the river, and then we were on 'Huntley-
Brinkley,' and we got famous and people bugged us, and we were met by a
jazz band from Preservation Hall when we got to New Orleans, and it was all
different than what we thought") makes for a wonderful tale, but in the end
it only goes to show how inextricably art and life are linked both in their
clarity and in their confusion.

Because at the heart of Lee's Hollins experience, of course, was her writing. The stories that she composed to start off with, and for which she received encouraging Cs, dealt with "stewardesses living in Hawaii and evil
twins," nothing to do with Grundy or the mountains or the world she came
from, until she was assigned a story by Eudora Welty and then, in her sophomore year, heard Welty read. She has described the impact of the experience
in a number of different ways, including the manner in which Welty disarmed
a passel of academics seeking to know how she had come up with the powerful symbol of a marble cake. "Well," declared the author, "it's a recipe that's
been in my family for some time." A response that would have had to delight

Lee Smith, who revels in "the things of this world" while raging against abstraction to this day. Probably, though, her first response was her truest. "It was like a *revelation,* really, kind of like, oh, well, OK, well, I can write about just *anything.* I can write about the people that I knew growing up and everybody I heard my daddy talking about—I mean, I can write stories about this!"

She devoured Welty's work, and the work of James Still, a transplanted Alabamian who had come to Knott County, Ky., in 1932 to "keep school" and whose 1940 *River of Earth,* an Appalachian *Grapes of Wrath,* she discovered all by herself under the S's in the Hollins library. "At the end of the novel," Lee has written, "I was astonished to read that the family was heading for—of all places!—Grundy! . . . I read [the] passage over and over. I simply could not believe that Grundy was in a novel! . . . Then I finished reading *River of Earth* and burst into tears. Never had I been so moved by a book. In fact, it didn't seem like a book at all. *River of Earth* was as real to me as the chair I sat on, as the hollers I'd grown up among."

What she had found in these writers was not just an echoing voice but an echoing *sensibility.* The first story that she wrote after her revelation reflected this newfound sense of kinship. "It wasn't even a story, it was just a sketch. It's funny, my last image of leaving Grundy to go to Hollins was, I kept waiting for my dad to come home from the dime store so we could drive over. And some of my aunts were over there, too, and they were having what I felt was this totally interminable conversation about whether my mother had colitis or not, and it just went on and on, and I thought my father would never come, and I would be stuck on this porch forever. So I just wrote a little sketch about some women sitting on a porch and talking about whether one of them had colitis. And then later, in the next course, I wrote something about this club we'd had in my neighborhood when I was a kid, and it later turned into my first novel."

The Writing Life—"I was strangely fortunate in that I was published when I was real young, but I didn't pay any attention to it. I was married and having babies in Alabama [Lee's two sons were born in 1969 and 1971]. I didn't know anybody in New York; I didn't even know my agent. I mean, I was an idiot. I was just totally immersed in my writing and my babies, and it didn't occur to me that it should be any different."

She published three novels with Harper & Row in rapid succession, her third, *Fancy Strut,* a hilarious account of the small-town misadventures engendered by the theme-park staging of a sesquicentennial celebration, which was the direct result of two years of reporting for the Tuscaloosa News. But then, under the influence of events in her own life and out of a sense of wanting to return to her "mountain material," she wrote a disturbing fourth novel, *Black Mountain Breakdown,* about flight and freedom and the impossibility of ever getting out—and no one wanted to publish it.

"Harper & Row wouldn't touch it, and then my agent didn't want to handle me either. So I sent the book around to about 20 publishers, and it was turned down, and everybody said, 'This is so dark, this is so depressing—bleuu!' This was a very difficult period of my life.

"I was having a hard time even sustaining the idea that I might be a writer, and I decided I needed to find an agent that I could talk to, a woman agent, so I went to New York, and I thought I had found one, but she went to Tibet to find herself, and I never heard from her again. Finally, my great good friend, Roy Blount, hooked me up with Liz Darhansoff [her agent to this day], a woman I could really relate to, that I loved—she taught me something about taking myself seriously. I mean, I had always taken my *work* real seriously, but she read *Black Mountain Breakdown* and she liked it, and she called up on the phone, and she has this real Northern voice, real businesslike, and she said, 'Well, send me some clips.' And I said, 'What do you mean, clips?' She said, 'Reviews, I mean reviews of your earlier books.' And I said, 'Well, I don't think I have any.' And she said—I'll never forget this, this was kind of a turning point for me, *'Well, how can you expect me to take you seriously if you don't take yourself seriously?'* And I said, 'Good point.' "

Black Mountain Breakdown was finally published in 1980 by G. P. Putnam's Sons, seven years after she first started sending it out and the same year as her divorce from her first husband, poet James Seay, with whom she had moved to North Carolina in 1973. In the meantime, she had begun her exuberantly informal, semi-obsessive documentation of the mountain material—the life, the people, the family bonds, the alternating push-and-pull of the past, the landscape amid which she had grown up and to which, it seemed, like Crystal, the broken heroine of *Black Mountain Breakdown,* she was inexorably drawn. *Black Mountain Breakdown* was not the direction in which she ultimately wanted to go. For all of its disturbing power, the novel failed to capture the vitality of the mountains, the *life* that Lee was driven to celebrate in all of its splashy colors, in all of its messy, beautiful, ugly, anarchic reality. To find that, she had to go home.

Almost without being aware of where it was taking her, she began taping relatives, neighbors, friends, "anybody that would talk." Weren't they, wasn't she self-conscious? I ask, from the depths of my own self-consciousness. "Are you kidding?" she says. "They loved to talk." As for herself, it became "my hobby, my avocation, I began to get addicted to 'going around.' And it made me realize—well, it made me doubt the possibility of ever getting it right from an omniscient point of view. I mean, in any given novel. And, finally, I began to get a sense that it's the storyteller's tale, that the storyteller tells the story the best he or she can, but that it's always according to the needs, or the vision—and the particular *angle* of vision—of the storyteller. And so the events themselves don't mean as much to the story as that it's coming out of somebody. And when I did decide I wanted to deal with some of this Appalachian material and history, it seemed to me: Who knows what happened in the past? Who can ever say?"

That was the genesis of *Oral History*, a 1983 novel that incorporated a chorus of diverse voices and remains one of her most ambitious undertakings. It offers the complex interweaving of myth and experience, a fragile web combining lyrical realism with gritty lyricism in a form that is very much, and very originally, its own. And yet it is framed by what Lee describes as the most "ramshackle" of devices, as a city girl named Jennifer goes back to her people, her unexplored "roots," for an oral history project for her professor, Dr. Bernie Ripman. At the beginning of the book she leaves her tape recorder up on top of Hoot Owl Mountain, deserted now because it is thought to be haunted, and the 250-page body of the novel is made up of the ghostly voices that the tape recorder captures.

"Well, you see, after my third novel, the sense of the well-made novel falls apart. It really does. But that was also—you see, I was trying to be a certain way, and finally my marriage wasn't going to work out, and I wasn't going to be able to be that way, you know, and my sense of reality and the world and politics and everything was just—I just had to drop, I guess, the well-made novel as a means of expression."

She began the book in the third person. "I started writing just straight, standard English, but one of my main intentions was to document and transcribe the mountain speech that I had grown up hearing. But when I wrote it down accurately, it sounded so stupid, juxtaposed alongside the proper English; it made them all sound like they were on *Hee Haw*. And it made it sound like I was condescending to my characters. So finally, I just realized this wasn't going to work at all, and I decided to let each person speak for herself or himself, and that was the only way I could do it. And just pray that the language that they were using was close to the way it had been. 'Cause you never really know—but it *had* to be their own voices, the characters' own voices, and not me talking about them."

Listening to Voices—The novels and stories poured out of her. *Family Linen* was a multi-generational comedy mystery; *Fair and Tender Ladies,* an epistolary novel, is her most beloved book, touching in a way that narrowly avoids sentiment by means of the same comic ferocity that has increasingly come to dominate her work. To date there have been at least four babies that Lee knows of who have been named for the novel's heroine, Ivy Rowe. What seems to have captured the imagination of her readers is Ivy's indomitable tenacity, her dedication to forward motion in the face of life's many obstacles, a quality that echoes Lee's own philosophy.

Women come up to her all the time to tell her how they have been inspired by Ivy, to let her know how Ivy's example gave them the strength to go on, something I witnessed one evening at dinner when a woman who recognized Lee from her book-jacket photograph tentatively approached. She had read the book when her mother was dying, she said, and it had meant so much to her. In a way this doesn't seem to surprise Lee all that much, because Ivy gave her the strength to go on, too; it was written at a time when her own mother was dying, she tells the woman, and she faced other domestic crises as well. Writing the book helped her to keep *her* life together.

In 1990, she won a Lyndhurst Prize to study the history of country music as background research for the novel that would become *The Devil's Dream.* It is the story of a family like the Carter Family in many respects, recounted through several generations up to the present day. Once again it is a conflicted tale in which success carries within it the seeds of failure; the very independence of Katie Cocker, its contemporary heroine, who directs her own life, who produces her own records, doesn't come without a price. Empowerment is always at the expense of connection. It's the eternal conundrum of country music, it's the eternal conundrum of life: As you sing a song that arises from a particular place, "what you want, of course, is to be successful, and as soon as you're successful . . . that's never your place again. You're always singing of home, but you're never home. And there's something about that—I think I feel like that about a lot of things, this intense ambivalence. To me that is the perfect ground for fiction."

That ambivalence was extended into real life with the publication of *The Devil's Dream.* For Lee it represented something of a crisis of self-definition.

Up until that time she had steadfastly resisted pushing herself in the market-place, both for practical reasons (she had two boys at home) and because she still clung to the idea that it was her job to write, not to promote. "But with *The Devil's Dream,* I felt like if it was marketed in the right places, in the right way, that it might really sell. I mean, I know my other work is weird, it's very regional, I'm obsessed with things that nobody else cares about, but here I felt like, this music is universal, there are a lot of people interested in it—people in all walks of life. But I think the publisher's perception was that people who are interested in country music can't read. And the people that can read would never presume to be interested in country music. They were just really uninterested, *really* uninterested in this particular book. And I really got my feelings hurt, because they didn't care at all.

"So *The Devil's Dream* kind of broke my heart, and it made me just about decide, well, I'll just forget about, you know, selling. But then two of my best friends, Susan Ketchin and her husband [the novelist] Clyde Edgerton were upset that nothing more was being done for the book, so for a reading I was going to do in Raleigh, they said, 'Well, we're going to sing some songs.' And it was just so much fun, we had so much fun, and other people started asking us to do it, and we got up this *Devil's Dream* show, and it was hysteri-cal. We did it on campuses, we did it in Nashville at the Southern Festival of Books, and, of course, I got to dress up in a glitter outfit, even though I can't carry a tune. So we just had the best time in the whole world, and it ended up—I was kind of pissed off, but finally the publishing of it was so much fun, because we did this show."

Pilgrim's Regress—The new book is, as Lee likes to say, "profoundly weird." The primitive Pentecostal world that it portrays, whose practices and premises *Saving Grace* simply presents as a given (the story is told by the daughter of a serpent-handling preacher, who doubts her faith but never her father's power), represents both "what terrifies me and fascinates me the most about the South in a certain way. I see it both ways. I see it as real attractive and also very, very dark. It's all about giving over yourself, giving up yourself, issues that to me somehow also have a lot to do with being a woman, and particularly a Southern woman. It's that desire to affiliate, you know, that terror of being on your own and thinking that you shouldn't be on your own. I mean it's always easier to do what you're expected to do and get with the group that will tell you what to do—I'm not articulating this at all, but there's something about that kind of religion, that kind of fundamental religion, and that kind of father, that is both totally compelling and desirable, and terrifying, to me: *then you don't have to make any decisions—ever."*

From the opening passage of the novel to its bleak conclusion, you never doubt the voice or the winning, disturbing humanity of the main character. "Oh, I just loved Gracie so much. In a certain way it was like giving birth to a terrible child." Much of the narrative consists of Grace's stubborn struggle to deny her heritage ("I am and always have been contentious and ornery, full of fear and doubt in a family of believers"), and her embrace of it in the end can be taken as either triumph or failure, or both. In the end, like all of Lee Smith's books, it is nonjudgmental and non-categorizable; there are "no big sociological explanations," there are no more explanations in fact that there were for Eudora Welty's cake. It is all, as Lee sees it, just another manifestation of experience, "these people are doing this because they want to feel that passion, they want to feel God move on them directly—which I think is [the same reason] why I write. It's like this woman told me one time, she said, 'Honey, I don't know, all I can tell you is, when you have the serpent in your hand, the whole world has got an edge to it.' Isn't that great? I mean, you know what she means—that's really true."

She wrote the book in a fever, breaking off from the story cycle that was going to be her next book when Gracie's voice started calling to her and then refused to be still. "I didn't mean to write this novel, I knew it wouldn't be something that my publisher would want, or anything, really, that I wanted to write, but sometimes a voice will just come to you so insistently—you know, it was almost like automatic writing once it started." She has always looked for inspiration in her reading, sought out a familiar, appropriate touchstone for each book, and for this book it had to be Flannery O'Connor. She went to Milledgeville, Ga., last spring for the annual Flannery O'Connor Festival, reveled in the landscape and in rereading all of O'Connor's work, returned home and wrote nonstop until she finished, delivering the manuscript to her publisher a year early: "So I never felt like I wrote it, actually—it just came like *eeuuh,* and all I could do was just kind of keep up."

Lee's Voice—And so here she stands, once again on the brink of publication, on the brink perhaps of wider fame, about to start a publicity tour of the South by automobile with her husband of 10 years, journalist Hal Crowther (his collection of syndicated columns, *Unarmed but Dangerous,* is being published at the same time as *Saving Grace*). She has just been awarded a three-year Lila Wallace-Reader's Digest Writers' Award, and she will use it both to support her writing and to maintain her commitment to the Hindman Settlement School in Knott County, Ky., where she will teach writing workshops in the adult learning program for those who can read and story workshops for those who can't. There is a musical adaptation of *The Devil's Dream* that has just opened in Raleigh (an earlier one-woman presentation of *Fair and Tender Ladies,* played Grundy High School before going to New York City), there are Grundy connections to maintain, maybe even brandy to be sipped with James Still. And while she will undoubtedly miss her students at North Carolina State (from which she has taken a three-year leave of absence after 14 years of teaching), you have the feeling that everywhere she goes she will be teaching—and learning.

"Very few of your students will actually become writers, but the ones that don't, you know, have had a chance to really express things, to hear things that they wouldn't have heard otherwise, to have been in this very special relationship with a group of people. To have read together and to have talked about things that mean so much to them. I mean, it's a wonderful thing, it's a wonderful sort of *process* to be engaged in together. And I just think you have to understand, if you're a young writer, that it's a life, you're embarking upon a life, and everything else is going to have to fit in around finding you the time to do it. It's a life, and it won't ever be a living probably, it's just a process, and the product is really not all that important for a long, long time.

"I don't write anything unless I am totally moved by it. I mean, it's a totally emotional experience for me. It's never a rational experience. And it's always something I feel deeply ambivalent about. I don't know. I just think when you're young, you're more arrogant, and you think that you can fathom out the truth, and then the older you get, it's like the more paths go off into the forest, and you can't, you just can't find your straight way.

"A lot of times for me it has really just been like salvation to write. Because, you know, real life is real chaotic, and you can't control what happens to anybody—even the people you love the most. Terrible things are going to happen to them. Terrible things are going to happen to you. And you can't control any of it. But to write is to order experience, to make a kind of ordering on the page, no matter how fragile it is. And it is, of course, profoundly, deeply satisfying—even though it's not real. It's like prayer, I think."

Interview with Lee Smith

Charline R. McCord / 1997

From *Mississippi Quarterly,* 52:1 (Winter 1998–99), 89–119. Copyright © 1998–99. Reprinted by permission of *Mississippi Quarterly* and Charline R. McCord.

The following interview with Lee Smith took place at her home in Hillsborough, North Carolina, on Sunday, May 18, 1997, about 10:20 a.m. With me was Reta Washam, a friend, fellow writer, and court reporter. Lee's husband, Hal Crowther, met us in the driveway, and Lee soon came bursting out the back door waving mail she was carrying to the mailbox. Lee first gave us a tour of the renovated turn-of-the-century two-story home she and Hal recently purchased, and which she said was reportedly once owned by the town undertaker. Afterward, she led us out to a delightful one-room guest cottage, situated between the main house and the swimming pool, which she thinks probably once served as a mortuary. A very lively interview that lasted about an hour and a half took place in the guest cottage/former mortuary, complete with fireplace, quilt-covered bed, and an animated Lee Smith resting on a futon.

McCord: Barry Hannah spoke in Clinton [Mississippi] not long ago and he said, "I guess I was in college before I even knew what a writer was." So there was this sense that he had not planned to write—that he was perhaps in limbo, not knowing what he would do. I found it interesting that you started writing so young, as did Ellen Douglas. Very young.

Smith: I grew up in a family of world-class talkers. They were wonderful talkers and storytellers, both the women and the men. I was an only child, and so I heard all this adult conversation all the time. I was always taken where these wonderful stories were being told. So I really did grow up on stories. My mother was a wonderful storyteller, not just my daddy and all the men in the family who were known for it. And I read all the time. I was a compulsive reader. I think I went naturally from reading to writing little stories, quite often like the ones I was reading. You know, I'd read a horse book and I'd try to write a little horse story. It was a natural outgrowth of the reading. I don't know if I'd had a twin sister or other children really close to me in age at home there all the time, whether I would have developed in such a single-minded way.

153

My father encouraged me. He used to pay me a nickel. He built me a writing house. In that film [Lee Smith video produced by KET, The Kentucky Network] there's a picture of the little writing house, which is still there on the river bank. And I'd go out there and write and he'd pay me a nickel if I'd write a story. So my parents were very encouraging although they were not really readers.

McCord: Do you still have any of those childhood writings?

Smith: I do. I have them. They're just—they're really embarrassing. I have a whole bunch of them because my father saved them, you know, and so I do. I was just up in Grundy [Virginia] for the weekend and the town has done this thing which was totally embarrassing. They put this marker in the town that says *me* on it, you know, which is really—it's not the kind of thing—it's totally embarrassing and sort of *horrifying*. I told them, "This is like when I used to work for the newspaper in Tuscaloosa, they were always saying so-and-so has been funeralized." This is like being funeralized. But you can't say no or everybody thinks you're a terrible person. And, you know, it's a town and a part of the country that has been put down and if they want to have a marker, by God, and be proud of something, you want to be encouraging.

McCord: Sure.

Smith: But anyway we were talking about writing as a child, and several people had these—I used to publish a little newspaper in my neighborhood. It was in big block print and was named *The Small Review*. And I would write little editorials if I didn't like what the neighbors were doing. [Laughter]

McCord: Well, now, it really *was* nice of them to put up that monument, wasn't it? [Laughter]

Smith: [Laughter] I know. So several people had these copies of *The Small Review*. That neighborhood is still intact, everybody who lived there when I was growing up. You know, I'm fifty-two, and they're all still there except for—

McCord: The young people, I bet.

Smith: Yeah, the young people left. There's all these older folks.

McCord: When did you start drawing the maps and creating character sketches and outlining and doing all that preliminary detail work in preparation for writing?

Smith: I always liked to draw and I keep thinking it's something I'm going to probably go back to. I've always drawn detailed maps of places. Places are very important to me and to be able to physically place my stories in a house and a landscape and a state is *really* important.

McCord: Did you do that before Hollins?

Smith: Well, I think it was Louis Rubin that got me into being much more specific about the characters, about writing all these things down and really knowing what you were doing. And I think—it's really interesting how he taught. I'm still not sure how he taught exactly. But mainly just by acting like what you wrote was worth reading. And every now and then he would make a suggestion and one was that if your characters are being inconsistent, why don't you just write down as much as you can beforehand? So I've always done that ever since.

McCord: Let's talk about Louis Rubin for just a minute. Yesterday he was inducted into the North Carolina Literary Hall of Fame.

Smith: Right

McCord: And in *The Chapel Hill News* they quoted you as saying, "I would never have been a writer if it hadn't been for Louis. He was a wonderful, inspirational teacher in large part because he took us and our work seriously, as if it deserved that." Did you also get your teaching philosophy from Louis Rubin—the idea that if you read your students' works as if they're worth being read, sooner or later they will be?

Smith: I hope so. I think I was enormously fortunate to have happened upon Hollins College, to have happened upon a place where writing was prized and taken seriously and where student work was prized and taken seriously. And I've always felt like if you are fortunate in any way, then your duty is to pass it on.

McCord: Is it true, as the paper says, that you still call Louis Rubin "regularly for advice and encouragement"?

Smith: I call him a lot, especially for information. And he always knows. I just called him to find out where a line of poetry was from and it turned out to be William Blake. I thought it was Wordsworth. I don't really call him for advice on writing fiction, but I will call him just about all kinds of things. Right now I need to call him because I want—I've forgotten where a line is—something about somebody talking about Faulkner and the influence of Faulkner on Southern writing, and someone said, "Well, who wants to be on the track when the Dixie Limited is coming through?" You know what I mean? I've heard this and I can't find it anywhere and I know if I call Louis, he will know.

McCord: Did everyone think of Rubin as invincible, as "Mr. God," as Doris Betts said?

Smith: Yeah, in the classroom. There's something he knows and it is how to read a manuscript, and what to say to you—which is often a question rather than a comment—that he's just better at than anybody. I mean, he's really, really good at it. I think that outside the classroom, you don't think of him as Mr. God entirely because he is so focused. He's really a genius with the written word and he's totally accessible to his students. Therefore, he doesn't engage in small talk, for instance, in the way that other people engage in small talk. So, when you're talking about writing or literature, yeah, you would think of him as Mr. God. Even though later, maybe I've come to hold different opinions about some writers. There are a number of ones that I like that he doesn't like. You know, we can hold different opinions now.

McCord: Friday's *Chapel Hill News* also says that Rubin said he never saw the difference between writing, editing, teaching, and reading. That they're all part of the same activity. Do you agree with that?

Smith: No. I don't agree with that.

McCord: No? So you can disagree with Mr. God. [Laughter]

Smith: Yeah. I just don't agree with that.

McCord: How does Lee Smith grow up in Grundy, Virginia, and hear these stories and see these people and know these mountains and become a writer, and yet Lee Smith's next-door neighbor sees and hears and knows the very same things growing up and becomes a beautician? Where is the difference? Rubin talked about the love of language—that you can't *give* someone a lively imagination and a love of language.

Smith: Right. And I think a lot of that really does have to do with your very earliest childhood experiences. I was really privileged to be around these people who could really tell a story. To be taken to church and hear the King James Bible. To be soaked in this wonderful kind of—I mean, there's a paucity of language in a number of homes.

And I love to teach, but I can't teach too much and still write anything that's worth reading because I do think—I agree with him [Rubin] in one way—it's all the same activity in the sense that you only have so much energy—I do put as much creative energy into reading my students' work as I do into something I'm working on. So I've been very lucky because I don't teach full time anymore, and I haven't for a while. But if you're teaching four classes or three classes and you're also trying to write your own stuff, you just don't have the creative energy left over.

McCord: How much are you teaching?

Smith: Well, right now, I'm *not* because I'm in the last part of this Lila Wallace-*Reader's Digest* award. I just got back from eastern Kentucky, right up next to Grundy where I'm from, where I have been doing writing workshops with adult literacy students. So it's a different kind of writing, a different kind of teaching.

McCord: Is that the Hindman School?

Smith: Yeah. I was just up there for ten days. And I do other sorts of workshops, too; next year, Hal [Crowther, Lee's husband] and I are going to do a residency for a month at a college in Virginia. But I'm not teaching regularly and won't until next year.

McCord: If I came to you as an eighteen-year-old student, and I sat down in your office at North Carolina State and told you that I thought I wanted to be a writer, what guidance would you give me?

Smith: *Read!* To me that's the most important thing. I think so many times young people mistake the desire to be *heard* with the desire to write, you know? I think that a lot of times they just want to express themselves, but they don't want to write fiction.

McCord: They may not have the discipline for it?

Smith: Yeah. They don't understand that it's a craft and it takes years and it's hard and most of it's boring. I mean, only that initial rush that you get with a first draft is really exciting. After that, there's just so much of the business of writing and revisions that it's more like slogging through mud. So I would just say, "Read."

McCord: And read specifically what?

Smith: Well, I think that's where it is really exciting to be a teacher, because I think the most important service the teacher performs, often, is to read work in progress and then tell the young writer some things that she might like to read or he might like to read. It's like a young man who just turned up with this amazing manuscript, you know? Just this week. He's never read *anything*. I said, "This is like a combination of Larry Brown and *Confederacy of Dunces.*" He's never read either one. He's never read Charles Portis. He's never read *Norwood,* and yet his style is quite similar. I said, "What you need first is to edit this thing with a chain saw, you know? You really do." [Laughter] He hasn't read anything at all like what he's come up with. And I think that when he *does* read *Norwood,* when he *does* read *Confederacy of Dunces,* he'll understand, maybe, how to get a little more control. When Louis Rubin gave me Eudora Welty to read, it was really important to me. It was a turning point. And then I happened myself upon James Still, who's an Appalachian writer that was an enormous influence on me. If you read the right works, the ones that are right for you, then all of a sudden you see whole areas of your own life or your own experience or things that you know about as *fiction.* You understand that they could be fiction.

McCord: Has there been anything about your life that you have not been able to write about?

Smith: Oh, yeah, you bet. Tons of stuff. The book that I have coming out in early September [*News of the Spirit*] is very—it's funny, because in a way my short fiction tends to be more contemporary, you know, and more urban. It's not very urban, but it's less—

McCord: It's not like *Oral History.*

Smith: No, it's not. The stories are not autobiographical, but they are more the way I've lived my actual life. They are not set back in time in the mountains.

McCord: I have a date of August 1 that your new book is coming out.
Smith: It's changed, I think, to September.

McCord: And I have conflicting titles. *News of the Spirit* is one title I was given. Is that correct?
Smith: That's what it's going to be. I wanted to name it *We Don't Love with Our Teeth,* but they won't let me. [Laughter]

McCord: It's on the Internet as *We Don't Love with Our Teeth.*
Smith: It's on the Internet?

McCord: Yes.
Smith: That is hysterical. See, we don't do the Internet, so we don't know what's on the Internet. We've got to learn how to do it. I mean, this is ridiculous.

McCord: The advice to read if you want to write—would that be the same if the would-be writer was fifty years old instead of eighteen?

Smith: Yeah. I just think it's really important to read the work of other people who are coming out of similar experience and/or a similar place, because then you see what your possibilities are. I think it's really helpful. One of my younger students really wanted to write, but I don't know what she was writing. She was writing all this sort of very stilted, fancy stuff, and I made her read Jill McCorkle. Because those were lives—particularly in *Crash Diet*—the lives of those girls were lives she could really identify with. And somehow she had thought that as a Southern writer she had to be writing about some old lady in an old house somewhere that she knew nothing about. So reading *Crash Diet* really opened her up; she went on to write some very good things.

McCord: How do you get published today? If you don't know a Louis Rubin, if you don't have anybody to give your manuscript to, what do you tell your students? Do you help them with publication?

Smith: Oh, yeah. If they've written something that's really good, I really believe that it's my duty to try to help them a little bit. To steer them toward a particular editor or agent and, you know, drop a line to that person. And I don't do it unless I think that they're at a point where it would be helpful to them to publish. But it's gotten so awful, Charline, as you're aware. So many fewer serious novels and collections of stories are being published. You know, now that the publishers, so many of them, are no longer independent— they're owned by big conglomerates and they have to—they're publishing schlock. It's gotten real hard. So I'm very wary of even suggesting publication for a long time with any young people, because I think they have to understand that they have to have a day job. And that they have to get their primary satisfaction from the writing.

McCord: From the creation itself.

Smith: From the creation itself—and if it's published, that's gravy.

McCord: Kaye Gibbons talks about how much she dislikes the fact that she spends as much time running a business as she does writing. Is that a big part of your life now, running this writing business?

Smith: Well, now, this is interesting. This is something Hal and I are trying to figure out right now. I told you we've just gotten an assistant. We have not ever—either one of us—paid enough attention to that aspect of writing, because we just don't care. I mean, to me, what really, really interests me is whatever I'm writing now, whatever idea I've got going, and I don't give a damn after it's done. This is probably to my detriment, because I haven't paid that much attention to business, and I haven't done this, and I haven't done that, and I don't answer letters necessarily, and I'm always in a panic, you know—and also I like to teach, so I keep doing that, and that's putting energy maybe somewhere that's not good for your, quote, *career*. But I love to teach. I don't know. I do understand that I should be running this business, so we have hired this wonderful person and we're trying to do a little bit better at that part of it, because it *is* a part of it. If you don't answer people and you don't put yourself forward and you don't do all this kind of stuff, then why would—I remember years ago when I first contacted the agent that I still have. I'd published three books and then nobody would take the fourth one. This agent, Liz Darhansoff said, "Send me all the reviews of your first three books." And I said, "Well, I don't have them." I had been sitting down in Alabama having babies, you know, and writing, but I didn't save stuff like that. And she said, "Well, why should you think that I would take you seriously if you won't take yourself seriously?" Which really hit me. It went "Ding!" you know.

McCord: Kaye spoke as if it was a real burden, that she never meant to be running a business, but by virtue of being somewhat successful, it had just turned into that and I can see where that would not be, necessarily, a writer's strength.

Smith: I think that's absolutely true because it's the other side of the brain. The part of your mind and your soul that leads you to write fiction is the complete opposite of the part that makes you savvy at marketing yourself, and at public appearances, and all that kind of thing. And people lose that first part—I mean, you see that happen all the time, that they get too public, and then they're not writing their best work.

McCord: Do you still write in longhand on yellow pads?
Smith: Yes.

McCord: I found that so interesting because that is something I got from the law firm. For years I wrote on yellow legal pads. And it had to be the *yellow* legal pad; it couldn't be the white or the gray.
Smith: Right. Oh, yeah.

McCord: You don't ever write at the computer, then?
Smith: Unh-unh.

McCord: Do you go to the computer with—
Smith: I don't have a computer.

McCord: You don't *have* a computer? Gosh, you're really *not* into the Internet, are you? You're *quite a ways* from the Internet. [Laughter]
Smith: Right. I mean, I'm a *ways* from it. And you know, the thing I don't understand is—like when I write, it's real messy and it's on a yellow pad and I will—maybe there's a word or a phrase that I'll mark out three or four times, but I like to keep what's been marked out, so I can go back to it. And if you're on the computer, how could you do that? And then I type, and I cheat, because for the last version I do have somebody that types for me. Peggy Ellis has been typing for me a million years, and she does now put it on a disk, so that if there are last-minute changes, like somebody's name or something, we can run it through and do that.

McCord: Yes, I've often found that I line through things, and then I'll go back and like my first word better.
Smith: Right. So I want those. I want to hang onto those first drafts. And I like to do the typing since I tend to be too fast.

McCord: In what way?
Smith: Well, just in general. I tend to write too fast and think too fast, and I think that having to do longhand and then just hunt and peck slows me down and that's good for me. I think I write too much anyway and I don't want to write faster or more.

McCord: Is a part of writing in longhand the need to see this creation emerging in your own handwriting?
Smith: Yes, I think so, particularly because what really appeals to me is a very strong character, a very strong voice, which is always a specific, human voice. And it's physical. I mean, I have a real physical sense of writing and I need to do it with my own body. I don't need to have a machine between me and whoever it is that's coming off the page, which is always a person, a very fully alive person.

McCord: That's interesting.
Smith: So I don't want anything between that messes it up.

McCord: I read that you almost never revise.
Smith: Well, that's not true. [Laughter]

McCord: I figured it wasn't. But there is an interview where you talk about what you were just describing—where the voice is coming through and it's almost like transcription.

Smith: Well, that's true. There have been several books that I have almost not revised at all. And it is always when there's a very strong character who seems to be spewing the story. One was *Fair and Tender Ladies* and one was *Saving Grace*. I just didn't revise. And certain sections of *Oral History* were the same way. I didn't really revise—the ones that are spoken in monologues in the first person.

McCord: Yes. I can see that.

Smith: But then again, see, I think all writers are different and I have to say that, unlike many writers I know, I spend an awful lot of time, Charline, doing what I think of as prewriting. I mean, instead of writing and writing and the story becomes clear as you write, I spend so much time with my little legal pads thinking through the characters and thinking through the things that are going to happen and figuring all this stuff out and making hundreds of pages of notes before I start writing.

McCord: So you're mapping out a strategy for the writing.

Smith: Yeah. I think what happens with most people in the revision process—a lot of it anyway—I've already done it in the prewriting phase. So it's not that I don't revise; I think it's more that I do a lot of stuff up front.

McCord: How do you think of your writing—do you think of it as a gift from God, like the "gift-song" idea that I read about in your work?

Smith: Yeah, I do. I think of it as a great—as an *enormous* gift. It just has *made* my life—I just feel very privileged. I feel very blessed. And it has made my life so rich and so interesting. It's like Anne Tyler said—she writes to have more than one life. I feel like I've been able to do that. I've been able, for instance, to write *Saving Grace*, which is a very emotional book for me. These are experiences I would never have. This is a person I wouldn't ever get to be, if I hadn't been able to write that book. I don't know what people are thinking about in traffic, for instance, if they're not writing a story.

McCord: [Laughter]

Smith: Do you know what I mean? I mean, at a red light, what is in their minds?

McCord: They're thinking about the Lee Smith book they just read. [Laughter] Do you ever make notes in the car?

Smith: Sometimes. But I mean, it gives you this whole parallel life. You've got your own life which is oftentimes full of terrible things or whatever. And then you've got this other parallel life where you can either have the awful thing happen or not.

McCord: Yes, or even fix it.

Smith: Or fix it. Or, you know, you can kill somebody off. [Laughter] There are all kinds of things that can happen. So it's a great and interesting thing.

McCord: You talked about encouraging other writers. Is it really exciting to find a talented writer among your students?

Smith: Oh, yeah, it really is. And it's so very—actually, it's much more seldom than you think.

McCord: Can you encourage them too much?

Smith: Yes, you can encourage them too much. And I don't ever really encourage anybody too much. But the thing that happens is, so often, the ones that have a great deal of talent or a real ear don't have the necessary drive. Or the ones that have this desire—this enormous drive and desire— have a tin ear. They have a very clichéd sense of story. So it's actually very seldom that the two go hand in hand. I've had some students that I thought were really wonderful writers, who went on to do something else. They just happened in there on their way to medical school, or whatever. And I believe they're probably better doctors since they ran past me. It's a big commitment. I'm not one of these people who believes if you're going to be a writer, then you will be a writer—no matter what. I don't think that at all. I think the rest of your life has got to fall in place so that you're able to write. And you've got to make it happen.

McCord: You have said that Flannery O'Connor and Eudora Welty were strong influences, particularly because you read their works and knew the kinds of people they wrote about. What else did you get from them, aside from identifying with the characters?

Smith: Well, from Miss Welty—I think the element of myth, particularly in *The Golden Apples,* that she has. The sense of characters as being larger than life. And the sense that—I don't know, this enormous *grace,* in the telling of very simple things. And then with Flannery O'Connor—I *do* take a darker view than Miss Welty. And I'm real comfortable with Flannery O'Connor's point of view.

McCord: Yes, and you sometimes share her brand of humor.

Smith: Well, I often think, "Oh, yes. Okay." Because I think that's the other side. I'm aware that people will talk about me as being a comic writer. And I'm glad if I can make anybody laugh. But the other side of that is you invariably take a real tragic view. And, if you really do take a tragic view, it's really hard not to be funny sometimes. I mean, you're either going to kill yourself or you're going to make a joke. Like Barry Hannah—he's a good example, I think. He's often very funny.

McCord: I read that at about age thirty-two you decided to take yourself seriously as a writer. You had three books out by then and maybe some awards to your credit. What kind of validation did you get at that point that made you—

Smith: I think it was that I *didn't* get any. [Laughter] I think it was a *lack* of validation. You know, I had been very lucky. I didn't even realize how lucky I'd been, early on, to have published the first three books, which had not sold worth a damn. And part of that is my fault because I hadn't paid any attention to them whatsoever.

McCord: You didn't even keep the reviews.

Smith: I didn't keep the reviews. I just sat down there in Alabama having babies, and having a good time. Having a real interesting life. I didn't even know my agent in New York. I just didn't do the business of being a writer. I didn't do it at all. And then I wrote this fourth novel, *Black Mountain Breakdown,* which was very dark. And since the first three hadn't sold, I just had a lot of trouble selling it. I got to the point where I was either going to have to take myself seriously and dig in my heels and *do* this, or forget it. I was really on the verge of forgetting it. In fact, I had applied to go to graduate school in special education.

McCord: Were there other times, besides that period when you were having trouble marketing *Black Mountain Breakdown,* when you got discouraged and thought you might not write?

Smith: Well, no, I never thought—I thought I might not *publish,* which is different. I had been writing since I was a little child and I never thought I might not write. I had been teaching high school English, and I had been teaching creative writing here and there, but it wasn't enough to make a significant contribution and I was thinking, well, okay . . . but I was counting on publishing a little bit along, you see. And if that suddenly didn't seem

possible, I just felt like I was going to have to become qualified and be able
to make more of a living, you know.

McCord: Is *Fair and Tender Ladies* still your favorite book?

Smith: I think it is, because it meant so much more to me due to the
circumstances that I was going through at the time I wrote it. But, you know,
I don't know. I've written some things in the new book that I really like—
particularly something named, oddly enough, "Live Bottomless," which no
one has read. Except Dave Smith is going to put it in the *Southern Review.*
It's a whole novella. It's real long. You know, I have written very little of
what you would call autobiographical fiction. But this is about something
that really did happen to me and I've been wanting to write it ever since I
was twelve, which is when it happened. I really enjoyed writing it. It's not
actually about my parents, but—I don't know, I feel very strongly about it at
the moment, because I just finished it in time for it to go in.

McCord: Who's your favorite character that you're created so far?

Smith: Probably Ivy Rowe. But I like Katie Cocker in *The Devil's Dream.*
I had a lot of fun doing *The Devil's Dream.*

McCord: Ivy is definitely my favorite.

Smith: Yeah, I think she is. But then I also like Birdie in *The Christmas
Letters.*

McCord: Yes, I do too. In an interview with Rebecca Smith you said, "I
don't give a damn if I've got a reader. As soon as you think about your reader
you're dead, as far as I'm concerned. I can't imagine considering the reader."

Smith: Yeah, that's still true.

McCord: Is your feeling the same for critics?

Smith: Yeah, exactly.

McCord: You're not influenced by what the critics say?

Smith: Well, I don't usually read what the critics say, but every now and
then I do and every now and then they have a damn good point. I subscribe
to a whole lot of regional magazines, and there's a copy of the *Appalachian
Journal* that just came a couple of days ago, and I was flipping through and,
to my surprise, I found a review of *The Christmas Letters,* although it's
certainly not an Appalachian thing. But it was a really good review—a favor-
able review, somebody who really liked it, but it said, "Unfortunately, a lot

of her characters are beginning to sound alike," which hit me hard. That is absolutely true.

McCord: I can see where that might happen over time.

Smith: Yeah, of course, you can see where that would happen over time, but it shouldn't. And if you're somebody that writes for the sheer pleasure of writing, which is essentially what I do, you've got to remember that these people are having to read this stuff, and they don't want to read the same damn stuff.

McCord: So that was something to think about?

Smith: I thought that was a very, very good point, because I'm just getting ready to think about another—I'm thinking—I can't decide which of two novels to write next. I'm really going to remember that criticism. When somebody makes a point that's truly valid, you know it.

McCord: I'm going to erect a little monument here to Lee Smith, so just be patient with me while I do it.

Smith: Oh, dear.

McCord: You have a reputation that precedes you. Everywhere I go I've heard about the generosity of Lee Smith. Jill McCorkle told me that she was in your first creative writing class—

Smith: She was so great.

McCord: —at Chapel Hill and that you were so encouraging. She said you were always telling them they didn't have to wear a tight black turtleneck and chain smoke and drink bourbon to be a Southern writer. [Laughter] Carolyn Haines told me that she heard you speak at the University of Alabama and you were "inspirational—not snotty or self-absorbed like some other writers, but very giving, very generous with your knowledge and enthusiasm." She says you were "truly wonderful." The fact that I'm here talking to you further validates all that they've said because you didn't know me.

Smith: Well, I had met you. And I knew Reta.

McCord: In *The Devil's Dream,* Dawn Chapel hangs up on Katie Cocker without telling her who her agent is.

Smith: Oh, right. Yeah.

McCord: And Katie says, "No matter how big I get, I will always remember this moment. I will always try to be nice to the kids coming up in this business and treat them decent, not like Dawn Chapel did me. It's a great feeling to help another artist who's really struggling as a newcomer. And I know what it means to a new artist for someone else to just speak up for them a little bit." That sounds like Lee Smith talking.

Smith: Well, I think that's true.

McCord: Did you ever have a rude, uncaring experience similar to Katie Cocker's?

Smith: No, no. Actually I didn't. But again, as I said, I was very, very fortunate. Almost everybody else I know has had some horrible incident like that—some horrible experience.

McCord: I'm curious about your study in France. You were there for a semester?

Smith: Yeah. Actually, I got kicked out of Hollins while I was there. I went to France on probation, you know, because I was *always* on probation. [Laughter]

I was. I was there, I guess, from December through May. And then I stayed out all night—I mean, just because I missed the Metro—big deal. But, this was the kind of thing—in those days, you know—

McCord: So the trip over was in association with Hollins?

Smith: Yeah. It was Hollins Abroad. We lived with a French lady and everything. And I was already on probation. So I got kicked out.

McCord: Out of Hollins?

Smith: France *and* Hollins! It was very traumatic. I traveled around on my own for a while and had a wonderful time and then I came back home and my father was just beside himself, because he was really living vicariously, to some degree, through me. He'd never left that little town, you know. He was just so pleased that I'd gone off to Hollins, and so pleased that I'd gone to France, and he didn't believe that I'd gotten myself kicked out. And he was *furious*. He made me go to bed and told everybody I had mono. [Laughter] And so I called Louis Rubin from bed and said, "Louis, I have to lie here and act like I have mono. What am I going to do?" And he called and got me a job in Richmond on the newspaper, with James J. Kilpatrick, the right-wing conservative columnist. So I got on the bus and went over there and got a room in a boarding house for $8.00 a week, and worked for the newspaper. That's how I got into the newspaper business.

McCord: And you didn't get to finish your semester?

Smith: No, unh-unh. I graduated by the grace of God. They gave me credit for working on the paper, and I was writing a novel, too, by then.

McCord: And every once in a while a French word still shows up in your work.

Smith: Yeah. I loved it. I loved France. I loved being there.

McCord: What's it like being married to another writer?

Smith: I think it's helpful. At least, with Hal. He is so often completely absorbed in what he's writing that he understands when I'm that way. He's really not jealous of the time I need to spend doing it, because he also needs to spend a whole lot of time reading and writing and thinking about it. Sometimes it can be disastrous, if there's jealousy, or whatever.

McCord: Your works are replete with redheads.

Smith: Oh, that's interesting.

McCord: Why are there so many redheads?

Smith: See, again, I just think that's like not spending enough time to think up something new, different. I think if you write a lot you do run a risk of repeating yourself. But also I had these redheaded cousins growing up, who were like my sisters. They're my first cousins, Randy and Melissa. They are both redheads. And I really admired them.

McCord: Red hair usually implies more spirit, spunk, more everything, you know.

Smith: Yeah, yeah.

McCord: You've also often got a simple-minded character.

Smith: I guess so.

McCord: And you write about them with a great deal of compassion. They know more than people give them credit for knowing. And you treat them very well.

Smith: Yeah. Well, I've always had—I mean, in my own family, there's been a whole lot of mental illness. I had an Uncle Tick who was, I guess, simple, or whatever, who always lived with my grandmother—he was real sweet and real deep, in a funny kind of way. There's a lot of that in the South—in Grundy, too. Not just in my own family. I feel right at home here; there's this one guy, Eddie, who walks all over Hillsborough every day. You'll see him if you're around here long enough. He walks and walks.

McCord: Yes, we have one of those, too; I guess every town has one.
Smith: Yeah.

McCord: I'm interested in your female characters in conjunction with an idea I'm working with of the "anti-belle." These are characters that step outside the traditional role for the Southern female. They just can't conform or they refuse to—or they just don't give a damn.
Smith: That's right.

McCord: Brooke Kincaid is an anti-belle. I know you said *Something in the Wind* is awful, but I found it, and I was so glad I did.
Smith: But I liked her. I was very young when I was writing that and there's a way in which she's certainly—they're all autobiographical in a sense, you know. Her spirit, in a way, was like mine.

McCord: One of the first things we learn about her is from Charles, who, before he died, told her: "The thing that is the matter with you is you are not a lady." Later, she writes in her notebook, "I'm the only one who knows I am different." And she develops a split personality, so that she can imitate what is Southern and what is successful as a Southern female.
Smith: That's probably pretty autobiographical, which I never thought about, because I haven't read it again, because it's so *awful*. But, that's the way I felt. My mother was from eastern Virginia, and she was always trying to raise me to be a lady, but then I had this wild mountain family on the other side. So there was this pull, always.

McCord: Other anti-belles in your work: Susan Tobey could be—
Smith: Yeah.

McCord: She's sort of a budding anti-belle in *Dogbushes*. At the end you create that wonderful picture of her in the mismatched outfit—the yellow dress and the red shoes, and she has become a damaged princess. In *Fancy Strut* there were several possibilities. Sandy, in particular, who is having an affair with Bob Pitt. She does these crazy, unladylike and *unSouthern* things, like at the Piggly Wiggly when she traps Bob with her cart and tweaks his privates. She winks at him in church, and that kind of thing. Are these feisty, anti-belle characters meant to challenge mens's ideas or notions of what a Southern female ought to be?
Smith: Well, I think, Charline, that when I was writing them—when I've written them, I've just *written them*. I mean, they're not meant to mean any-

thing. That's just—there are just these women or men who appear really strongly in my mind, and they do what they're going to do. I mean, they're not—you know, I don't know what they're meant to do.

McCord: They're not meant necessarily to break the mold—
Smith: No.

McCord: —or to challenge women to be different in the South or—
Smith: The only thing I have ever written with an actual idea of a theme was *Black Mountain Breakdown*.

McCord: Right, and that was passivity.
Smith: Um hmm.

McCord: Ruthie Cartwright is also the type.
Smith: Um hmm. Yeah.

McCord: Monica Neighbors is the type. There are several characters that fit the anti-belle mold.
Smith: I can see where you—but, see, I don't think—I was very much struggling with that, because in my first marriage, I was married to somebody who was a little bit older and also from Mississippi.

McCord: And he had these expectations?
Smith: You bet. Absolutely. And I had expectations for myself. I thought, "Well, I've been sort of a wild girl," but I was going to somehow become a wife and have lovely little dinner parties and use all the silver. And so I did that. But I was very uneasy. I was struggling all along. There's nothing I love more than to set the table. I love to set the table just as much as I like figuring out a short story, so I always feel that—

McCord: That you're pulled in both directions?
Smith: Yeah, yeah. Absolutely.

McCord: Let's talk a minute about *Fair and Tender Ladies.* You've said that book wore you out, and it wrung me out. I held up well until Oakley died. When Oakley died, I put the book down and just boohooed. And right in the midst of that a friend called me and said, *"What on earth is wrong with you?"* I blubbered, "Oakley died." And she screamed at me, *"Oakley who?!"*
Smith: [Laughter]

McCord: For two days I could not pick that book up. I finally said, "Okay. You know Oakley's dead. Now you can go back to it. You'll be okay." But I cried through the rest of that book, about the last forty-five pages or so.

Smith: I can't read it.

McCord: You still have not reread that ending?

Smith: Unh-unh. I was unable to write the ending because my mother was so sick, and I had the sense that she was going to die if I wrote the end. You know, it was like O. Henry's story of the last leaf on the tree. But then she did die, and then I wrote the end. So it's all intermingled in my mind.

McCord: For Ivy Rowe memory seems to be both a blessing and a curse. She says that she thinks the most important thing is "Don't ever forget—that a person cannot afford to forget who they are or where they came from—even when remembering brings pain." That's another time when I thought Lee Smith was talking.

Smith: Oh, I think that's absolutely true.

McCord: In *Saving Grace* there's Travis Word, and there are other men in your works who are almost too good to live with. They're just too good.

Smith: Yeah.

McCord: Why are there no women who are too good? I can't remember any—a lot of the women run off with other men.

Smith: That's true. I don't know. Some of them are—like—well, like Agnes in *Black Mountain Breakdown*—

McCord: She's dutiful, but she's not married.

Smith: Or Ora Mae in *Oral History.* I don't know. I mean, there are some who are good—but they're so sanctimonious—

McCord: Yes. Too heavenly minded to be any earthly good.

Smith: Oh, that's great. That is a wonderful line. Yeah.

McCord: There is a type like that.

Smith: I haven't really had a woman character that's exactly like that. I mean, they've been so sanctimonious that they've finally been insufferable, I think. Most of them are obsessed with doing good and having everybody know how much good they do.

McCord: Is there something about the Southern makeup that's truly unique?

Smith: Yes, I think there is, and I think it does have to do with what we've just been talking about, which is the sense of narrative. No matter how much the South urbanizes and changes, still there is a sense of narrative. There is a way of expressing oneself that remains peculiarly Southern, and it does have to do with just simply talking a lot. It has to do with transmitting information in the form of anecdote. You know, telling stories. And I think this remains the same. I think that's peculiarly Southern.

McCord: And wanting to connect people to people.

Smith: Yeah. Wanting to connect people to people, and also wanting to mythologize ourselves. Families that tell stories about themselves. My own children talk so much they wear me out sometimes. And they will make a big story out of anything. I was talking to two fraternity boys the other day, for instance—unlikely mythologizers. And they were telling me all these big stories about the different characters in the fraternity house, and everybody had a nickname, and was this, and was that. It's a kind of mythologizing that I think still goes on—whether it's my neighbor telling me about the different people who live on this street, or whatever. I mean, it is very much a sense of narrative.

McCord: Is guilt still the great disease of Southern womanhood?

Smith: I think it is. It's certainly *my* great disease. I think it's just kind of free-floating—you know, if you don't bat it off, it'll attach itself to you. [Laughter]

McCord: Is there a sisterhood at work among female writers, a support system between yourself, say, and Jill McCorkle, and Kaye Gibbons, and others?

Smith: Oh, yeah. I think so. Absolutely. And I don't think it's true among male writers.

McCord: I noticed acknowledgements in your books—to Jill McCorkle and to Kaye Gibbons—for different things. But you're right. Barry Hannah once told me, "If you want to write, stay away from other writers."

Smith: Well, I don't agree. I think it's real helpful to know other writers, because it helps you to feel okay about what you're doing. About leaving the dishes in the sink. In the South, and particularly right here in North Carolina, we have had a tradition of women writers who are teaching. You know, like Doris Betts. Or Jesse Rehder years ago, who was a famous woman writing teacher at Carolina. Daphne Athas. So many writers have been in the classroom here. And this is really, really helpful to young women who are in those classes.

McCord: Sure it is. And now you get invited to be in the classroom. Mary Hood was just up at Ole Miss.

Smith: Yes. So a young woman sees other women who are a little bit older, who are writers, and you think, well, maybe I could do that. That was one great thing about Hollins, all the writers who were around there. Julia Randall, the poet, was another one of my teachers who was wonderful, always writing, and clearly involved in a life of the mind.

McCord: Do you feel like you grew up in a "Christ-haunted" or a "Christ-centered" South?

Smith: Christ-haunted. We all went to church all the time, though my parents were not Sunday School teachers or anything. I was very religious as a child, and very obsessed with it. But we were not—it was not like being the minister's daughter or—we were not quite as religious as some of the other families I knew.

McCord: In the Notes at the end of *Saving Grace,* you say, "In a way my writing is a lifelong search for belief." Did you work out any of your religious feelings and concerns while writing *Saving Grace?*

Smith: Yeah, I think I did. As a child, I had several real mystical experiences, where I thought I heard the voice of God call my name and different kinds of things like that. "Tongues of Fire" is a story that's fairly autobiographical. And so is *Saving Grace*—I've always been completely obsessed with the very dramatic, more compelling kinds of religion. I am drawn to them as much as I'm terrified of them. And the reason I'm terrified is because of the loss of identity. I mean, if you give yourself over completely in this mystical sense, then who's left? Who are you? If you're born again, then who are you? Where did you go? This is a kind of identity struggle in a way for me.

McCord: But you didn't grow up in that?

Smith: No. The Grundy Methodist Church was a very staid little church. I had this boyfriend in the Church of Christ and I was always going to everybody else's revivals and getting saved.

McCord: The Church of Christ was charismatic?

Smith: In Grundy, it was, yeah. And then there were various Pentecostal churches and Holiness churches and so on.

McCord: You said you were going to write about evil. Have you done that yet?

Smith: I don't think I really have. I have a lot of trouble because, for instance, I get a character like Virgil Shepherd in *Saving Grace,* and then I realize somewhere along that he didn't really mean to be *really* evil. The better you get to know somebody, it's really hard to see them as purely evil.

McCord: He just had a weakness in his character—a flaw.

Smith: Yeah, but he wasn't purely evil. So I have yet to do that. Have you seen *Sling Blade?*

McCord: No.

Smith: God, you've got to see that movie. It is just amazing. There is a character in there, the one that Dwight Yoakam plays, who is a great evil character. But I think it's easier to do an evil character in a film or on the stage. When you're writing a novel about them, you get so far into their minds, into their heads, that you find other things about them that are not entirely evil. This is true once you get to know anybody. They become very hard to classify.

McCord: Do you feel like you've had it all? You've had the husband, the home, the children, the writing career, the teaching. You've been a journalist.

Smith: No. [Laughter] Well, I still haven't really written anything that came out the way I thought it would.

McCord: Well, writing takes its own turns, I think.

Smith: Oh, I think it does.

McCord: I was hoping you weren't about to say you hadn't written the one book that you thought you were really capable of producing, because that's *Fair and Tender Ladies* for me.

Smith: Well, I'm glad you think that because I like that book a whole lot and I love Ivy, but I just always think, God, there's always so much stuff that I wish I could have done. Could do. My head is full of novels.

McCord: Is there a piece missing in your life puzzle, then, at this point? Is there something else still to be done, other than creating more fiction?

Smith: Yeah, I think there's a whole lot. I've been so obsessed with writing, and with family concerns, too. So I've never been to Europe since I was a girl, for instance. There's a lot of that kind of stuff that I would like to do. I'd like to take some serious cooking lessons, too. I'm taking Spanish lessons right now, which is really fun. I'd like to start painting again. I used to paint as a girl, and draw. But it's not that I feel I've missed doing anything. I mean, I would much rather have been real involved in my family and my writing, but just every now and then I think, well, you know, there's some other stuff I'd like to try.

McCord: You mentioned that your dad had died. I knew your mom died. When did your dad die?

Smith: He died in 1992.

McCord: He ran the Ben Franklin in Grundy?

Smith: Up until his death, and he was in the process of closing it when he died—closing it not because of his age, but because it was not making any money, and he was too good a businessman to run it at a loss. We didn't know what he was going to do with himself when he couldn't go down to the story every day.

McCord: Had other stores come in, like Wal-Mart?

Smith: Well, the town itself was dying. The coal business had run out.

McCord: So what family is left in Grundy?

Smith: Not very many. Only some distant cousins. After his death, I gave the dime store to the town, and it's now a teen center. Me and my first cousin, Jack Smith, owned it together. But they're going to flood it, we hear, for flood control. Flooding is caused by strip mining, and Grundy has had two big floods—one in '57, and one in '77. They're looking for another one this year—every twenty years, see. They plan to flood the dime store and also the house that my parents always lived in, where the lady evangelist lives now.

McCord: I'm amazed at the distance you can cover in a work like *Oral History* or *Fair and Tender Ladies*. You cover so much in terms of time and generations and family events, life events, the connections of people, and somehow you keep the reader straight on all this.

Smith: [Laughter] I'm not sure that I do. See, you're a devoted reader.

McCord: Well, I started at book one and read you all the way through and found that you always did this miraculous tying up at the end where you brought everything together in this wonderful way and I wondered if you really worked especially hard on those endings?

Smith: Unh-unh.

McCord: Writing the ending is just like writing the rest of the book?
Smith: Yeah.

McCord: There's something that happens at the end of one of your books that is just rather amazing to me.
Smith: Well, I always think that's one of the things that is infinitely pleasurable about writing fiction. Because unlike in life, where things end up in all kinds of ways that you can't control and things are irrevocable—in a novel, you can work on it and make it at least, if not happy, sort of aesthetically balanced. But I don't really know the whole ending until I get to it, though sometimes I'll write the last line of a book and put it up on the wall. I'll just tape it up and kind of aim toward it, but I don't really know how I'm going to get there.

McCord: That's not a part of your outlining and charting out of things? You don't always know the ending?
Smith: I know *generally,* but I don't really know exactly. I'm always surprised. Like with *The Devil's Dream,* I remember, it was going to be that everybody was going to get together and make an album. But that's all.

McCord: You didn't know how they were going to get together.
Smith: Exactly.

McCord: Did you know that R.C. would not come?
Smith: No.

McCord: I was disappointed that R.C. wouldn't come. That he chose to kill himself instead.
Smith: Right. That really surprised me. [Laughter]

McCord: And I'm not happy that Ivy Rowe is dying at the end of *Fair and Tender Ladies,* but gosh, what a wonderful book that is.
Smith: I did know the last line of that, but I didn't know she was going to die. I don't know. You just never—it's always like walking through a door.

McCord: *The Christmas Letters* has that same movement through several generations, and that wonderful ending where the granddaughter has become the writer and is wearing the robe, the mantle, of her mother.
Smith: Right.

McCord: Great things happen in your books. You and Hal have a reading this afternoon. What will you read?

Smith: I don't know. It's to benefit this umbrella organization for people with developmental disabilities of all kinds, and so one of us better read something about give some money.

McCord: [Laughter] I don't think you've written anything about "give some money."

Smith: No. I think what we've decided is that—Hal wrote a column at Christmas that was really good, called "A Nation of Scrooges." It's an appeal to the conscience sort of thing. How America has become—how we've all become so complacent, I think, since George Bush. You know, it's okay to be rich and to keep it all, and to be greedy is okay. There's a horrible way in which our attitude toward wealth has changed. Particularly in the '90s, I think, it's very much the workaholic ethic. These young people have a different sense of money.

McCord: They worked for it and they'll spend it.

Smith: Right, exactly. Hal questions that. And so I think he might read that and I might just read a little medley of women's voices.

McCord: In *Saving Grace* there is a scene where Grace goes in and finds her mother hanging, and she has the one shoe that has dropped off and Grace gets on her knees and is kissing that foot. That is a wonderful scene—

Smith: I don't know where that came from. I don't have a clue. Again, I don't have a clue where Grace came from. Except I do often think there are these parts of your personality that you're not giving voice to in your life. I have this orderly kind of life, you know. And yet here is wild, haunted Grace running around. I think she's another part of myself that never has a voice in the real world. You don't know where this stuff comes from, actually.

McCord: Do you ever cry when you write a scene like that?

Smith: Oh, yeah. Oh, yeah. Writing is really emotional for me. It's much more like going to the movies than it is like doing a thing. I mean, engaging in an activity. And, in fact, for me to get ready to write is much more like figuring out how I'm not going to be interrupted and just clearing the decks, and then letting it all happen. Making sure it can happen.

Lee Smith at Home in Appalachia

Jeanne McDonald / 1997

It's one of your standard plots: young girl leaves Appalachian hometown for big city, only to discover that home, after all, is the place that holds the key to her future.

That's what happened to Lee Smith.

Thirty-two years ago, as an undergraduate at Hollins College in Roanoke, Virginia, Smith, now 53 and the author of nine novels and two short story collections, came across a book that changed her life. It was James Still's *River of Earth,* the story of a Kentucky family struggling to survive when their crops fail and the mines close. Near the end of the novel the family heads for Grundy, Virginia, the small mountain mining town where Lee Smith grew up. Seeing the name of Grundy in print for the first time, Smith began to look at her hometown from a new perspective. Her discovery was an epiphany in the sense that the mountain that had seemed to imprison her throughout her childhood suddenly became her chosen stamping ground. After that, there was stopping her.

There had never been any question that Smith was already a writer, but until the moment she finished Still's book, her convoluted plots had been based on stewardesses' adventures in Hawaii and the machinations of evil twins. After reading *River of Earth,* Smith realized that truth makes a stronger story than anything that can be dreamed up, and she was suddenly struck by the wealth of stories and characters she had left behind in Grundy.

Years later, she recorded her reactions in a feature article in the *Raleigh News & Observer.* "Suddenly, lots of the things of my life occurred to me for the first time as stories: my mother and my aunts sitting on the porch talking endlessly about whether one of them had colitis or not; Hardware Breeding, who married his wife, Beulah, four times; how my uncle Curt taught my daddy to drink good liquor; how I got saved at the tent revival; John Hardin's hanging in the courthouse square; how Pete Chaney rode the flood. . . . I started to write those stories down. Twenty-five years later, I'm still at it. And it's a funny thing: though I have spent most of my life in universities, though I live in Chapel Hill and eat pasta and drive a Toyota, the stories which present themselves to me as worth the telling are most often those somehow connected to that place and those people."

As they say in the South, Lee Smith has never met a stranger. Five minutes after you meet her, you are exchanging intimate secrets and discussing weighty things—metaphysical issues, humanity, the really important stuff. Smith demonstrates an empathy and involvement with the concerns of others that are so sincere, you realize immediately that she herself has been on the same emotional plateau at one time or another. Her lively blue eyes are as friendly and approachable as a cool lake you can wade into, and her smile and expressions seem completely implicated with everything you are telling her. No wonder her characters are so real, her subjects so genuine. Lee Smith *understands*. She *listens*. And after her discovery of James Still, Smith began listening even more intently to the stories told in Grundy, taping them and writing them down. She coaxed her mother to retell tales from the past that she might have forgotten, talked to her father about ghost stories and legends of the region, and prompted her Aunt Kate to tell her version of the truth.

"Writing comes out of a life lived," James Still said once in an interview. "For me, ideas are hanging from limbs like pears, from fences like gourds. They rise up like birds from cover." So it was for Lee Smith, who began to incorporate all those true tales and anecdotes from Grundy into her novels. Last year, at the beginning of her ninth novel, *Saving Grace,* she quoted these lines from T.S. Eliot's "Little Gidding":

> We shall not cease from exploration
> And the end of all our exploring
> Will be to arrive where we started
> And know the place for the first time.

During the writing of her fourth novel, *Oral History,* another revelation occurred. Smith discovered that the device of using first-person narrative gave her characters dignity and removed stiffness from the dialogue. Now she had place, story, *and* voice, the voice that had been in her head, in her ears, on the tip of her tongue, for years. The rhythms of the native dialect came naturally to her.

Even in the novels she had read as a child, Smith had fallen in love with the Southern literary voice. "Of course," she says, "it was impossible not to be influenced by Faulkner," and it was from novels like *The Sound and the Fury* and *As I Lay Dying* that she got the idea of multiple narrators, even though Faulkner's Deep South settings, with their Spanish moss, ruined columns, and crumbling old mansions, were a world apart from Grundy's dark hills and poverty-ridden hollows. There were no black people in Grundy, either. For Smith, Faulkner's world was so alien, it might as well have been a foreign country. The voices of Grundy that already existed in her head were reinforced by the characters in Eudora Welty's "Shower of Gold" and Flannery O'Connor's "Everything That Rises Must Converge." Although Smith is often compared to both these Southern writers, her own reading taste is broad and eclectic. She lists Virginia Woolf's *To the Lighthouse* as the "perfect novel," is an avid reader of poetry, and, with tongue in cheek, calls Shakespeare "real good." Smith could never be labeled as a "grit-lit" writer who reduces poor white Southerners to generic caricatures. She brings to her characters a decency and dignity that makes them as credible as any memorable character in English literature. Some people, however, equate Southern dialects with ignorance—in both characters *and* authors. Smith recounts an episode that occurred early in her career, when she gave a reading at Columbia University. As soon as she began to speak, several people got up and walked out of the auditorium, put off, she assumed, by her thick Southern accent. Others call her accent "lilting," "charming," and *Newsweek* summed up the impact of her work in a review of her fifth novel, *Fair and Tender Ladies:* "Her work is about the moment when, as you look at or listen to a work of naive art, it stops being a curiosity and starts to speak to you in a human voice."

Lee Smith made a giant leap into the mainstream when *Oral History* was published. With that novel, she became the titular queen of the new Southern regional movement, which Peter Guralnick, writing in the *Los Angeles Times Magazine,* defined as a "simultaneous embrace of past and present, this insistent chronicling of the small, heroic battles of the human spirit, a recognition of the dignity and absurdity of the commonplace." Guralnick includes among the movement's members Larry Brown, Kaye Gibbons, Cormac McCarthy, Jill McCorkle, Jayne Ann Phillips, Anne Tyler, and James Wilcox. Though they may have varied literary styles, all these authors, like Smith, write stories with an exceptionally strong sense of place.

"In the South," Smith says, "sense of place implies who you are and what your *family* did. It's not just literally the physical surroundings, what stuff looks like. It's a whole sense of the past. Even if I write a short story, I have to make diagrams of what the character's house looks like and where the house is in relation to the town." In fact, Putnam recently returned to her a map she drew when she wrote *Oral History,* depicting not only the physical setting for the novel, but also the geographical relationship of all the characters.

Oral History is the virtual prototype of the modern Appalachian novel, but it is also the book that broke Lee Smith out of the regional mold. "Lee Smith," says Guralnick, "is the latest in a long line of Southerners who transform the region's voices and visions into quintessentially American novels." Other novels by Smith that celebrate the "small, heroic battles of the human spirit" followed soon after: *Family Linen, Fair and Tender Ladies, The Devil's Dream,* and, in 1996, *Saving Grace.*

Smith's first novel came out of her senior thesis at Hollins College under the tutelage of Louis Rubin, who later founded Algonquin Press. *The Last Day the Dogbushes Bloomed,* published by Harper and Row in 1968, was an impressive beginning for such a young writer, but there was a period early in her career when the initial momentum broke down. "Harper and Row had published my second and third novels [*Something in the Wind,* 1971, and *Fancy Strut,* 1973], when my wonderful editor, Cass Canfield, retired. I was young, living in Alabama, and my books had lost money for the publishers. I had been published in *Best Writing From American Colleges,* had won a Book-of-the-Month Club Writing Fellowship, and I had a good agent, Perry Knowlton. But nobody would take my new novel, *Black Mountain Breakdown.* Not even my agent believed in it."

To further complicate matters, Smith realized that her marriage to her first husband, poet James Seay, was disintegrating, and she had two young sons to care for. From 1973 to 1981 she taught high school English and a variety of other courses and had actually enrolled in graduate school for training as a special education teacher when her friend Roy Blount, Jr., helped her find the New York agent who still represents her work—Liz Darhansoff—and her literary career took off again. "Faith Sale at Putnam became my editor and remains my editor after all these years," says Smith, "and that ended the nonpublishing streak." She handled the temporary defeat as cheerfully as she handles all obstacles: "I have never had writer's block," she says wryly, "but I have definitely had publisher's block."

Meanwhile, back in Grundy, nobody had ever doubted Lee Smith would grow up to be a famous storyteller, especially not Smith herself, who says she had been "romantically dedicated" to the grand idea of being a writer ever since she could remember. Like Karen, the teen-aged narrator in her story "Tongues of Fire" (in the short story collection *Me and My Baby View the Eclipse*) who Smith says is closest to her autobiographical double, she often pictured herself "poised at the foggy edge of a cliff someplace in the south of France, wearing a cape, drawing furiously on a long cigarette, hollow-cheeked and haunted."

As soon as she was able to spell, Smith started writing stories. "I loved it," she said, "because everything happened just the way I wanted it to. Writing stories gave me a special power." Her first "novel," written on her mother's stationery when Smith was eight years old, had as its main characters her two favorite people at the time—Adlai Stevenson and Jane Russell. The plot involved their falling in love, heading west in a covered wagon, and converting to Mormonism.

At the age of 11, Smith and her best friend, Martha Sue Owens, published a neighborhood newspaper, *The Small Review,* which they laboriously hand-copied for 12 neighbors. Articles from the newspaper show evidence of Smith's budding talent for detailed observation as well as her curiosity about people's idiosyncrasies. Her controversial editorial, "George McGuire Is Too Grumpy," exacted an apology to the neighbor across the street, but it was indicative of Smith's dedication to truth in writing. For example, in the novel, *Fancy Strut,* she writes, "Bob and Frances Pitt stayed in a bridal suite in the Ocean-Aire Autel at Fort Walton Beach, Florida, on their honeymoon, and had a perfectly all right time; but do you know what Johnny B. and Sandy DuBois did? They went to the Southern 500 at Darlington, South Carolina, and sat out in the weather on those old hard benches for three entire days, watching the cars go around and around." In another story, "Life on the Moon" (in *Me and My Baby View the Eclipse*), she writes: "Lonnie took the rug and the E-Z Boy and his clothes and six pieces of Tupperware, that's all, and moved in with a nurse from the hospital, Sharon Ledbetter, into her one-bedroom apartment at Colony Courts."

It is these "particulars of life" that are "splendidly observed," said reviewer Caroline Thompson, writing in the *Los Angeles Times* at the publication of *Black Mountain Breakdown:* "They would make a Carson McCullers or a Flannery O'Connor proud."

Smith already knows her characters intimately before she sits down to write the first word of a story. In order to keep her work spontaneous, she rarely revises, which is lucky, because she still writes first drafts in longhand.

But she knows exactly what her characters are going to do because, she says, they tell her. In fact, she describes herself as the medium through which those characters speak. For her, voices are "easy to do. There's always a human voice that's telling me the story." It is easy for us as readers to accept her declaration that she is merely the vehicle for her characters' stories when we see how accurately she gives voice to those poverty-stricken daughters, wives, and mothers who live in the mountain "hollers" she knew when she was growing up in Grundy. Her empathy and her innate ability to recreate the events of their lives and the cadence of their voices are factors that help the reader understand—even love—those women who marry young, are weighed down by poverty and children while they are mere children themselves, and who usually die never having seen the world beyond the shadowy mountains where the sun rarely shows itself before noon. Most of Smith's novels deal with women whom *Publishers Weekly* called "spirited women of humble background who are destined to endure difficult and often tragic times." She draws her women so thoroughly—Crystal Spangler in *Black Mountain Breakdown,* Florida Grace Shepherd in *Saving Grace,* Ivy Rowe in *Fair and Tender Ladies*—that by the time you have finished her novels, you feel as if you have made two new friends—the character and Lee Smith herself.

Until Smith began to write novels, most southern heroines, like Scarlett O'Hara, were from privileged families. Poor white women remained in the background, unexamined and unworthy of star billing. But Smith changed all that by exploring their hearts and minds and resurrecting the dignity of Appalachian women. *Saving Grace* is the perfect example of a story and voice that Smith says "possessed her," much as Ivy Rowe's had in *Fair and Tender Ladies.* In fact, she was so involved with Ivy, a character she says helped her deal with the death of her own mother, that she was reluctant to give up the manuscript when her editor declared the book finished. Grace had already been speaking to Smith for a while when she went to the annual Flannery O'Connor Festival in Milledgeville, Georgia. She returned home to Chapel Hill, reread all the O'Connor works she could find, submerged herself in a torrent of writing, and delivered the manuscript to Putnam two years early. "I got taken over by Grace," she says. "It was the most compelling narrative that had ever come my way. But even when it was finished and I went to the post office to mail the manuscript to the publisher, I still hadn't thought of a name for the book. While I was waiting in line, the wife of the local pediatrician came in. 'What's the book about?' she asked me. 'And what's the main character's name?'

" 'Grace,' I told her," recounts Smith.

" 'Well, there's your title, Lee,' she said. 'Call it *Saving Grace.*' And I did."

One reason so many southern fans identify with Lee Smith is that she tells a story in the same convoluted way that they themselves do, using intimate asides, gossipy digressions, and personal references, just as any friend would tell a story in ordinary conversation. "The way Southerners tell a story is really specific to the South," Smith says. "It's a whole narrative strategy, it's an approach. Every kind of information is imparted in the form of a story." Ask for directions in the South? She laughs. "It's not just *turn left.* It's *I remember the time my cousin went up there and got bit by a mad dog.* It's a whole different approach to interactions between people and to transmitting information."

There is a fine line between the exaggerations and embellishments with which Southerners give details and what they define as a story. "My father was fond of saying that I would climb a tree to tell a lie rather than stand on the ground to tell the truth," says Smith. "In fact, in the mountains where I come from, a lie was often called a *story,* and well do I remember being shaken until my teeth rattled and [given] the stern admonition: 'Don't you tell me no story, now.' " But Smith was a precocious and imaginative child, and her dramatic views were reinforced by books that gave her an insight to the outside world that few others in Grundy were privy to.

Though none of her large extended family ever read novels, Smith discovered literature early. "Not for entertainment or information," she says, "but to feel all wild and trembly inside." Her favorites were "anything at all about horses and saints. Nobody ever told me something was too old for me because they didn't know, see? They hadn't read them. I read stuff that would have made my mother die—*Mandingo,* Frank Yerby, *Butterfield 8,* lots of John O'Hara. And *Raintree County* put me to bed for two days. I had to lie down."

Smith gave these same books to Florida Grace Shepherd to read in *Saving Grace,* and that is how Grace, like Smith, learned that there was much more to explore in the world. Still, it is the people Smith grew up with who provided most of the material and background for her characters: the minister and his wife, her grandmother, her friends who lived in the hollers, or the women who worked in her father's dime store and talked about babies being born "with veils across their faces." Although her characters may be eccentric or bizarre, they are always believable, and their dimension emanates from Smith's ability to slip into other people's hearts and minds. Even when her characters are flawed—shallow or evil or crafty—she gives the reader something to love in each one. Their weaknesses and vulnerability make them seem real, and every single one of her characters is that kind of person you can still meet in southern Appalachia today. You can still find the Randy Newhouse of *Saving Grace* at any roadside tavern in the South; you can still hear Travis Word preaching at any Southern fundamentalist country church; and you can see Virgil Shepherd on religious TV on any day of the week. In order to make these characters realizable, Smith gives them dignity. "Smith has great empathy for the poor," said *Publishers Weekly* in a 1996 review of *Saving Grace,* "uneducated country people who yearn for a transcendent message to infuse their lives with spiritual meaning."

A review of *Saving Grace* in *The New York Times Book Review* complained that Smith had made her characters "dangerously close to cliché," but anybody who has grown up in the South recognizes in Smith's stories his cousin, or an eccentric neighbor, or the man who runs the grocery store down at the crossroads. And Lee Smith knows human nature. When she wants more information for a story, she dives in headfirst. For background on *Family Linen* she took a job as a shampoo girl at a local beauty shop to learn firsthand how her characters' lives would play out.

Nothing is too demanding or exhausting for Smith. She is a woman who loves her work. In conjunction with her latest award—a Lila Wallace-Reader's Digest grant, which gives her a generous financial stipend and a three-year sabbatical—she chose to affiliate with the Hindman Settlement School in Kentucky, where, ironically, James Still was librarian in 1932. Besides the connection with Still, Smith is attracted to the area because it reminds her of Grundy, and she feels an affinity to the people there. She has been working with writing students at Hindman's Adult Learning Center and at other eastern Kentucky schools.

Smith has also been the recipient of the Robert Penn Warren Prize for Fiction (1991), the Sir Walter Raleigh Award (1989), the John Dos Passos Award for Literature (1987), the North Carolina Award for Fiction (1984), and a Lyndhurst Prize. She left Hollins College in 1967 with a bachelor's degree in English and $3,000 from her first major award, the Book-of-the-Month College English Writing Contest Prize, and embarked on a career that has spanned 30 years.

The affiliation in Kentucky has excited and energized Smith. "Watching people express themselves in language," she muses, "is like watching them fall in love." She is particularly excited and inspired by the older participants in her workshops, especially the ones who have only recently learned to read and write. For the first time, she says, they are able to express on paper the scores of stories that have been stored in their heads for years. And—lucky for them—they have Lee Smith to help.

"I love to work with older writers," says Smith. "At North Carolina State University I have lots of older graduate students, but it's good to get out of the academic community where people are always deconstructing texts and talking about symbolism. This experience in Kentucky puts the emphasis on communication and how thrilling it is to read and write."

For both Smith and the adults enrolled in the literacy program, the ultimate fulfillment is seeing their words in print for the first time. "The publishers are Lila Wallace, Kinko's, and me," says Smith with a laugh. "We've already printed two autobiographies in batches of 1,000 and we're selling out." Some of the manuscripts are being used by other writing workshops as models of how writing can be taught in the community.

Next year Smith will return to teaching at North Carolina State University in Raleigh. She and her second husband, Hal Crowther, a syndicated journalist and columnist for *Oxford American* magazine, have recently bought an old house in Hillsborough, North Carolina, eight miles from their former Chapel Hill home. They've also purchased a cabin in Jefferson, North Carolina, where Smith grows dahlias and roses and nourishes 20 apple trees. The cabin and the surrounding woods remind her of Grundy and her roots and the people who have been her greatest source of inspiration.

But while she's living other areas of her life, plots are still buzzing around in her head, and she rarely takes a vacation from her stories. Louis Rubin, Smith's former writing teacher, has said of her: "Lee's a real writer. She writes all the time. She writes when she's down. She writes when she's up—that's just her way of dealing with the world."

"I write fiction the way other people write in their journals," Smith says. "It helps me keep track of time so I can see what I'm up to." Often, writing helps her work through real-life trauma. It's her personal brand of therapy, the way she deals with whatever emotional ups and downs she inherited from her beloved manic-depressive parents. She never discussed their illness while they were alive, but it's something she is dealing with openly and honestly now. "Sometimes when I look back at something I've written, I remember what was going on in my life at that time, and I see how I worked it out through the writing." The deaths of both her parents in recent years and their constant history of depression have been overwhelming, but writing, she says, has actually helped her to work through and come to terms with such obstacles. Now, life generally seems balmy. "I want more time with Hal, more years," Smith says adoringly of her husband. (The two met at Duke University's Evening College, where both were teaching writing courses.)

Smith never loses her enthusiasm for teaching classes and workshops. Although she firmly believes that such programs have given rise to a proliferation of good writers, "the terrible paradox," she says, "is that even though there are more good writers now than ever before, publishers are publishing less literary fiction. In fact, almost nobody who is a good literary writer ever makes it any more." Among those who have made it, a few of her current favorites are Richard Bausch, Larry Brown, James Lee Burke, Clyde Edgerton, Ellen Gilchrist, Toni Morrison, Lewis Nordan, and Anne Tyler.

Smith's project that she calls "a stocking stuffer" was published by Algonquin in the fall of 1996. Although most of her books have been published by Putnam, she has always wanted to do a project with Algonquin editor Shannon Ravenel, her old friend from Hollins. Like *Fair and Tender Ladies,* which is an epistolary novel based on actual letters Smith found at a garage sale, *The Christmas Letters* is a novella composed of actual Christmas letters from three generations of women in the same family. But the resemblance stops there. "The new book also involves recipes," she says. "I guess I could tell my entire life story through food. You know how we went through that phase using Cool Whip and cream of mushroom soup? And then we went on to fondue, then quiche? Now it's salsa." Recently she has also been busy promoting her newest book, *News of the Spirit,* a collection of short stories and novellas released in September by Putnam, and is working on new stories.

Smith has come full circle, from discovering James Still's novel and becoming a friend of the author himself at the Hindman Center in Kentucky, to seeing her first novel, *The Last Day the Dogbushes Bloomed,* recently reprinted in paperback by Louisiana State University Press as part of a series of Southern reissues. Now she is working on the songs and stories of Florida Slone, a ballad singer famous around Knott County, and participating in a workshop for public school teachers in Kentucky. Meanwhile, she has donated her father's former dime store in Grundy to the town for use as a teen center. And with all this boundless energy and enthusiasm for life, Smith continues to write incessantly and to support the work of others. She is fascinated by the writing of Lou Crabtree, a woman in her 80s in Abingdon,

Virginia, who, like everyone else who meets her, has become Lee Smith's friend. "Until LSU recently published her collection, *Stories from Sweet Holler,* Lou had been writing her whole life without any thought of publication," says Smith, with her usual exuberance. "Once I said to her, 'Lou, what would you do if somebody told you that you weren't allowed to write anymore?'

" 'Well,' Lou replied, 'I reckon I'd just have to sneak off and do it.' "

So would Lee Smith: she'd just sneak off and do it.

Index

Adams, Shelby Lee, 108
Alcott, Louisa May, 143
Algonquin Books, 34, 141, 181, 187
"All the Days of Our Lives" (in *Cakewalk*), 42–43, 54–55
Appalachian culture, xiv–xv, 5–6, 67, 78–80, 86–87, 95–96, 104, 105, 106, 141, 148, 184–85; change in, 50, 58–59, 86, 96, 97, 111–12; effect of television on, 7, 50, 58, 96; institutionalization of, 5–6; preservation of, xiii, 5–6, 9, 50. *See also* Appalachian folklore; Appalachian language; Appalachian storytelling; Southern culture
Appalachian folklore, xiv–xv, 5–6, 10, 13, 19–20, 33, 57, 86–87, 91, 95–96, 97–98, 111–12, 117, 147–48. *See also* Appalachian culture; Appalachian storytelling
Appalachian landscape, 4; change in, xii, 6–7, 58; claustrophobic feel of, 54–55, 144; destruction of, 97; exploitation of, 8–9. *See also* Appalachian region; South
Appalachian language, xiv, 6, 13, 33, 45, 51, 78, 90, 96–97, 111–13, 141, 148–49, 156, 178–80, 183; change in, 7, 58–59, 96, 111–12. *See also* Appalachian culture; Appalachian literature; Appalachian storytelling
Appalachian literature, ix, xi–xii, xiii–xiv, 1–3, 12–14, 27, 51, 58, 59–60, 74–75, 79, 87–88, 96, 105, 106, 111–12, 114, 158, 181; difference from southern literature, 50–51, 60, 74–75, 79; Smith's work as part of, xi, xii, xiv, 12–13, 27, 58, 59–60, 74–75, 111–13, 141, 147–48, 178–81. *See also* Appalachian language; Appalachian storytelling; Southern literature
Appalachian region, ix, xiii–xiv, 13, 49, 78–80, 97, 108, 111–12, 141; change in, xii, xiv, 3, 6–9, 50, 58–59, 86, 96–97, 111–12; difference from South, 55; exploitation of, 8–9, 97; "outsiders" vs. "insiders" in, 9; romanticization of, 9; scholarly approach to, 5–6; social class in, 11, 52–54, 79, 142. *See also* Appalachian landscape; South
Appalachian storytelling, xi, xii, xiii, 6, 57, 59, 86–87, 95–96, 105–06, 115–16, 117, 140, 156, 178–79, 183; women and, ix–x, xiv–xv,

106, 108. *See also* Appalachian culture; Appalachian folklore; Appalachian language
Appalachian Studies, as academic field of study, 5–6, 9, 59
Appalachian women, xi–xii, xiii–xv, 3, 4, 6, 66–67, 105–06, 115–16, 183; as storytellers, ix–x, xiv–xv, 106, 108. *See also* Gender roles, in Appalachia and South; Southern women
Arnow, Harriette, 13, 51, 87–88, 145
Artist figures: in Smith's fiction, 9; women as, xii–xiv, 20, 35, 40, 43, 62–64, 66–67, 106
Athas, Daphne, 172
Atlantic Monthly, The, 17

Ballads, xiv, 51, 105
Barnhill, Sheila, 105
Barth, John, 48, 101
Barthelme, Donald, 16, 18, 46, 47
Barthes, Roland, 120
Basso, Hamilton. *See View from Pompey's Head, The*
Bausch, Richard, 26, 187
Betts, Doris, 15, 138, 156, 172
"Between the Lines" (in *Cakewalk*), 40
Bingham, Jennifer (character), 6, 11. *See also Oral History*
Black Mountain Breakdown, xi, 1, 2–5, 10, 11, 14, 15, 18, 25, 38–39, 58, 95, 170, 171, 182; as Appalachian novel, 8, 96; as cautionary tale, xii, 15, 32, 41; condensed *Redbook* version of, 15–16; critical reception of, 1; diary/ journal device in, 4–5; as feminist novel, 41; publishing history of, x–xi, 30–31, 100–01, 147, 164, 181; rape in, 32, 119–20; research for, 86–87. *See also* Spangler, Crystal
Blount, Roy, 31, 48, 142, 147, 181
Book of the Month Club, ix
Book of the Month Club Writers Fellowship, 29, 181, 185
Borges, Jorge Luis, 46
Brontë, Charlotte. *See Jane Eyre*
Brown, Larry, 141, 158, 180, 187
Buchanan County, Va., 91, 96
Burke, James Lee, 187
Burlage, Richard (character), 9, 11, 24, 39, 70, 74, 137. *See also Oral History*